Macmillan Building and Surveying Series

List continued overleaf

List continued from previous page

Macmillan Building and Surveying Series
Series Standing Order
ISBN 0–333–71692–2 hardcover
ISBN 0–333–69333–7 paperback
(outside North America only)

You can receive future titles in this series as they are published by placing a
standing order. Please contact your bookseller or, in the case of difficulty, write
to us at the address below with your name and address, the title of the series
and the ISBN quoted above.

Customer Services Department, Macmillan Distribution Ltd
Houndmills, Basingstoke, Hampshire RG21 6XS, England

Building Maintenance Technology

Lee How Son and George C. S. Yuen

Building Department,
Ngee Ann Polytechnic,
Singapore

MACMILLAN

First published 1993 by
MACMILLAN PRESS LTD
Houndmills, Basingstoke, Hampshire RG21 6XS
and London
Companies and representatives
throughout the world

ISBN 0–333–48992–6 hardcover
ISBN 0–333–48993–4 paperback

A catalogue record for this book is available
from the British Library.

This book is printed on paper suitable for recycling and
made from fully managed and sustained forest sources.

10   9   8   7   6   5
03   02   01   00   99   98

Printed in Hong Kong

Contents

Foreword

Some six years ago I was privileged to meet Lee How Son and George Yuen, when I was engaged as a United Nations Consultant to advise Ngee Ann Polytechnic, Singapore, on the development of building courses. Since then I have been closely involved with the authors as an External Examiner and I soon became very impressed by their thorough understanding of the technological aspects of building maintenance, the high standard of excellence that they achieved in their lecturing and examining work, and their dedication and enthusiasm. Hence I was delighted when they agreed to write a book on this subject in the *Macmillan Building and Surveying Series*.

There can be no doubt as to the immense importance of this subject to architects, surveyors, contractors, maintenance personnel, building owners and many other related professions. In addition, the text has been skilfully produced to provide a wealth of information in a systematic and readily assimilated format, supported by numerous high quality and very informative diagrams, aimed to assist the many students concerned with this subject in a most helpful and enlightening way.

The numerous building defects, many of them with major implications for the building owner, which occur daily, bear testimony to the great need for an authoritative and detailed exposition of this subject. Lee How Son and George Yuen have accomplished this task in a truly workmanlike and very professional manner, identifying the defects, their characteristics and causes, and the remedial measures required to rectify the problems that can arise, in this lucid yet detailed exposition.

I believe that this book will have a universal appeal and that it will, in the fullness of time, become the recognised text in this important and developing area of building work. Any book which assists in the improved maintenance of buildings must be of great value, and this text will help significantly in this task by providing a sound technological base and a better understanding of the underlying problems and their prevention or cure.

Professor IVOR H. SEELEY
Series Editor for the *Macmillan Building and Surveying Series*

Preface

In *The Seven Lamps of Architecture*, John Ruskin wrote: 'When we build, let us think that we build forever'. This statement may well have been true in the nineteenth century. But in the context of modern times, it is hard to believe that we can ever create Ruskin's Utopia of maintenance-free buildings.

Surprisingly, building maintenance has been a much neglected sector of the building industry universally. Because of its non-glamorous nature, it is unlikely to attract the attention of the different parties in the building process compared with new construction. Architects, for example, seldom have an extended interest in the buildings they designed beyond their defects liability period, nor do they retain a long-term responsibility for their maintenance. Owners, on the other hand, usually attempt to keep maintenance expenditure to the minimum, in the popular belief that maintenance costs invariably erode profits.

Admittedly, maintenance commences with the service life of the building and is the accepted responsibility of the owners. But it is also necessary to incorporate maintenance considerations at the design stage so that potential maintenance complications can be arrested at their source. Furthermore, the contractor has a duty of care in ensuring that he complies with specifications, drawings and instructions and supervises the progress of the construction diligently. In other words, effective building maintenance requires a conscious effort undertaken collectively by all parties of interest in the building.

While accurate figures are hard to come by, it has been estimated that the annual costs of building maintenance and repair in some developed countries already account for at least half of the total building market. This is the result of a gradually growing realisation that the existing building stock represents sizeable economic resources that must be managed and maintained efficiently to prevent their premature failure and to extend their useful life.

This scenario reinforces the importance of building maintenance. There is evidence of its increasing awareness by government departments, universities, polytechnics and professional bodies associated with building in the number of conferences and seminars and the amount of documentation on maintenance related issues all over the world. Nevertheless, the main problem now lies in giving increased emphasis to the teaching of building maintenance technology at both degree and diploma levels.

Building maintenance technology essentially deals with the study of the occurrence of building defects and the remedies which such defects would require. It involves the application of the principles of the physical sciences to the process of determining the effects on building performance produced by both human and environmental factors. This book is an attempt to present as logically as possible the events that occur from the onset of symptoms of defects to their ultimate rectification. One outstanding feature of our book is the generous use of illustrative diagrams which we believe should help the reader along. Most of these diagrams are extracted or adapted from authoritative sources which we have acknowledged separately.

It is also intentional on our part to exclude aspects of building maintenance management in this book since the subject matter is sufficient to warrant a separate text.

Finally, it should be made known that this book is the culmination of our many months of motivated research and documentation. Although both of us have been involved in the teaching of building maintenance technology in a polytechnic in Singapore for many years and have practical experience in building diagnostics and estate management, this is our first attempt at writing. However, it is hoped that our efforts will go some way towards producing a single comprehensive textbook on the subject that both building students as well as practitioners will find useful. It is also our hope that the book will provide the yeast for more research and documentation on the area of building maintenance technology.

LEE HOW SON
GEORGE YUEN
Singapore

Acknowledgements

The authors and publishers wish to thank the following who have kindly given permission for the use of copyright material:

Butterworth-Heinemann Ltd for Table 14.2 from T. A. Oxley and E. G. Gobert, *Dampness in Buildings*, 1983;

Chapman & Hall Ltd for Table 2.2 from W. H. Ransom, *Building Failures*, 2nd Edition, E. & F. N. Spon, 1987;

The Chartered Institute of Building for Table 7.3 from G. Taylor, Maintenance Information Service Paper No. 87, 1981, reprinted in *Managing Building Maintenance*;

Palladian Publications Ltd for Table 6.1, D. Higgins, 'Diagnosing the causes of defects or deterioration in concrete structures' and Table 7.1, D. Higgins, 'Repairs to cracks in concrete' in *Concrete Repairs*, Vol. 1, Eyre and Spottiswoode, 1984.

We are also greatly indebted to the many individuals and organisations to whose works we have made reference. Details of these references are given at the end of the appropriate chapters.

Tables and figures from Building Research Establishment publications are reproduced by permission of the Controller of Her Majesty's Stationery Office. Copies of the digests and other papers mentioned in the book are obtainable from the Building Research Establishment, Bucknalls Lane, Garston, Watford, Herts WD2 7JR.

Extracts from BS 5250: Part 1: 1989 are reproduced with the permission of the British Standards Institution. Complete copies of the standard can be obtained through National Standards bodies.

We are grateful to the Royal Institution of Chartered Surveyors for their consent to the reproduction of RICS copyright material, particularly from Malcolm Hollis, *Surveying Buildings* (third edition); and the Controller of Her Majesty's Stationery Office for permission to use figures from Property Services Agency, *Defects in Buildings*.

Our special thanks and appreciation are accorded to Professor Ivor H. Seeley, Emeritus Professor, Nottingham Trent University, and Series Editor for the *Macmillan Building and Surveying Series*, for his constant encouragement and valuable guidance, comments and advice that were instrumental in the completion of this book; and to Ngee Ann Polytechnic, Singapore, for providing the conducive environment necessary for academic staff to excel in areas of research and other development programmes.

Finally, it must be mentioned that it is truly impossible to name all the people who influenced and contributed to the preparation of this book without overlooking some. To all these people we express our sincere gratitude.

Every effort has been made to trace all the copyright holders but if any have been inadvertently overlooked the publishers will be pleased to make the necessary arrangement at the first opportunity.

1 Overview of Building Maintenance

Buildings are expected to exist for a long time, regardless of whether or not they have actually been designed and constructed properly to do so. The building industry is responsible for maintaining, improving and adapting the existing stock of buildings in addition to the production of new buildings. The maintenance and retrofitting market has grown rapidly and is bound to continue growing. The standard and level of maintenance of buildings in any country is invariably directly related to the strength of its economy. As countries become more developed, they are disposed to require higher standards from buildings, as with other aspects of life.

1.1 Definition of Maintenance

Maintenance is defined in BS 3811: 1984 as 'The combination of all technical and associated administrative actions intended to retain an item in, or restore it to, a state in which it can perform its required function.'

To 'retain' implies that defects are prevented from developing by carrying out work in anticipation of failure. To 'restore' means that minor defects are allowed to occur before they are corrected. In order that an item or facility can perform its required function, some degree of improvement is needed over the life of the building as standards of comfort and amenity rise.

1.2 Concept of Building Maintenance

In our society, organisations are set up to carry out a whole range of activities. In order that these activities are carried out efficiently, vari-

1

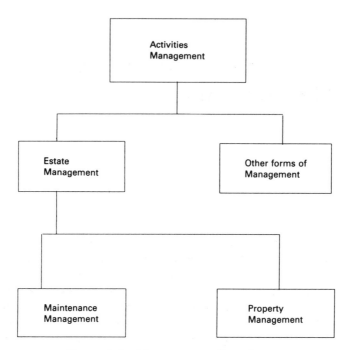

Figure 1.1 Management flowchart

ous forms of management have developed (see figure 1.1). For example, estate management involves the financial management of buildings and land as well as the administration, improvement, retrofitting, adaptation and expansion of the built assets.

Estate management embraces two main forms of management: Property Management and Maintenance Management. Property Management can be defined as an economic service designed to create the greatest possible net return from a land and its buildings taken together over their remaining economic life. Maintenance Management, on the other hand, involves the organising of resources to deal with the problems of maintenance within an estate to obtain maximum benefits from the investment (see figure 1.2).

Maintenance Management can be further divided into Building Maintenance Technology and Building Maintenance Management proper. The former essentially deals with the study of the occurrence of building defects, such as deterioration of building finishes and fabric and the remedies which such defects would require. It involves the application of the principles of the physical sciences to the process of determining the effects on building performances produced by the intrinsic properties of building materials, the loading distribution of the building structure and other related factors.

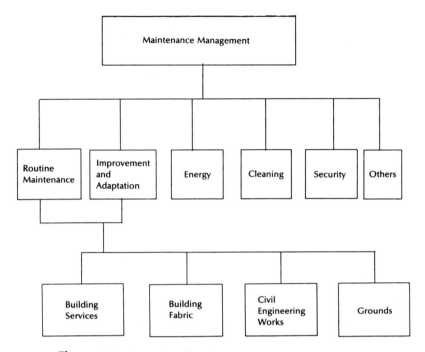

Figure 1.2 Aspects of maintenance management

In contrast, Building Maintenance Management should properly be regarded as describing how a system of maintenance effort could be organised to deal with the problems of building maintenance as a whole. It recognises that, aside from locating and rectifying defects, an effective programme to curb maintenance costs must start with the design of the building itself and must eventually justify itself, not only in terms of minimising the costs of maintenance, but also in maximising the benefits of the investment. This means that financial considerations and techniques play a vital role.

1.3 Role of Maintenance in the Building Process

The performance of any building can be affected by decisions taken and actions performed at any stage of a building project, from its initial conception to its final demolition. This reflects the importance of maintenance throughout the life of a building.

The building process starts when a brief is provided to the designer, stating his requirements and constraints. The client should determine his maintenance objectives, such as economy and efficiency. A maintenance policy is then formulated to allow the objectives to be achieved.

A skilful design can reduce the amount of maintenance and also make it easier to carry out the work. Major decisions at this stage include, among other things, selection of materials, forms of construction, orientation of building and user requirements.

The construction stage is the most vulnerable to the occurrence of defects. It requires, therefore, a high level of supervision to ensure good standards of materials and workmanship as well as correct detailing and specification.

Maintenance is needed throughout the entire period that the building remains in use or occupation, so that the various facilities are kept to a standard consistent with overall policy. Feedback is important to indicate success or otherwise of design, in terms of satisfactory user requirements and maintenance objectives.

Finally, a decision has to be made regarding the future of the building and this depends very often on its condition. A survey is carried out to determine the cost of repairs and adaptations before the building is demolished and redeveloped.

1.4 Nature of Maintenance

The proper maintenance of buildings covers many aspects of work which may be divided into four categories. Firstly, there is the planning and execution of day-to-day maintenance, which includes such activities as servicing and cleaning and the inspection of facilities and components. The frequency of cleaning varies. For example, floors are usually swept daily and polished weekly; and painting done every 3 to 5 years.

Secondly, rectification work may be needed quite early in the life of the building because of design shortcomings, inherent faults in the use of materials or faulty construction. These shortcomings often affect the performance of the component.

Thirdly, there is the need to consider the replacement of costly items in a building (see table 1.1). Thus, the flat roof coverings to an apartment block may be relaid or the air-conditioning system in a hotel may be replaced once every 10 years.

Finally, maintenance may also embrace aspects of retrofitting or modernisation. This sector of the market is concerned with alteration, addition and enhancement to existing buildings on both a small and large scale. Retrofitting work includes all work designed either to expand the capacity of a facility or to enable the facility to perform some new function.

Table 1.1   Renewal cycles of selected categories of building (Source: Chow, K. F., *The Construction Agenda: Development of the Construction Industry in Singapore*, Construction Industry Development Board, Singapore, 1990)

Facilities / Components	Public housing	Condo-miniums	Retail	Hotels	Office	Airports
Upper floors	10[A]	—	—	—	—	—
Roof: i. Construction	20[B]	—	—	—	—	—
ii. Coverings	10	10	7	10	10	5
Stairs	5[A]	20[B]	—	—	10	10
External i. Walls	5[A]	25[B]	5	10–15	15	5
ii. Painting	5[A]	10[A]	5	10–15	15	4
Windows	10	15[B]	10	—	—	10
Doors i. External	5	25[B]	7	7–10	10	10
ii. Internal	—	10	10	6	—	10
Games court resurfacing	—	2–3	—	—	—	—
Ironmongery	—	20[B]	7	6	8	5
Wall finish	5	—	7	4	5	5
Floor finish	5	10	7	6	12	2
Ceiling finish	—	25[B]	7	—	6	5
Decoration: i. External	5	3–5	5	5	3–5	1
ii. Internal	5	1–2	5	6	10	1
Sanitary fittings	—	5	7	20	10	5
Water/Sanitation	—	10	5	3	10	10
Air-Con. i. Cooling tower	—	10	10	10	10	—
ii. Chiller	—	10	10	10	10	—
iii. Ducts	—	10	10	10	10	—
Electrical i. Wiring	20[A]	10–15[B]	10	20	12	—
ii. Fittings	20[B]	10–15[B]	10	6	6	—
Drainage	15[B]	10–15[B]	7	20	15	—
External works	10	3–5	10	10	15	—

[A] Minor replacements. [B] Estimated figures.

1.5 Characteristics of Maintenance Sector

In developing countries, the construction sector usually ranks among the largest sectors of the economy and is typically characterised by high levels of investments in new buildings and infrastructure facilities. As a country becomes developed, new construction will slow down and the upkeep of existing buildings and other facilities becomes increasingly more important. The size of the maintenance sector will depend on the building stock and infrastructure facilities. In addition, new economic activities and new social needs generate new demands which can be met either by building new facilities or improving existing ones. Therein lies the impetus for renovation and retrofitting demand.

Like new construction, building maintenance and retrofitting are the most labour-intensive of industrial activities. However, unlike new construction, the nature of maintenance and retrofitting does not readily permit mechanisation.

It is recognised that the maintenance and retrofitting sector is a service sector. Clients expect prompt reaction to their needs with a professional and competent approach. They also expect co-operation in the execution of the work to minimise disruption of the building. It is required of the operatives that they must not only be trustworthy and friendly, but must also be multi-skilled and flexible.

The market is also a competitive one, serving industrial, commercial and public sector clients. Competition comes from both small builders as well as the in-house resources of the bigger clients themselves.

The very nature of building maintenance involves jobs that are invariably of short duration, often lasting no more than part of a day. The maintenance manager, therefore, needs exceptional managerial ability to manage a labour-intensive service which can rely on only a small future workload at any given time.

Generally, maintenance and retrofitting operations are perceived as being more difficult than new construction. Frequently, they are considered to be a 'Cinderella' industry that consequently does not attract the better people at both the supervisory and operational levels.

1.6 Growth Factors

The construction industry needs to manage maintenance and retrofitting in a way that matches its ability to manage new construction, because the former will be an increasingly sizeable task. The reasons for the continuing growth of the maintenance and retrofitting sector are as follows:

1 Ageing Stock of Building

The most direct determinant in developed countries is the increasing stock of buildings which will have to be maintained or retrofitted. For example, expenditure in this sector averaged about 21 per cent of overall spending on construction each year in Singapore; 33 per cent in the United States; and 35 per cent in Europe. In Canada, it has been reported that the volume of renovation work accounts for some 63 per cent of total residential construction in the industry.

2 Obsolescence of Buildings
Regardless of the state of the property market, commercial developments face increasingly keen competition to attract new tenants and retain existing ones. Property owners will want to upgrade their buildings to prevent their obsolescence. In addition, easier access to private financing and lesser regulatory requirements may make retrofitting a better proposition than redevelopment.

3 Advent of New Technologies
With the advent of new technologies, changes and modifications to existing buildings are required to meet new demands. For example, the introduction of computer-aided manufacturing in factories inevitably initiates demand to change factory layouts and storage facilities. Such changes are likely to be carried out by renovation and retrofitting of existing buildings.

4 Rising Social Expectations and Aspirations
The natural increase in aspirations and purchasing power will expand the market for higher standards of both maintenance and retrofitting work, already particularly evident in residential premises. At the same time, rising social affluence will also generate demand for restorative retrofitting of archaic buildings and structures.

5 New Legal Developments
New legal developments, particularly in the law of occupiers' liability and the tort of negligence, continue to impose an increasingly heavier burden on building owners to maintain and keep their premises safe. These developments will push for higher standards and a greater degree of professionalism and thoroughness in the execution of maintenance and retrofitting work. Furthermore, mandatory inspection of buildings under their Building Control Act, in some countries like Singapore, will raise demand for maintenance, diagnostic work and repairs.

6 Environmental Issues
From the environmental point of view, it may not be acceptable to demolish buildings. This means that, in some cases, maintenance and modernisation will be a better alternative than massive demolition, because of the high costs involved to take protective measures against pollution.

Apart from the effects of building materials on the environment, there is the additional problem of the 'sick building syndrome' inside buildings which may result from inadequate maintenance.

1.7 Issues to be Addressed

The immediate issues which the industry has to address will be those pertaining to the problem of upgrading the quality of maintenance and retrofitting work. Briefly, some of the principal issues in Third World nations are:

1 Raising Maintainability Awareness
It should be noted that maintenance expenditure usually constitutes one of the most critical items of operating expenses in most facilities. In order to keep it in check, it is important that the whole construction team understands the long-term implications of design decisions relating to such matters as detailing, selection of materials and components and provision of access for maintenance purposes.

It is necessary, therefore, to have a structured mechanism to make sure that inputs on the technical aspects of maintenance are adequately channelled back to the designers. The appointment of a maintenance expert at the design stage of a building may go a long way to ensure that maintenance problems have been carefully studied before the design is finalised.

A lot of work has also been done to promote concepts such as life cycle costing. If such data are available as part of a set of project evaluation criteria, it will definitely increase maintainability consciousness.

2 Contract Documentation
If facilities are to be maintained well, maintenance standards must be defined with better precision. However, the nature of maintenance work may not allow industry-wide specification. It is sufficient that owners and their consultants are aware of their requirements and are able to state them clearly in the maintenance and retrofitting contracts.

3 New Contract Form
Some new standard contract form may have to be formulated, especially for major renewals. Existing standard forms of building and engineering contracts may not be suitable because the great majority of renewal contracts are small in value and are unlikely to be administered by the full team of architects, engineers and quantity surveyors.

4 Manpower Development
There should be accurate projections of manpower requirements of the various technical and management levels. At the professional level, there is a need to increase the pool of local architects and engineers who are competent to undertake and oversee retrofitting works.

In the area of maintenance, the training needs may be considered at two levels. The first relates to the training of managers in property maintenance who would be expected to co-ordinate and manage maintenance contracts against prescribed budgets and constraints. The second relates to supervisory training of maintenance personnel involved in building maintenance and repairs, maintenance of mechanical and electrical services and cleaning.

5 Accreditation
The primary advantage of accreditation would be to accelerate the need for upgrading standards in the maintenance and retrofitting industry. However, there is a price premium to be paid for these services.

Related and Further Reading

British Standards Institution. *BS 3811: 1984 Glossary of maintenance management terms in terotechnology.*

Bushell, R. J. *Preventing the Problem – A New Look at Building Planned Preventive Maintenance.* Chartered Institute of Building, UK, Information Service 11 (1979/80).

Chartered Institute of Building, UK. *Maintenance Management: A Guide to Good Practice* (1982).

Chartered Institute of Building, UK. *Managing Building Maintenance* (1985).

Chow, K. F. *The Construction Agenda: Development of the Construction Industry in Singapore.* Construction Industry Development Board, Singapore (1990).

Chudley, R. *The Maintenance and Adaptation of Buildings.* Longman, London (1981).

Edwards, J. P. The economic significance of building maintenance to industry and commerce. *Department of the Environment Third National Building Conference, 1971.* HMSO, London (1972).

Gibson, E. J. (ed.). *Developments in Building Maintenance – 1.* Applied Science Publishers, London (1979).

Greaves, M. J. and Motha, P. *Building Maintenance and Estate Management – An Overview.* UNIBEAM, Journal of the School of Building and Estate Management, National University of Singapore, Singapore (1986/87).

Lee, R. *Building Maintenance Management*. Granada, London (1981).

Mills, E. D. (ed.). *Building Maintenance and Preservation*, Butterworths, London (1986).

Stone, P. A. *Building Economy*. Pergamon, Oxford (1983).

Thomas, M. The new system of mandatory structural surveys for buildings in Singapore – strategic maintenance planning, opportunities and practical issues. *Structural Survey*, Vol. 8, No. 3, p. 303 (1990).

2   Causes and Agents of Deterioration

Building demands many skills in planning, design and construction, and the selection and use of many materials and techniques. After the building is completed, it has to meet various requirements, withstand the rigours of the climate and, at the same time, it is expected to last for many years, preferably with minimal maintenance. It is not surprising that defects and failures occur frequently. Consideration must be given, therefore, at every stage of the building process, of ways of reducing the incidence of defects and prolong the durability of the building.

2.1 Primary Causes

2.1.1 Design Deficiencies

Design is the pre-planning process of knowledgeably selecting materials and determining their relative positions in a construction to produce a building with predictable performance. To ensure predictable performance, the designer must possess a good knowledge and understanding of material properties, as well as of the interactions that building materials will have with their environment in service.

Many of the subsequent maintenance problems are directly attributed to decisions made at the design stage of the building. These decisions can be broadly classified into several categories.

1 Approach to Design
Many maintenance problems arise where design is sound in principle but has a low probability of satisfactory achievement in practice. Some designers fail to realise that their design can be too complex for site

conditions and can present problems of buildability.

The designer must be fully aware of the client's needs. Defects often occur because of a lack of understanding of how a building is to be used. It is a designer's responsibility to find out the requirements of the building type. Very often, the client's own maintenance staff can provide some assistance, but unfortunately this advice is rarely sought.

The owner of a proposed building understandably wants value for money. Economy should be achieved through measures that do not compromise on safety, performance and durability.

Inadequacies and faults also result from the owner's and designer's attempts to provide too much with insufficient money. It must be the designer's responsibility to decide how much to provide within the available budget. He should also advise the owner of the effects upon maintenance costs of using certain materials or techniques, so that the owner can decide whether he prefers lower initial costs and high future maintenance costs, or vice versa.

2 Selection of Materials

The choice of design details in relation to the materials to be used, and in relation to the proposed use of the building and its environment, is probably the factor most affecting the risk of defects and failures. Many materials are satisfactory in some conditions but not in others. The designer must either design to suit the materials available or, for a required design, choose materials which may be expected to perform satisfactorily with that design in the given environment.

The choice of materials will be governed mainly by the following factors:

- Their ability to withstand the effects of the climate.
- Their ability to fulfil their design function.
- Their reaction with surrounding materials.
- Their ease of maintenance and/or replacement.
- Overall economic acceptability.

The designer's task is to find a successful solution to the above factors by using materials which have acceptable physical and economic advantages over other materials being considered. He must know how the various materials will weather and react with one another. It is also necessary to consider the likely behaviour of combinations of different materials in use, for there are many examples of such combinations which give rise to problems that arise from chemical interaction or differential movement.

Designers must bear in mind that innovation is likely to give rise to greater risks than traditional buildings using traditional and tested materials.

Materials tend to deteriorate as soon as they are used in a building because of the following factors:

- Environment, which comprises a complex number of variables such as air temperature, rainfall, wind and atmospheric gases.
- Design, which includes details that prevent contact between certain materials which could be harmful and the factors which produce deterioration.
- Workmanship, such as faulty assembly, can frustrate the satisfactory performance of an otherwise well-designed component.
- Intrinsic properties of the materials, which determine the physical and chemical changes of the materials during their lifetime use.

The incorrect selection and specification of materials by designers will lead to construction and maintenance problems which include:

- Mismatch and misfit problems from the use of different materials having different characteristics, shapes, textures and fixings.
- Chemical interaction occurring between the materials themselves or as a result of an aggressive environment.
- Structural failure when there is a reduction in the ability of the material to withstand designed loads.
- Premature or accelerated damage due to the use of unsuitable materials.
- Construction difficulties, particularly when excessive support systems or highly skilled labour are required.
- Difficulties in repairing or replacing very complex materials if these are used in the original design.

3 Environmental Factors

The performance of a building may be greatly affected by a host of environmental factors. The factors arising from above ground conditions will usually include climate, atmospheric conditions, atmospheric pollution and exposure conditions; below ground factors will include nature of subsoil, drainage and site stability.

- Weather conditions, such as sunlight, wind, rainfall, temperatures and atmospheric humidity, have profound effects upon the durability of materials and their behaviour. Some which have high durability in warm, dry conditions would have a reduced life in very humid conditions, and vice versa.
- Stability of a site may be affected by chemically aggressive soils or groundwater, inadequate drainage as well as large-scale seismic movements.
- Different exposure conditions within the same climatic zone may result in varying severity of rain penetration and, hence, different

effects upon durability of materials. For example, a building situated on an exposed hilltop may behave very differently from a similar building in a developed urbanised area.

4 Building Shape and Form

Building maintenance consumes a large proportion of material resources. Particular attention should be paid to designing buildings which will cut down maintenance expenditure in the future. The influence of building shape and form on maintenance expenditure can be summarised as follows:

- Generally, maintenance costs are higher for high-rise buildings than for low-rise ones of similar shape. The main reasons for this trend include the higher proportion of services like lifts and lighting; more communal areas; problems of accessibility for redecoration and repair; and the usual computation of maintenance costs per dwelling.
- Complex-shaped buildings are more expensive to maintain because of additional costs incurred in providing temporary support systems, slower working rate and higher overheads.
- Older buildings are also more expensive to maintain because of the need to replace or repair more components which have reached their useful and economic lifespans. The effect of age on high-rise buildings is even greater because of a higher proportion of services to be overhauled or replaced.

5 Orientation of Building

The orientation or arrangement of the axis of a building is a way of controlling the effects of the sun, wind and rain since the sun is regular in its path and favours the southern aspects of buildings in the northern hemisphere.

The building may be orientated to capture the heat of the sun or, conversely, it may be turned to evade the solar heat in the tropics. Orientation may also be used to control air flow circulation and reduce the disadvantages of wind, rain and snow when prevailing currents are predictable.

It can be seen that the orientation of a building can be maximised to control the local climate. But other factors must also be taken into account. For example, the character of the local terrain may have some influence on the final orientation of the building by the way in which undulating ground, trees and adjacent buildings create shade and reduce or intensify the effects of the wind.

6 Design and Maintainability

In designing for maintainability, many designers are often trapped in a dilemma: whether 'form should follow function' or 'function should follow form'.

Designers are often criticised for giving too much emphasis to aesthetics at the expense of maintainability. It is difficult to argue against functionalism even though everyone acknowledges the fact that aesthetic value is equally important. It is for this reason that so much criticism has been directed at the design of the Pompidou Centre in Paris.

Maintenance considerations during the design and planning stages from the building services point of view are intimately related to architectural considerations. There must be continuous interaction between the architect and the engineers in the initial planning as well as in the final design of the building. The architect must accord a healthy respect for the needs of mechanical and electrical services in a building. Likewise, the engineers must reciprocate with an equal respect for the architect's concern for aesthetics, form and flow of movement.

Some examples of poor decisions which tend to give rise to maintenance problems include:

- Inadequate provision of space around plant and equipment for proper maintenance to be carried out.
- Keeping ceiling space low in order to maximise ceiling height at the expense of inefficient ductwork for air-conditioning services.
- Failure to provide accessibility to ceiling space for the purpose of maintenance.
- Locating wet pipes above electrical rooms.

On the other hand, there are examples of buildings where serious planning at the design stage has produced remarkable buildings in terms of maintainability, such as:

- Good planning of access routes so that bulky equipment can be easily replaced.
- Adequate floor-to-floor height provided in basements for the movement of heavy equipment.
- Good layout of equipment in plant rooms to maximise the utilisation of space and for maintenance to be carried out without difficulty.
- Provision for building automation systems.

2.1.2 Construction Faults

The site personnel can be just as guilty of promoting deterioration of buildings by bad workmanship, inadequate supervision and the substitution of poor materials, components or fixings. In view of these problems, there is a constant need for stringent control of both the work on the site as well as the materials used for the construction.

1 Control of Work on Site

Careful supervision of building work at all stages is necessary to complement good designs, specifications and detailing by the designers. However, even where the contractor is trying to follow the drawings and specifications closely, it may be difficult to ensure that workmanship is of an adequate standard. The reasons may be due to the following:

- Increasing difficulty in recruiting workers with the necessary skills for an industry which is often associated with a poor working environment and a high accident rate.
- Lack of a properly trained workforce who can appreciate the importance of good construction practice.
- The increase in the number of complex projects in recent years requires careful coordination between the contractor and services sub-contractors.
- There may be an over-emphasis on quantity rather than quality of construction, particularly in developing countries where the urgent need to fulfil housing programmes is a political issue.

2 Control of Materials

The materials used in building are normally purchased according to the specification, or to be similar to an agreed sample. It is necessary that the contractor should arrange for all deliveries and documents to be checked carefully to make sure that the materials delivered to the site comply with the specifications or samples. Sometimes it may be desirable to test the samples in addition to visual checking.

Materials which do not comply with the specifications should be rejected. This may cause delays and added cost. The contractors may be tempted to substitute inferior materials rather than have such delays. This should only be allowed with the agreement of the designer.

2.1.3 Lack of Maintenance

The client's brief for a new building often determines the long-term maintenance needs of the building. The brief should indicate performance requirements and possible changes in use, as well as the future policy for operating, cleaning and maintaining the building.

The role of the designer includes that of providing advice to the client on maintenance matters so that the performance and durability of the building itself, and of the fittings and equipment, can be enhanced.

Even after the building is completed, the effects of deterioration can be minimised by a serious commitment towards maintenance by the users of the building. For example, the failure to allocate sufficient financial resources for maintenance may have serious implications on the standard of maintenance for the property. Any delay in attending to the problem by indifferent users can also heighten the problem of deterioration. Similarly, the use of inferior materials may accelerate the deterioration of the materials and increase maintenance costs.

2.1.4 Change of Use of Building

Buildings are normally designed for a specific use. During the design stage the designers will make provision for that use only. These provisions may be for space layout, floor loading requirements, acoustic standard, thermal transmission and type of finishes, services, fittings and equipment.

Serious defects arising from certain actions of the users of the building may sometimes occur even if these actions are within the original intended use of the building.

The problems are worsened if there is alteration or change of use by the owners or users without the designers being consulted beforehand. For example, the implications upon space configuration, fire precautions and increased floor loading are not often appreciated.

2.1.5 Vandalism

Vandalism is caused by wilful damage to the building or structure. It has its roots in the social fabric of the country. But other factors can increase the incidence of vandalism: lack of security, wrong choice of materials, poor space layout, poor lighting arrangement and failure to promote awareness of social responsibility.

Any act of vandalism will affect the aesthetic appearance of the material or component and reduce its lifespan. The end result is higher maintenance costs.

2.2 Weathering Agents

2.2.1 Solar Radiation

Solar radiation is received at the surface of the earth both directly and as diffused long-wave radiation. The intensity of solar radiation reaching the earth is lost because of reflection, scattering and absorption of the radiation by water vapour, ozone, air and dust particles (see figure 2.1).

Ultra-violet radiation is of shorter wavelength belonging to the

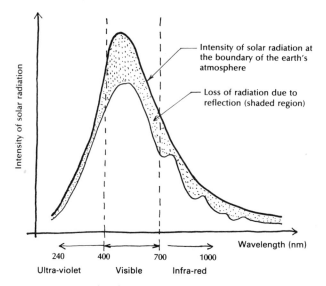

Intensity of solar radiation at the boundary of the earth's atmosphere

Loss of radiation due to reflection (shaded region)

Intensity of solar radiation

Wavelength (nm)

240   400   700   1000

Ultra-violet   Visible   Infra-red

Figure 2.1   Intensity of solar radiation received by earth's surface

region beyond the violet end of the visible spectrum, while infra-red radiation is of longer wavelength beyond the red end of the visible spectrum. Solar radiation affects building materials in two ways: photochemical reaction and thermal movement.

1 Photochemical Effects
Many of the polymers present in organic materials are composed of long-chained molecules. Only ultra-violet radiation possesses sufficient energy to break the primary bonds of these materials. The only chemical effect of visible and infra-red radiation is to speed up the rate of deterioration caused by other agents.

During the attack by ultra-violet radiation, the main chain of the polymers may be broken in isolated locations or reactive areas in large molecules may react with other chains. The resultant cross-linking of the molecules makes the material harder and more brittle.

Exposure to ultra-violet radiation can also cause changes or loss of colour of the organic materials, particularly the blues and greens. A good example of this is the yellowing and surface delamination of glass fibre reinforced polyester sheets.

Most building materials are opaque and are, therefore, susceptible to attack by radiation. But the radiation absorption coefficients vary considerably from material to material, depending on the colour and texture (see table 2.1).

Table 2.1 Absorption coefficients of various colours and materials

Surface (clean)	Absorption coefficient (%)
Aluminium	10–20
White-washed surface	10–15
White oil paint	20–30
Light coloured paint	35–45
White marble	40–50
Medium grey	60–70
Dark coloured paint	65–75
Bricks, concrete	70–75
Glossy black paint	80–85

2 Thermal Effects

Solar radiation is absorbed when it strikes a material. As the material warms up it expands and, as it cools off, contracts. The extent of dimensional change in each material depends on its coefficient of thermal expansion (see table 2.2).

A further effect of temperature is the change in viscosity that occurs in liquids and in some organic materials, such as bitumens and sealants. As the material is heated it becomes 'thinner' and flows more easily. As it cools it thickens and at a sufficiently low temperature it can be quite brittle.

Most chemical reactions increase in rate with increasing temperature. For example, the degradation reactions responsible for the breakdown of plastic sheets are initiated by ultra-violet radiation, but the rate of deterioration is largely dependent on temperature.

Solar radiation causes a surface to heat up fairly quickly. Rain falling subsequently on a heated surface can cause severe quenching shock to the material and may result in tension cracking, especially on roofing membranes.

2.2.2 Moisture

Moisture is the principal agent of deterioration and is probably also the agent with the greatest influence on the properties of materials. It can exist in the form of solid (snow and hailstones), liquid (rain) or vapour.

In many cases, moisture is a prerequisite for physical, chemical or biological reactions to take place. Examples include:

- Changes in relative humidity can lead to dimensional changes in materials, with deformation, crazing or cracking.

Table 2.2   Thermal expansion of some common building materials
(Source: Ransom, W. H., *Building Failures*, Spon, London, 1981)

Material	Approx. coefficient of linear expansion per °C ($\times 10^{-6}$)	Unrestrained movement for 50°C change (mm/m)
Bricks and tiles (fired clay)	5–6	0.25–0.3
Limestone	6–9	0.3 –0.45
Glass	7–8	0.35–0.40
Marble	8	0.40
Slates	8	0.40
Granite	8–10	0.40–0.50
Asbestos cement	9–12	0.45–0.60
Concrete and mortars	9–13	0.45–0.65
Mild steel	11	0.55
Bricks (sand–lime)	13–15	0.65–0.75
Stainless steel (austenitic)	17	0.85
Copper	17	0.85
GRP	20	1.0
Aluminium	24	1.2
Lead	29	1.45
Zinc (pure)	31	1.55
PVC (rigid)	50	2.50
PVC (plasticised)	70	3.50
Polycarbonate	70	3.50

- Rain, especially when driven by strong winds, can erode and dissolve certain soft materials.
- Water rising from damp ground into walls by capillary action can cause flaking and cracking of wall decorations.
- When water freezes in the pores of materials such as bricks, stones and concrete, stresses are produced which may cause spalling of the surface.
- Presence of moisture can promote corrosion of metals, efflorescence and other chemical reactions.
- Moisture also creates an environment for fungal growth as well as attack by insects in organic materials.
- Giant hailstones can cause damage to glass surfaces and roofing tiles.

Most materials also absorb moisture to some degree. The direct effects of moisture on building materials can be volumetric, a change in mechanical properties, the developing of certain forces that can cause distortion or deformation, a change in electrical and thermal properties or a change in appearance of the material.

2.2.3 Wind

Wind can cause direct physical damage by the removal of parts of a building. It can cause dampness by driving moisture into or through a building fabric and excessive heat losses from the interior of a building by uncontrolled air changes.

Wind pressure varies according to the direction and intensity of the wind and affects the vertical, inclined and horizontal surfaces according to their locations (see figure 2.2). The consequent compression and suction forces may result in the loading or lifting of the structure. For these reasons, a careful study of the effects of wind on a building and the effects of adjacent buildings which can cause deviation of air currents becomes necessary during the design stage. The effects are more significant with increasing height and exposure of the building.

Suction forces tend to remove roofs or coverings along the vulner-

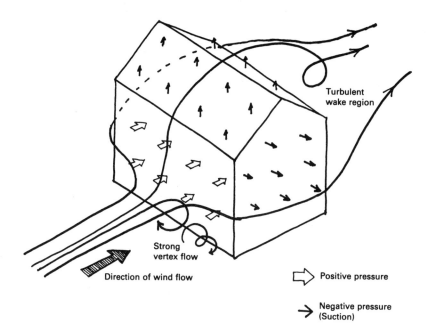

Figure 2.2   Typical pattern of airflows and resulting pressure on an isolated building

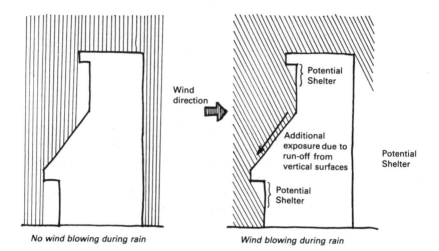

No wind blowing during rain   Wind blowing during rain

Figure 2.3   Effects of rainfall under windless and windy conditions

able edges of a building. There have been reported cases where whole roofs were lifted off because of very strong winds.

2.2.4 Driving Rain

Raindrops tend to fall vertically but if there is a steady wind it will carry the drops along with it at the same speed, provided that the raindrops are of the same size. Unfortunately, this seldom happens in practice and some consideration is necessary to establish the relationship between rainfall and wind speed (see figure 2.3).

Driving rain is rain carried along at an angle to the vertical by wind so that it impinges on the vertical surfaces of the building. The effect of driving rain is that the vertical surfaces facing the wind now receive rainwater, albeit at an angle. The run-off from the vertical surfaces will increase the loads on any abutting horizontal or sloping surfaces unless the water is drained away separately.

When a droplet of rain driven by wind strikes the building surface, it disintegrates and its kinetic energy may force part of the droplet into the pores of the material used in the construction. The remaining parts may either bounce off into the surrounding air, adhere to the surface by molecular attraction or be absorbed into the material by capillary action. The accumulation of moisture within the material may cause expansion of the material while slower surface drying causes contraction at the surface. The resultant stresses set up may lead to disintegration of the surface layer.

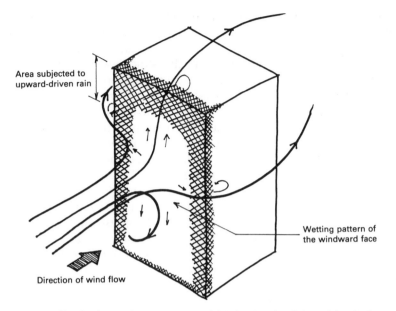

Area subjected to
upward-driven rain

Wetting pattern of
the windward face

Direction of wind flow

Figure 2.4   Typical wetting pattern of high-rise building block facing
the prevailing wind

Tall buildings can receive more rainwater on their walls than on their
roofs, particularly in cases where the building is facing the prevailing
wind. Because of this, rain is often driven vertically up the face of the
building, making it necessary to use constructional details clearly different from those applied to lower buildings (see figure 2.4).

In addition, the facades facing the prevailing wind are subject to a
greater amount of rainwater which cleanses them in the process. Some
of this water is carried by the wind circulating over and around the
building and becomes concentrated on parts of the facade where the
wind abruptly changes its direction, such as the upper parts and corners of buildings.

2.2.5 Atmospheric Gases

Atmospheric gases include sulphur dioxide, carbon dioxide, oxygen
and ozone. In the presence of moisture they contribute to the formation of acids that attack certain materials such as metals, concrete,
other cementitious products and stones. Often it is not only the gases
themselves that can cause damage but the products of the reactions
may also be reactive towards other materials.

Vast quantities of sulphur dioxide are given out by the burning of
fuel in factories. This gas, together with other hydrocarbon emissions

from power stations and other industrial pollutants, form what is generally known as acid rain. Its injurious effects on building materials include erosion of limestones and brickwork and corrosion of metals.

The presence of carbon dioxide in the atmosphere is generally beneficial in reacting with lime products to form a protective carbonated layer. However, if carbonation is allowed to proceed as far as the reinforcement in concrete, for example, it can have serious consequences in causing the accelerated corrosion of the steel bars.

Oxygen can cause oxidation of organic materials such as paints, plasters and sealants, and is particularly severe on unprotected steelwork. Because of its high concentration in the air and its high reactivity, this gas is potentially the most damaging.

Ozone, which is an unstable modification of oxygen, is very much more reactive towards organic materials. Though ozone is present only in traces, it plays a major role in the degradation of rubber, mastics, bituminous compounds, paints and plastics, which can result in their embrittlement and eventual failure.

2.3 Chemical Agents

2.3.1 Corrosion

Corrosion is the result of the instability of some metals which tend to achieve a more stable state by combining with certain environmental elements such as air, water, soil and carbon dioxide.

Atmospheric corrosion means an oxidation process where the metal combines with oxygen in the air to form rust. The process is usually accompanied by expansion of the metal which can affect adjacent materials.

Electrolytic corrosion is sometimes referred to as electro-chemical corrosion and is the result of contact between two dissimilar metals or between a metal and a non-metal, the condition being that the second material should be more electro-positive than the material affected. The presence of moisture is essential for this form of attack, where the potential difference between the metals will set up a galvanic action.

2.3.2 Sulphate Attack

Sulphates are salts which are naturally present in industrial wastes, gypsum products, clay bricks, flue condensates and in some groundwaters.

In persistently damp conditions, sulphates will react slowly with tricalcium aluminate (a constituent of Portland cement and hydraulic lime) forming a compound called calcium sulphoaluminate. This reaction causes the cement mortar or render to expand and eventually disintegrate.

2.3.3 Crystallisation of Salts

Soluble salts may be present initially in certain building materials or may be conveyed into them by movement of moisture from the ground or adjoining materials. They may also be formed by the action of acid gases in the atmosphere on the constituents of building materials.

When moisture gets into a material and evaporates from the surface, the concentration of the salt in solution increases until finally it crystallises out. If this occurs within the pores of the surface layer and not on the surface, it may cause gradual erosion or flaking. On the surface it is referred to as efflorescence which causes some surface disfiguring only. If crystallisation takes place below the surface, it can cause more serious problems.

2.4 Biological Agents

Attack by rodents, insects, fungi, algae and plants may cause serious deterioration in various parts of a building.

Rodents may cause considerable damage to timber and other organic material. Insect attack is generally confined to timber, but some other materials derived from organic fibres or pulp may also be affected.

Fungal attack occurs only in the presence of sufficient persistent moisture. Fungi are parasitic and attach themselves to surfaces which supply nutrients. Attention to the problem of moisture exclusion will take care of this cause of deterioration generally. When the risk cannot be totally eliminated by design, there remains the second line of defence of pre-treating all vulnerable materials with suitable fungicides.

Algae, being chlorophyll-bearing, grow on walls of buildings to which they are transferred by wind as spores. Algal growths resemble dirt deposits on external paint surfaces and porous concrete. In the early stages of attack they can be washed off but moulds may penetrate and damage the films.

Plant life in the form of ivy, moss and lichens, if allowed to develop, will cause deterioration of the material surface and the jointing materials. The damage is done by the penetration of roots into crevices as they grow to extract moisture from the damp materials. In addition, lichens and mosses can produce acidic waste which can increase the problem of metallic corrosion, particularly of embedded components.

2.5 Mechanical Agents

Mechanical agents are those which tend to impose a physical force on the building. They can be static and permanent, such as ground pressure, or static and temporary such as a transient load. Alternatively, the force can be dynamic such as wind or vibration.

The design of structural elements should take into account all the possible actions of predictable mechanical agents impinging on a building.

Mechanical forces which act on and within components do manifest themselves as building defects. Examples are:

- Frost action through the formation of ice crystals within components already saturated with water.
- The combined action of rain and wind in forcing pollutants into the building materials.
- The erosion effect of wind on the external fabric.
- Abrasion, especially to such items as floor finishes.

For durability of materials, the following two points need to be considered. Firstly, agents do not act uniformly, that is to say, individual agents have differing effects on different materials. For example, plastics are not attacked by corrosion, fungi and insects but are susceptible to damage by ultra-violet radiation. On the other hand, timber is affected by both agents.

Secondly, the extent of any damage is likely to vary according to the nature of the attack. For damage by corrosion, for instance, the duration of the attack is the critical factor; whereas in the case of thermal movement, the intensity of the agent is the dominant consideration.

Related and Further Reading

Ashton, H. E. The weathering of organic building materials. In Burgess, R. A., Horrobin, P. J. and Simpson, J. W. (eds.), *Progress in Construction Science and Technology*, Medical and Technical Publishing Co., UK (1971).

Bessey, G. E. *Avoiding Faults and Failures in Buildings*. Overseas Building Note 177, Building Research Establishment, UK (1977).

Building Research Establishment, UK. *Wilful Damage on Housing Estates*. Digest 132 (1971).

Building Research Establishment, UK. *Durability of Materials for Tropical Building*. Overseas Building Note No. 12 (1972).

Building Research Establishment, UK. *Roofs, Roofing and the Wind*. Current Paper 75/74 (1975).

Building Research Establishment, UK. *Control of Lichens, Moulds and Similar Growths*. Digest 139 (1977).

Chartered Institute of Building, UK. *Building Better Buildings – Maintenance at Design Stage*. Maintenance Information Paper No. 3 (1978).

Chaston, P. Maintenance implications during the construction stage. *Proceedings of Seminar on 'The Construction Maintenance and Retrofitting Market – Opportunities and Implications'*. Construction Industry Development Board, Singapore (1985).

Chia, K. L. Maintenance considerations – Architect's role. *Proceedings of Seminar on 'The Construction Maintenance and Retrofitting Market – Opportunities and Implications'*. Construction Industry Development Board, Singapore (1985).

Chudley, R. *Maintenance and Adaptation of Buildings*. Longman, London (1981).

Eaton, K. J. How to make your building withstand strong winds. *Proceedings of Seminar on 'Low-income Housing'*, St Vincent (March 1980).

Freeman, I. L. Chemical interaction in building. *Building Technology and Management*, UK (January, 1964).

Freeman, I. L. *Building Failure Patterns and their Implications*. Current Paper 30/75, Building Research Establishment, UK. (1975).

Hng, H. C. Maintenance considerations during design and planning – the building services aspects. *Proceedings of Seminar on 'The Construction Maintenance and Retrofitting Market – Opportunities and Implications'*. Construction Industry Development Board, Singapore (1985).

Marsh, N. G. The effects of design on maintenance. In Gibson, E. J. (ed.), *Developments in Building Maintenance*. Applied Science Publishers, London (1979).

Property Services Agency. *Defects in Buildings*, HMSO, London (1989).

Ransom, W. H. *Solar Radiation: Thermal Effects on Building Materials*. BRS Tropical Building Studies No. 3, UK (1962).

Ransom, W. H. *Building Failures: Diagnosis and Avoidance*. Spon, London (1987).

Roberts, W. G. Innovation in materials and technology makes a major contribution to defects and failures in buildings. *Building Technology and Management*, UK (May, 1982).

Seeley, I. H. *Building Maintenance*, 2nd edn. Macmillan, London (1987).

Ward-Harvey, K. *Fundamental Building Materials*. Sakoga, Australia (1984).

Yates, T. J. S, Coote, A. T. and Butlin, R. N. The effect of acid deposition on buildings and building materials. *Construction and Building Materials*, Vol. 2, No. 1 (1988).

3 Diagnosis and Investigation Techniques

Even with reasonable care and management at every stage of a building process, defects do occur. Some of these defects are manageable, particularly if they are localised; other defects are more serious, take a longer time to show up and usually need expert investigation. There is, therefore, a need to understand why and how defects occur, what the immediate and long-term implications are, and what remedial measures are necessary to restore, maintain or extend the usefulness and safety of the building. Out of this need has arisen a relatively new discipline which is broadly described as 'building diagnostics'.

3.1 What is Building Diagnostics?

Building diagnostics involves a process in which relevant experts investigate the existing condition of a building, carry out the necessary tests, evaluate the data collected, make recommendations professionally, and predict the future performance of the building.

The process makes use of a variety of techniques, ranging from visual inspection to sophisticated instrumentation. These techniques are aimed at transforming measurable characteristics and properties of a building material or structure into valuable information appropriate to the building's condition and performance. In the final analysis, it is the correlation and interpretation skills of the expert that are the essence of the whole process.

It is obvious that building diagnostics involves experts from a wide range of disciplines, including structural engineers, architects, building surveyors and materials' specialists. In addition, testing specialists experienced in the use of sophisticated instruments are also available to give support services when required.

29

3.2 Need for Building Diagnostics

During the whole life of a building, there will be many occasions when the physical condition of the building may have deteriorated, thus affecting its continued use. It is useful for a building owner to know when such occasions occur so that he can call in relevant experts to arrest the problems in time.

Briefly, it is likely that a diagnostic assessment will be required under the following circumstances:

1 Persistent Defects
The presence of defects such as cracks and deformations are common in most buildings. Most of these are minor and localised, and could be rectified by regular maintenance. However, if the cracks and deformations persist in a manner that appears to worsen progressively or become widespread, a thorough building diagnostic assessment should be carried out to determine the causes of defects and ensure the safety and long-term serviceability of the building.

2 Ageing Structure
When a building ages, it may develop visually hidden defects such as decreasing concrete strength and corrosion of steel reinforcement. Usually, tell-tale signs may be detected such as minor deformations or discoloration. It is advisable that old buildings be checked periodically to determine the presence and effects of these hidden defects.

3 Change of Use or Rehabilitation
If a building is being rehabilitated or a change of use is planned, a diagnostic assessment should be considered. Such an assessment will examine the suitability of the new usage, particularly with reference to the adequacy of structural members to take the new increased loads, if any. The assessment will also reveal the extent of rehabilitation work required for the new usage of the building.

4 Sale of Property
Whenever there is any resale of a building, a diagnostic assessment could be initiated by the following interested parties:

- The prospective purchaser who needs to know the condition of the building, be it a house, factory, office or shop.
- The vendor in order to disclose to the purchaser the defects and their rectification, especially those works undertaken which are not available for inspection such as underpinning, alterations, damp-proofing or eradication of rot.

- The bank or financial institution that is processing the mortgage loan to the potential buyer. The report will enable the institution to have some knowledge about the condition of the existing building in order to approve the amount of the loan.

In addition, no responsible valuer should give a market valuation of the building without a thorough knowledge of its condition.

5 Budgeting Maintenance Costs
An assessment of the building will permit accurate budgeting of annual repairs and maintenance costs required as well as longer-term expenditure to upkeep the building. This is particularly important with older buildings and when funds are difficult to secure.

6 Post-crisis Assessment
Severe events such as a fire or overloading can cause damage to structural members of the building. In such cases, it is imperative that an assessment of the structural integrity and safety of the building be conducted before any reinstatement work is done.

7 Satisfying Statutory Requirements
In many countries, mandatory inspection of certain types of buildings is required. The main objective of such compulsory inspections is to ensure that buildings are structurally sound and safe to be occupied or used. It is usual practice for commercial and industrial buildings to be subjected to more regular inspections than residential ones.

It is clear from the above reasons that the scope of a survey required in all building diagnostic assessments is related to the nature of the defect, the accuracy with which the causes of the defect need to be identified, and the main reason for wanting to know why the defect has occurred. At a very simple level, the diagnosis may be based on a survey that consists of no more than a thorough visual inspection (often called a reconnaissance survey). At the other extreme, it may be necessary to undertake extensive opening up, site and laboratory tests and intensive data collection (called a detailed structural survey).

3.3 Approach to Diagnostic Assessment

In the normal approach, maintenance personnel would notice defects during their routine duties and alert the building owner. Depending on their training and experience, maintenance personnel could make some preliminary assessment as to the severity of the defects. If the defects are only minor, then a suitable repair contractor would be called in to rectify the defects. However, for major or recurrent defects such as excessive concrete spalling, severe cracking or serious water seepage, an independent building consultant should be engaged. For architectural defects, the consultant could be a building surveyor, architect or engineer experienced in such works. Sometimes a materials specialist could also give useful opinions. On the other hand, a professional engineer should be engaged for structural defects.

The consultant would prepare an assessment programme, conduct a building diagnosis and recommend necessary remedies (see figure 3.1). In the case of architectural defects, the consultant could have basic instrumentation to conduct the diagnosis himself. But for structural defects, a diagnostic testing expert would usually be necessary to carry out tests on the members as part of the diagnostic programme. Once the data have been collected and collated, a proper report should be drawn up for the owner. In most cases, the consultant's service could be extended to include preparation of specification and tender documents, selection of repair contractors and supervision of the repairs.

3.4 Principles of Diagnosis

The diagnosis of building defects has often been compared with crime detection or even forensic medicine. During the process of investigation, clues are found which must be analysed carefully; hypotheses have to be tested to determine which one best explains the causes of the defect. The whole process is never a simple straightforward one. By its nature, the process is iterative; the more unusual or complex the cause, the more will be the need to go back and repeat some or all of the stages previously completed.

The investigation required for the diagnosis of the cause(s) of a building defect has to be carried out thoroughly and systematically. Some points worth noting include the following:

- A list of the potential causes of a defect would be useful as a reference point to return to when unexplained symptoms are found or a diagnosis is challenged.
- Diagnosis must be done step-by-step in a methodical manner. But it is essential to recognise that even the most obvious diagnosis may still lead to the wrong conclusions because the symptoms, the investigation and the original assumption of potential causes may all be incomplete.
- In reality, defects are often caused by a combination of factors and

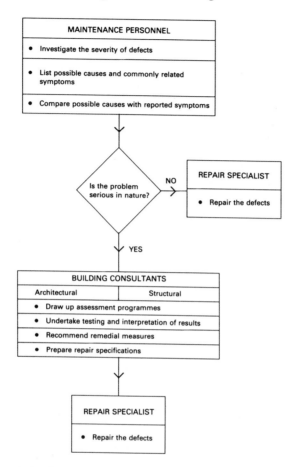

Figure 3.1 Systematic approach to building assessment

seldom by a single factor. Some of these factors on their own may not require remedial work, but where they are attacking the material in combination, may need urgent attention. Diagnosis should not be geared to discovering a single cause for a defect.

- Sometimes the cost involved in determining all the possible causes of a defect may not be justified for various reasons. In this case, it may be more prudent to embark on a replacement of the damaged material than try to find out all the possible causes.

In spite of all the patience, inquisitiveness and caution shown by the investigator, common pitfalls still exist that could lead to the wrong diagnosis of building defects. For example, inadequate or wrong information, inaccurate 'as-built' drawings and outdated records could all mislead the investigator into the wrong diagnosis of a certain defect.

3.5 Client's Instructions

Before undertaking a survey it is imperative that the purposes, nature and scope of the survey be ascertained. An exchange of letters with the client or the holding of a series of discussions will often be needed.

The client's requirements can range from the survey of a specific defect, such as a leaking basement, to a full survey of the whole building to assess its structural integrity.

In order to prevent misunderstanding, care must be exercised at this stage to advise the client of the limitations of access and the problems connected with the inspection. For example, if a large multi-storey commercial building is involved, the client must be aware of the cost incurred in inspecting each and every part of the building. It may be more suitable to select sample floors or units to reduce the time spent and, hence, make the fees more acceptable.

Immediately after agreement is reached, the surveyor or other investigator should follow this up by confirming in writing all relevant and important aspects such as:

- Purpose of survey, that is, whether a structural survey, valuation, redevelopment feasibility or any other survey is required.
- Agreed date of commencement of survey and expected date of completion.
- Statement of surveyor's intentions covering a range of relevant matters which include extent of inspection of building; extent of opening up of structure; any limitation of liability by surveyor; enquiries to be made to statutory authorities; and basis of calculation of professional fees and other reimbursements.

3.6 Process of Investigation

Having established the purpose and extent of the investigation and agreed on a basis for professional fees, a plan of action has to be drawn up to make sure that the investigation process can progress without causing unnecessary inconvenience to the occupants of the building. This process normally entails several steps.

3.6.1 Preliminaries

One important component of preliminary work needed is a documentation survey during which existing information on the building structure and the maintenance records may be obtained from design and as-built drawings, specifications, adjacent buildings, suppliers' records, contractors' test records during construction, records of defects and repairs, past and present usage of the building, loadings and subsequent alterations, if any. This historical overview of the design, construction and maintenance of the building may be a very tedious exercise, but nevertheless a very essential one.

Another essential preliminary activity is a site visit to assess practical restrictions such as access and safety requirements. This would enable the surveyor to have a 'feel' of the task in terms of its difficulty and extent of work involved.

3.6.2 Visual Inspection

On-site investigation should begin with a careful scrutiny of the building, relying mainly on normal human sensory perceptions such as sight, hearing, touch and smell. It is at this stage that many of the basic tools such as magnifying glass, hammer, scrapers, mirrors and binoculars are used. Graphic and photographic records may also be made of critical members for further analysis. Additional information may be obtained by conducting interviews with occupants and maintenance personnel.

From the visual inspection, valuable information may be obtained relating to workmanship, structural serviceability and signs of material deterioration. It is particularly important that the surveyor or engineer doing the survey be knowledgeable in these areas.

The visual inspection is an essential feature of the investigation process, leading to the selection of other subsequent testing methods. If no defects are detected or suspected, confirmatory tests could be carried out more economically on critical locations only.

3.6.3 Testing and Monitoring

There is a wide range of testing techniques available to suit the purpose and may be decided upon after the visual inspection has been completed. These techniques include:

- Non-destructive and semi-destructive methods.
- Chemical and physical analysis of materials.
- Destructive tests.

For large buildings involving thousands of structural elements, testing must be selective. It is not economical nor necessary to test every member. Critical zones or members could be sampled for testing purposes. Where no specific problem has been identified, a sufficient number of elements could be selected according to a statistical sampling technique in order to give a measure of confidence in the results obtained. An optimal number can be determined to give reliable results at a reasonable cost.

A combination of destructive and non-destructive methods should be used together to achieve more consistent and accurate results. The choice of testing methods will be influenced by the costs of the test and the extent of testing needed for the purpose. Accessibility must also be considered, together with the safety of the occupants, site personnel and general public.

Monitoring is a useful method of assessing the movement of building structures over a period of time and this can be done by measuring the widths of fractures or by taking vertical alignment readings of the structure with a theodolite from a datum position. Monitoring is time-consuming. The state of the building and the needs of the client must be considered before using them.

3.6.4 Exploratory Works

Exploratory works include the techniques of removing obstructions to facilitate a closer inspection of hidden parts.

These include excavation works to reveal the depth, size and condition of foundations to expose structural parts. In every case, damage will be caused and high costs may be incurred. They should generally be regarded as last resorts in elucidating causes and only employed where everything else has failed.

Identifying particular locations for removal or excavation requires careful planning to reduce the costs. In some cases, exploratory instruments will assist in reducing disturbance to a minimum.

3.7 Surveying Equipment

The surveyor requires certain items of equipment for use during his survey. The choice of equipment needed would depend to a large extent on the preference of the individual surveyor and the nature of the survey as instructed by the client.

3.7.1 Basic Equipment

General-purpose or basic equipment is required for recording data, marking measurements, making observations and simple opening up of a construction. The list includes the following:

1 Recording Instruments and Stationery
- Cameras: 35 mm, polaroid and video, together with flashlight to record observations. Subsequent study of the photographs and video-recording often reveals important information which was missed during the initial inspection.

- Sketch pads, notebook, clipboard, scale, coloured pencils, chalk and adhesive tapes for recording all data in sketch and written forms.

2 Measuring Dimensions
- Measuring tapes, rods and rules for measuring overall dimensions.
- Calipers for measuring widths of joints or cracks and small inside and outside dimensions of pipes and joints.
- Feeler gauges for measuring fine gaps and cracks.
- Plumb bob and line for checking verticality of walls.
- Spirit levels for checking slopes of roofs and floors.
- Compass for establishing the orientation of the building.

3 Access and Inspection
- Mobile hydraulic platform for inspecting claddings, fixings, sealants, tiled or decorative finishes of exterior facade of high-rise buildings.
- Folding ladder for gaining access to defects which are beyond reach.
- Binoculars for studying surface defects and details that are inaccessible.
- Magnifying glass and pocket microscope for identifying condition of surface finishes, debris in cracks, nature of holes and fungi.
- Mirrors for visual inspection of otherwise inaccessible exposed parts of a construction such as external window putties and underside of coping projections.
- Torch or some other light source for investigating dark areas such as roof spaces and cellars.
- Stopcock keys and drain keys.

4 Testing and Sampling
- Penknife, screwdriver, bradawl, hammers, pliers and other hand tools for exploring and excavating on a limited scale.
- Power drills for taking dust samples for further analysis.
- Plug top circuit tester for testing whether sockets are correctly wired.
- Thermometers for measuring air or surface temperatures.
- Whirling hygrometers for determining the relative humidity of the air.

5 Protection Equipment
- Face mask to reduce inhaling of dust.
- Goggles to protect eyes.
- Plastic gloves to handle toxic samples.
- Hard hat to wear in restricted areas.

3.7.2 Specialised Equipment

Specialised equipment would be needed where more accurate measurements and extensive opening up for observation and/or laboratory testing are required. Most of these items of equipment require trained personnel in their operation.

1 Damp Diagnosis
- Electrical resistance meters for measuring accurately within limited ranges the moisture content of timbers, plasters, stone, brick and concrete.
- A carbide moisture tester allows very accurate determination of moisture content in dust samples collected from walling materials.

2 Visual Inspection Probes
- Endoscopes, which are optical instruments with an integral light source for inspecting cavities and voids without extensive opening up.
- Borescopes come in a wide range of angles of views, lengths and diameters with several different attachments, including one for a camera.

3 Non-destructive Tests
- Cover meters to determine the location and sizing of reinforcement bars in concrete as well as giving guidance on cover to the steel.
- Ultrasonic pulse velocity meters for determining the quality of concrete, the presence of voids, cracks or other imperfections, and the assessment of concrete strength. The same equipment can also be used on metals and timbers.
- Half-cell potential meters for surveying reinforcement corrosion risk in concrete, based on the electrode potential of the steel.
- Rebound hammer for determining comparative surveys of surface hardness of concrete.
- Windsor probes for *in situ* strength measurement of concrete.
- Infra-red thermometers to record temperature variations within a building, for example, to detect leakages in heating systems as well as mapping delamination of wall finishes on building facades.
- Radar which measures the reflected signal of pulses fired into the concrete and is useful in detecting voids, reinforcement positions at larger depth and other defects which are associated with changes in the homogeneity of the concrete.

3.8 Sources of Information

The information needed in all diagnostic work should aim, first and foremost, to provide the surveyor or other investigator with relevant data relating to the actual materials and details that were used during construction, as well as the actual conditions to which the materials and the elements of which they form part have been exposed during and after construction.

The sources of information from which the data have to be collected can be wide and varied. For example, the information can be recorded, oral, from observation, published or from test results.

The main sources of information and the data they are likely to provide are as follows:

1 Drawings and Specifications
All drawings and specifications, including those produced by the consultants, specialists and sub-contractors, and used during the construction should provide data on the materials used and details of construction. But these documents do not necessarily include all the revisions made during construction.

2 Site Notes, Minutes and Reports
Apart from giving information on modifications made during construction, site notes, minutes and reports also give information regarding difficulties encountered during construction; the quality of workmanship achieved; and the precautions taken to protect the materials and the building subsequently from the weather.

3 Maintenance Records and Manuals
These documents contain reasonably accurate details of the construction, alterations and additions, maintenance, replacements and repairs. More importantly, the records should also contain materials used in cleaning and redecoration, and the history of all defects in the building.

4 Interviews
Interviews conducted by the surveyor or other investigator with any party connected with the design, construction, maintenance and use of the building can provide valuable information on a number of aspects associated with a defect. But such information should be treated with some caution because the party providing the information may not always be impartial.

5 Inspection

Inspection of the defect obviously provides the most important information, for it is during this process that the investigator uses his keen sense of observation, making use of sight, hearing, smell or touch. The observations made during the inspection usually have to be compared with other data collected by other means.

6 Published Information and Research Reports

There is a wealth of information available from many institutions noted for their research work. These organisations include both publicly and privately funded ones, for example, universities, polytechnics and trade associations.

7 Test Results

Tests and measurements of properties of materials may include moisture determination, chemical analyses of the composition of samples, and physical analyses related to structural properties and resistance to water or frost. Other readings taken on the site that may assist the surveyor in his diagnosis of the defect may be those of temperature of air or surfaces, relative humidity of the air, rate of ventilation and movement of cracks.

3.9 Reports

A report is a written document produced after some investigations to meet the client's requirements. The methods employed in the preparation of the report will depend considerably on the surveyor's own knowledge and experience. But there are a few points to note in writing a technical report.

First, the report must be simple, clear and concise. At the same time it must be technically accurate. The report should also be presented in a logical way and be written in a style that maintains continuity and is easy to follow.

A comprehensive report usually comprises the following parts:

- Title.
- Details of location of building or structure, type and use, client's name and name of engineer or surveyor and/or the firm engaged.
- Synopsis, which is a brief summary of the important information presented in the report.
- List of contents.
- Introduction, containing the history and subject matter of the report, the brief, and scope and limits of the work.

- Body, usually includes the background and history of the structure, details of inspections carried out, results and calculations, and all details of repairs.
- Conclusions, based on firm, reasoned judgements reached after careful evaluation of all the information obtained.
- Recommendations should tally with the rest of the report and usually include proposals for remedial work, regular maintenance inspections or inspections to detect further deterioration.

3.10 Recommending Remedies

Making creditable recommendations is a very difficult task as there are many alternative materials and techniques used in repair work. The client should be made aware of the cost implications, not only in terms of capital outlay but also the future maintenance costs. Very often the latter is overlooked in order to minimise the cost of repair.

The remedial work often chosen may belong to one of three general categories:

1 Patching Up
This recommendation is very often accepted because of apparent lower costs. But it should always be regarded as a temporary measure and employed only where the building has a limited functional or economic life and when more extensive rehabilitation or improvement works are planned in the near future.

2 Replacement of Parts
This should be the first consideration to give a permanent repair. However, the lack of suitable compatible materials, high costs or other difficulties may give rise to problems to make this recommendation unattractive. Sometimes there is no other alternative but to use this method in spite of the difficulties. For example, preserving the character and appearance of older buildings provides some incentives to carry out replacement of certain parts using limited resources of skilled operatives.

3 Complete Renewal
This last recourse is the most economic solution for buildings with a longer life, and the process can either involve removing existing parts for the entire area or providing a complete coverage over existing areas depending on adequate fixing facilities being possible.

In any one of these alternative courses of action, the faults need to be properly corrected to prevent a repetition of the same defects and only materials, components and techniques which are well tried and tested should be used.

Related and Further Reading

Addleson, L. *Building Failures: A Guide to Diagnosis, Remedy and Prevention.* Butterworth Architecture, London (1989).

Bowyer, J. *Guide to Domestic Building Surveys.* Architectural Press, London (1979).

Briffet, C. Structural failures – survey techniques and report procedures. *Proceedings of International Conference on 'Structural Failures'*, Singapore (1987).

Building Research Establishment, UK. *Assessment of Damage in Low-rise Buildings.* Digest 251 (1981).

Building Research Establishment, UK. *Simple Measuring and Monitoring of Movement in Low-rise Buildings Part 2: Settlement, Heave and Out-of-plumb.* Digest 344 (May, 1989).

Building Research Establishment, UK. *Why do Buildings Crack?* Digest 361 (May, 1991).

Building Research Establishment, UK. *Structural Appraisal of Existing Buildings for Change of Use.* Digest 366 (October, 1991).

Chappell, D. *Report Writing for Architects.* Butterworth Architecture, London (1984).

Construction Industry Development Board. *Building Diagnostics: A Guide to Non-destructive Testing Methods on Concrete.* Construction Industry Development Board, Singapore (1988).

Darbyshire, A. E. *Report Writing.* Edward Arnold, London (1970).

Gass, M. How to write better survey reports. *Chartered Surveyor* (October, 1981).

Hamilton, A. *Writing Matters.* Royal Institute of British Architects Publication (1988).

Hollis, M. and Gibson, C. *Surveying Buildings.* Surveyors Publications, London (1983).

Institution of Structural Engineers. *Appraisal of Existing Structures.* Institution of Structural Engineers, London (1980).

Melville, I. Surveys – perils, pitfalls and procedures. *Chartered Surveyor Weekly* (23 June 1983).

Mika, S. L. J. and Desch, S. C. *Structural Surveying.* Macmillan, London (1988).

Property Services Agency. *Defects in Buildings.* HMSO, London (1989).

Royal Institution of Chartered Surveyors, UK. *Guidance Note on 'Structural Surveys of Commercial and Industrial Property'* (1983).

Royal Institution of Chartered Surveyors, UK. *Practice Note on*

'Structural Surveys of Residential Property', 2nd edn (1985).

Seeley, I. H. *Building Surveys, Reports and Dilapidations.* Macmillan, London (1985).

Staveley, H. S. *Structural Surveys.* Chartered Institute of Building, UK, Maintenance Information Paper 15 (1981).

Staveley, H. S. and Glover, P. V. *Surveying Buildings.* Butterworth Architecture, London (1992).

4   Foundations

The most expensive building repair bills are often incurred with foundation failures. Where foundations are built on rock, there is very little chance of failure, provided that the rock is sound and solid. But because most buildings have to be built on other soils, which include materials of various origins, some movement and settlement must be expected.

The soil which supports the foundation is bound to be disturbed when the foundation trenches are dug and compacted, together with the increased loading due to the construction of the building. Other causes of movement and settlement may arise from trees, vibrations and chemical attack of the foundation concrete.

4.1 Movement of Soil

It is obvious that a building and its foundations interact with the supporting soil. The behaviour of any one depends on and influences that of the others. Thus, a good foundation design must take into consideration not only the type of structure to be supported but also the soil conditions.

4.1.1 Shrinking and Swelling of Clay Soil

Clays contain very fine particles which can hold a large amount of water. The water films between the particles are responsible for the characteristic stickiness which binds them together.

When water is removed from clay, the solid particles move appreciably together. Clay, therefore, shrinks when it is dried and this shrinkage is accompanied by an increase in its strength. Conversely, when clay absorbs water, the films thicken and the soil swells and loses its strength.

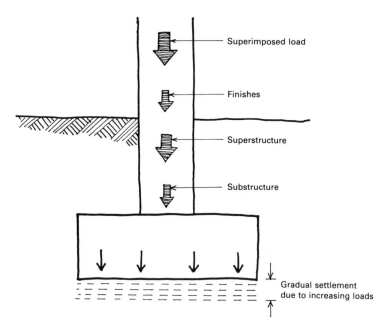

Figure 4.1   Settlement caused by consolidation of soil

Movements associated with shrinking and swelling are not found in sands because of the negligible amounts of water held between the larger particles. Soils of intermediate particle size, such as silts, have properties intermediate between those of sand and clay.

4.1.2 Consolidation of Sandy Soil

Any increase in the external pressure on a soil, for example, that imposed by a load, increases both the water and soil pressures. There is a tendency for water to be squeezed from between the solid particles and driven to other areas where the water pressure is less, while the soil particles are forced into closer contact with each other. As the soil is compressed, so the foundation settles (see figure 4.1).

This process of consolidation will continue until the water pressure falls to its original value and the forces between the soil particles have increased by an amount equal to the newly applied load.

Consolidation tends to be completed very quickly in the case of sands, once the load is applied, because the pore spaces are large. Clays, however, offer considerable resistance to the expulsion of water.

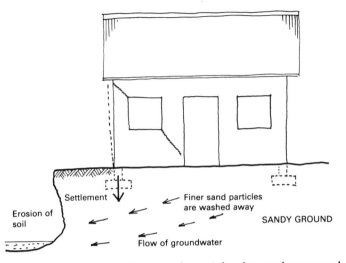

Figure 4.2   Washing out of fine sand particles by underground water

4.1.3 Organic Matter in Made-up Ground

Peats and other soils which contain a high proportion of organic substances from decaying vegetation vary greatly in volume as their water content changes. These soils are highly compressible so that they can even settle readily under their own weight. Made-up ground is an example of this type of soil.

The bearing capacities of sites filled by refuse and other similar materials are poor; they should not be used for construction purposes unless deep foundations passing through the fill can be designed and provided economically.

4.1.4 Loss of Ground in Sandy Soils

Dense beds of sands usually provide sound bases for foundations, but sometimes water can wash out the finer particles, leaving the coarser material in a less stable state (see figure 4.2). This happens, for example, when fine sands and silts are affected by water flowing underground from a higher ground nearby. Much of the bearing capacity of the sand may be lost in such circumstances.

4.1.5 'Swallow Holes' in Limestones

In chalk or limestone districts, cavities in the bed-rock can form by the action of subterranean streams dissolving the rock away. When the

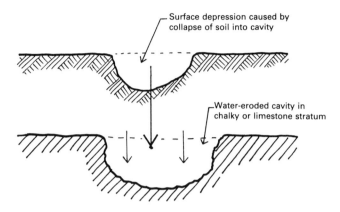

Figure 4.3   Formation of a 'swallow hole' in limestone

overburden collapses into a cavity, a 'swallow hole' is formed at the surface, causing serious damage to buildings above or near to the site (see figure 4.3).

4.2 Movement Due to Loading

Overloading of foundations can be caused by a number of different circumstances. The extent of the movement depends on the nature of the soil and the imposed loads.

It is possible that overloading may have originated from a faulty design which is inadequate to support the loads. Overloading may also arise when some alteration to the original design was made after the building was constructed. For example, the enlargement of a window or door opening can lead to a redistribution of the load to an adjacent section of the wall, resulting in increased stress on a part of the foundation.

Another cause of overloading is due to the building being used for a different purpose than that for which it was designed. For example, a dwelling house may be used as an office with heavy filing cabinets and other office equipment.

4.3 Other Causes of Movements

4.3.1 Effects of Vegetation

The extraction of moisture by tree roots in shrinkable clay will cause the soil to shrink. If this shrinkage takes place under the foundation,

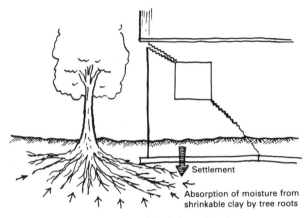

a. *Typical crack pattern caused by drying action of tree roots*

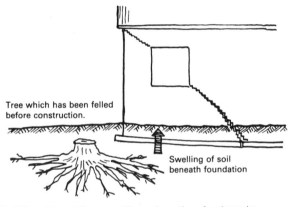

b. *Lifting of foundation caused by re-absorption of moisture by clay below foundation*

Figure 4.4   Effects of vegetation on foundations

there is a tendency for it to settle, thus affecting the stability of the building (see figure 4.4).

On the other hand, clay soil dried by the action of roots of trees which have been felled will tend to absorb moisture and swell, thus lifting the foundation of the building: a phenomenon commonly known as ground heave.

There are several ways of preventing penetration of new tree roots under a building apart from the obvious method of cutting down and poisoning the tree. One of these measures involves installing a physical barrier between the tree and the building using, for example, sheet steel or concrete.

4.3.2 Slopes and Excavations

Changes in pore water pressure can affect the stability of sloping ground. Such changes occur rapidly in granular soils.

The build-up of water pressure in the soil can happen in two distinct ways. The first and more obvious way is by inadequate provision or blockage of drains, for example, behind a retaining wall. The less obvious manner in which pore water pressure can increase is through the dissipation of negative pore water pressure, for example, that caused by excavations.

For clay soil to swell and lose strength, it requires an increase in moisture content. Freshly dug clay soil can stand without collapsing for quite some time because suction pressures are generated. But for a longer period of time and with an adequate supply of water, these negative pressures will dissipate, resulting in loss of strength. In this way, an apparently stable slope may become unstable (see figure 4.5).

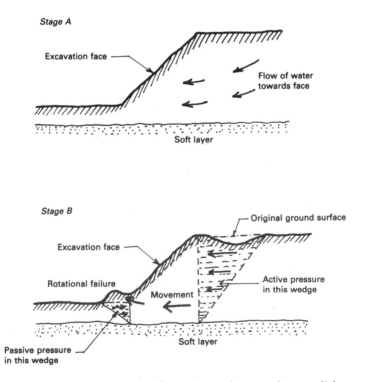

Figure 4.5 Stages in the formation of a translatory slide

4.3.3 Vibrations and Sudden Shocks

Vibrations may be caused by traffic or machinery. If the vibrations are prolonged and intense, they can affect the foundations of older buildings and structures by causing them to settle gradually. With modern construction, the problem is controlled because the foundations are designed to withstand ordinary vibrations.

An explosion can generate sudden shocks which can affect the stability of the building structure and ground support. The effects, however, may not be visible until some time later. For this reason, any building near to a site affected by an explosion should have its foundations carefully checked.

Various types of construction plant and equipment can also cause damage to the foundations of adjacent buildings and structures. For example, shock waves produced by pile driving can cause foundation movements, particularly if the building or structure is very old. For this reason, special care should be taken when condition surveys of neighbouring buildings and structures are carried out close to new developments.

4.3.4 Mining Subsidence

Buildings built above mine tunnels can suffer deformation as the ground subsides over the workings. Initially, when the tunnels are bored, the buildings tend to tilt. Subsequently, the tilt decreases but the settlement increases as the ground below it is affected.

The apparent signs of defects include random cracks on walls, sagging of arches and beams, and fracture of pipe joints. If the damage is not very severe, the building will gradually return to its vertical position, albeit at a lower level.

The general principles recommended for construction in districts vulnerable to subsidence caused by mining activities include the following:

- Structures should be completely rigid or completely flexible; simply supported spans and flexible superstructures should be used wherever possible.
- A shallow raft foundation is the best defence against tension or compression strains in the ground surface.
- Large structures should be divided into smaller independent units.
- Small buildings should be kept separate from one another; linkage should be avoided.

A technique that has been successfully used in Germany and The Netherlands provides for an articulated foundation to support a rigid superstructure. The foundation consists of three piers or pads with the superstructure constructed on columns resting on spherical bearings on the pads. In this way, the foundations are always kept in the same plane although they may tilt with the passing of each subsidence wave.

Another method uses patented jacking systems that incorporate several hydraulic jacks under the walls or columns. These jacks are connected to a central control system which automatically adjusts them individually as settlement takes place.

4.4 Differential Settlement

When settlement is uniform over the whole area of the building, it is very unlikely to cause any damage to the superstructure. Damage is usually the result of what is known as 'differential settlement' in which one side of a building subsides more than another, leading to cracks and stresses in the superstructure.

Wherever possible, differential settlement should be avoided by good design. For instance, in certain types of soil, such as shrinkable clays, it is better to use a more expensive raft foundation rather than an ordinary strip foundation because the former behaves as a whole foundation in resisting stresses.

The best form of foundation to resist ground movement is one that is sufficiently deep to penetrate below the zone where volume changes take place so that the building effectively rests on a more solid and stable formation. This is achieved by either driving piles into the ground or boring out a hole to the formation level and casting the piles in place. When there are signs, such as severe cracking or differential settlement of the foundations, the first step must be to identify the cause so that the likelihood of further settlement can be ascertained.

4.4.1 Effects of Differential Settlement

There are two main ways in which differential settlement can affect a building, namely (see figure 4.6):

- If the ends of a wall settle while the central part remains at its original level due to lighter loading or a stronger underlying soil, the cracks are wider at the top.
- If the central portion settles relative to the ends, the cracks are narrower at the top.

Buildings with additions are more likely to suffer damage from differential settlement than simple structures because the loading in the added part will probably be different, the type of construction may be

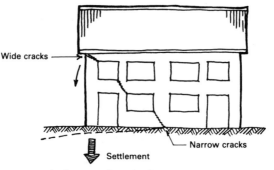

a. *Settlement at the ends of a wall*

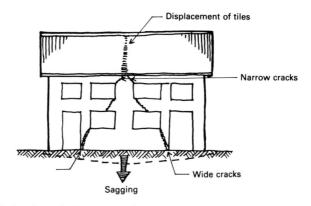

b. *Sagging under the centre section*

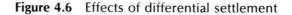

Figure 4.6   Effects of differential settlement

different or the foundations may have been taken down to a different level (see figure 4.7). It is also possible that the foundations of the main building may have been damaged during the construction of the addition. Although the bonding of new brickwork to the existing may help, it is not sufficient to resist any substantial stresses set up by differential settlement.

4.4.2 Types of Movement

The recording of variations in crack sizes over the length of the crack helps to reveal the part of the building which has moved and the part which is stable.

Rotation is usually the result of differential settlement. Horizontal movement on its own may be due to slippage on a sloping site. With a trench-filled concrete strip foundation, horizontal movement or out-

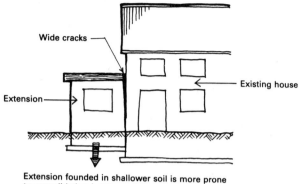

Extension founded in shallower soil is more prone
to consolidation (settlement) than the main structure

Figure 4.7 Effects of a new extension adjoining existing house

ward movement may have resulted from differential pressures being
set up by the shrinkage of clays to one side of the foundation. Pressure
on the other side, possibly due to expansion caused by variations in
ground moisture content, will result in horizontal movement (see
figure 4.8).

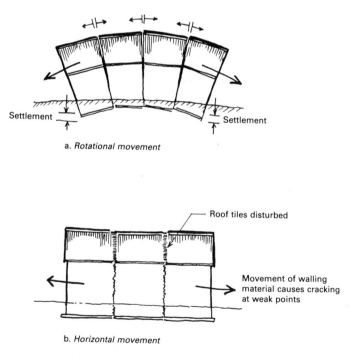

a. *Rotational movement*

b. *Horizontal movement*

Figure 4.8 Types of movement

4.5 Assessment of Foundation Defects

The first stage of any assessment of existing foundations involves identifying the overall form of the superstructure, the substructure, as well as the soil, and then determining how well they behave in combination.

While the superstructure can usually be examined quite easily, trial pits are generally needed in order to determine the condition of the foundations. According to BS 5930, the investigation should follow these guidelines:

- Visual inspection of the building and adjacent buildings, taking note of any cracking and distortion.
- Examination of old building and local plans.
- Examination of the geology, topography and water level records of the area, including nearby trees.
- Exposure of the substructure and foundations, often by trial pits and boreholes to assess the ground conditions.

4.5.1 Reporting Damage

BRE Digest 251 recommends the following procedure for assessment of damage in low-rise buildings:

- On a sketch of each damaged wall, draw the position and direction of any cracks. Distinguish, where possible, between tensile cracks, compressive cracks and shear cracks.
- Determine the approximate age of the cracks by interviewing the occupants.
- Where possible, measure or estimate the magnitude of any distortion or movement of the building, for example, tilting and bulging of walls or sloping floors.
- Report any impediments to the serviceability of the building, for example, jammed doors and windows.
- Report condition of the walls and finishes.
- Record details of the construction because this can have a very significant effect both on the degree and location of structural cracking.
- If foundation movement is suspected, additional factors must be considered.

4.5.2 Damage Classification

BRE Digest gives further guidelines for the classification of damage resulting from foundation failures (see table 4.1) as follows:

Class 1 Failures which affect only the *aesthetic* appearance of the building.

Class 2 Failures and cracks which affect the *serviceability* of certain parts of the building and which result in fracturing of service pipes, jamming of doors and windows, and breakdown of services in the building.

Class 3 Failures which affect the *stability* of the building and require extensive repairs to foundations.

The classification is extended by reference to a scale of 0 to 5 based on the ease with which repairs can be carried out. For example, categories 0 and 1 relate to minor damage in the form of hairline fractures of less than 1 mm in width and can often be easily camouflaged by normal redecoration.

Categories 2 and 3 embrace fractures visible from the exterior of the building which can be easily filled and dealt with during redecoration.

Categories 4 and 5 refer to more serious fractures over 15 mm in width. Such cracks can only be repaired by extensive and expensive methods, often involving stabilising the foundations.

Table 4.1   Classification of visible damage to walls with particular reference to ease of repair of plaster and brickwork or masonry (Source: BRE Digest 251: Assessment of Damage in Low-rise Buildings: with Particular Reference to Progressive Foundation Movement, HMSO, London, 1990)

Category (degree) of damage	Description of typical damage (Ease of repair in italic type)	Approximate crack width (mm)
0 (Negligible)	Hairline cracks of less than about 0.1 mm width are classed as negligible	Up to 0.1 [1]
1 (Very slight)	*Fine cracks which can easily be treated during normal decoration.* Perhaps isolated slight fracturing in building. Cracks rarely visible in external brickwork	Up to 1 [1]
2 (Slight)	*Cracks easily filled. Re-decoration probably required. Recurrent cracks can be masked by suitable linings.* Cracks not necessarily visible externally; *some external repointing*	Up to 5 [1]

continued on p. 56

Table 4.1   continued

Category (degree) of damage	Description of typical damage (Ease of repair in italic type)	Approximate crack width (mm)
	may be required to ensure weathertightness. Doors and windows may stick slightly	
3 (Moderate)	*The cracks require some opening up and can be patched by a mason. Repointing of external brickwork and possibly a small amount of brickwork to be replaced.* Doors and windows sticking. Service pipes may fracture. Weathertightness often impaired	5 to 15[1] (or number of cracks up to 3)
4 (Severe)	*Extensive repair work involving breaking-out and replacing sections of walls, especially over doors and windows.* Window and door frames distorted, floor sloping noticeably[2]. Walls leaning[2] or bulging noticeably, some loss of bearing in beams. Service pipes disrupted	15 to 25[1] but also depends on number of cracks
5 (Very severe)	*This requires a major repair job involving partial or complete re-building.* Beams lose bearing, walls lean badly and require shoring. Windows broken with distortion. Danger of instability	Usually greater than 25[1] but depends on number of cracks

Notes: 1. Crack width is one factor in assessing category of damage and should not be used on its own as direct measure of it.
2. Local deviation of slope, from the horizontal or vertical, of more than 1/100, will normally be clearly visible. Overall deviations in excess of 1/150 are undesirable.

4.5.3 Foundation Depth

It is important to investigate the depth of foundations of pre-1940s houses for it is not uncommon to find that apparently well-constructed houses have foundations no deeper than 400–500 mm. Investigations are particularly important if there are plans to add to the existing structure, for such shallow foundations would not be permitted under current regulations. The difference in levels between old and new foundations can increase differential movement, particularly in shrinkable clays.

4.5.4 Recognition of Damage by Tree Roots

In investigating damage caused by tree roots, it is essential to establish whether the soil is shrinkable clay. Although it is possible to rely on a geological map, the precise nature of the soil under the foundations must also be determined from excavations right down to the bottom of the foundations. This information will establish whether the foundations are in firm ground and not in any other soil of inadequate load-bearing capacity.

Where the foundations are exposed, it is essential to collect and identify any roots present under the foundations. Usually quite extensive excavations are required to ensure that representative samples are collected.

4.5.5 Recording of Cracks

The survey of the building which has been affected should include not only the sizing and location of the fractures but also a careful measurement of the variation in the level of the damp-proof course all the way around the building. This would indicate any variations in levels which could have resulted from ground movement or foundation failure.

Such a survey would have recorded any variations in the verticality of the external wall of the building. Once these variations have been plotted, the location and points of movement will be more clearly ascertained. If this information reveals that there is a problem, further investigation should be initiated to determine the type of construction originally used. A proper drawing prepared from the available information will give a picture of the type of failure (see figure 4.9).

4.5.6 Monitoring of Crack Movement

'Tell-tales' are normally installed to the exterior and interior of the building to monitor crack movements. The tell-tales should be of the type which record progressive movements and not merely indicate whether there is any movement. Care should be taken that the tell-tales are not damaged accidentally or wilfully.

One common type of tell-tales used for such purposes consists of metallic studs which are securely positioned on both sides of the crack. It is important that measurements are taken and checked consist-

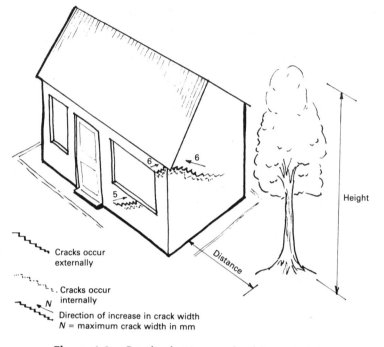

Cracks occur
externally

Cracks occur
internally

Direction of increase in crack width
N = maximum crack width in mm

Figure 4.9   Crack plotting on building sketch

ently from the same reference points on the studs. Crack monitoring
is a long and tedious process: it may take more than a year before a
report can be finalised.

4.5.7 Further Investigation

In some cases, it may be found that the cause of damage is related to
material shrinkage, decay or differential thermal movements. Such
failures very seldom exceed the damage categories of 0, 1 and 2.
However, if the failures are associated with ground movements, settlement, foundation failures, chemical attack on concrete or overloading,
the result could come within any of the categories in table 4.1.

Where failures exceed category 2, it is probable that they have been
the result of progressive ground movement. The investigator would
need to find the answers to these questions: Is the damage due to a
foundation fault or ground movement, and will the damage get progressively worse?

The investigation may require the excavation of trial holes to expose
the foundations, as well as the drilling of boreholes as close to the
foundations as possible.

If it is believed that the failures are attributed to foundation movement, it becomes necessary to determine the stability of the foundations.

Floor slabs may fail because of movement caused by poorly compacted hardcore. Such damage is usually confined to the slab at its junction with the external walls and with internal partitions carried on the slab. This type of problem usually occurs quite early after construction.

Chemical attack by sulphates can also cause failures. But such damage is rare in residential buildings because their foundations are usually sited above groundwater level. On sloping sites, instability of the ground is frequently seen in the form of fractures on roads, garden walls and services.

Where the building is near existing trees, the type of trees should be examined so that one can have a reasonable chance of assessing the likelihood of progressive movement. If the trees have reached or are close to maturity, minor shrinkage and swelling movements can be expected. Larger movements are only likely to occur in exceptional spells of dry weather.

4.6 Foundation Repairs

The technique of underpinning, whereby a new foundation is constructed beneath an old foundation or a new foundation is formed at a lower level to take the place of an old one, which has to be removed for some reason, has long been an established method of dealing with foundation problems. It is also necessary in cases where new buildings with foundations at a lower level are to be erected adjacent to old buildings.

Underpinning may be necessary for any of the following reasons:

- When there is excessive settlement of the existing foundation arising from uneven loading, action of tree roots, upheaval of soil or other causes.
- To permit the existing level of adjacent ground to be lowered, for example, where a new basement at a lower level is to be constructed.
- To increase the load-bearing capacity of the existing foundation.

In all cases it is necessary to consider two important factors before any work is carried out. Firstly, the loads supported by the old foundation must be temporarily relieved during the whole operation. Secondly, the work should be done in such a way that, once completed, the new foundation can support the whole load without any appreciable settlement in itself.

4.6.1 Preliminary Work

Before any underpinning work is to commence, some preliminary activities are necessary to ensure that a systematic, complete and effective repair system can be used. The preliminary activities include:

- Notifying adjoining owners of the proposed work, including all details of temporary supports to the existing structure.
- Carrying out a detailed survey of the site, the building to be underpinned and the adjacent structures or buildings to determine the reasons for the settlement, the depth of suitable load-bearing subsoils, and defects and structural weaknesses of these structures or buildings.
- Fixing glass slips or other 'tell-tales' across any vertical and lateral cracks so that any further movement affecting the cracks can be monitored.
- Periodic checking for any possible movement by taking readings of plumb bobs and levels.
- Reducing the loading on the structure as much as possible.
- Providing temporary supports by adequately shoring and strutting of openings in the structure or building.

4.6.2 Selection of Underpinning Method

The final choice of the most suitable underpinning method to be used depends on a number of factors which must be carefully evaluated and considered before a decision is made by the engineer. These factors are:

- Condition of existing structure or building to be underpinned, for example, poor condition of brickwork or masonry; effects of settlement which may be accentuated during the course of the repair; and in very old or badly damaged buildings or structures, strengthening by grouting up cracks and loose rubble masonry or tying in walls with tie rods or prestressing cables may be required.
- Building loads involved which will affect the complexity of the underpinning technique to be used.
- Depth to new bearing which depends on the level of suitable load-bearing subsoil available for the new foundation.
- Freedom to work, for example, in highly built-up areas, clearly certain methods which cause vibration and interruption of activities and services may not be suitable.
- The level of adjacent ground to be lowered.

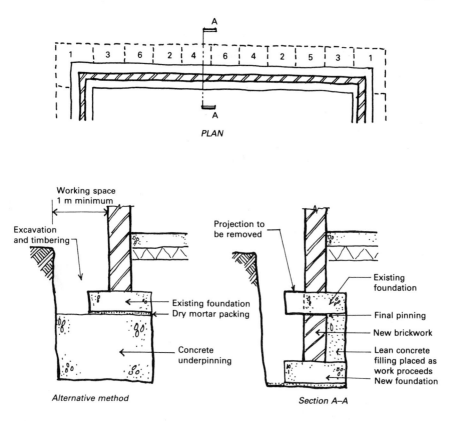

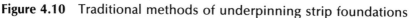

Figure 4.10 Traditional methods of underpinning strip foundations

4.7 Methods of Underpinning Strip Foundations

4.7.1 Traditional Underpinning

Traditional underpinning to walls (see figure 4.10) is carried out by excavating in stages alongside and underneath the existing foundation, casting a new foundation, building up to the underside of the existing foundation in brickwork or concrete, and finally pinning between the old and new work with a rich dry mortar. This method is not, however, used extensively nowadays.

The work should be carried out in sections in such a sequence that the unsupported lengths of existing foundation over excavated sections are equally distributed along the length of the wall being underpinned.

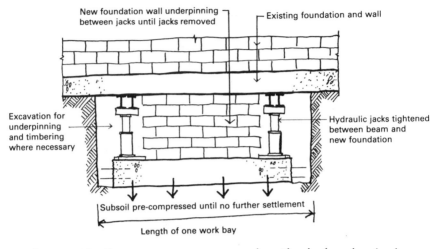

New foundation wall underpinning between jacks until jacks removed

Existing foundation and wall

Excavation for underpinning and timbering where necessary

Hydraulic jacks tightened between beam and new foundation

Subsoil pre-compressed until no further settlement

Length of one work bay

Figure 4.11   Pretest or precompressed method of underpinning

To prevent fracture of the existing foundation, damage and settlement of the walls, work should always be carried out in short lengths. The total length of unsupported walls should not be greater than 25 per cent of the total wall length. Generally, each bay length is about 1.500 m.

In this process, each bay is excavated and timbered or otherwise supported as necessary, after which the bottom of the excavation is prepared to receive the new foundation. To give the new foundation strip continuity, dowel bars are inserted at the end of each bay. Brick underpinning is toothed at each end to enable the bonding to be continuous.

4.7.2 Pretest Method

This method follows all the steps of the traditional method but requires an additional operation after the new concrete foundation has been laid (see figure 4.11). A hydraulic jack supporting a short beam is placed in the centre of the section under the existing foundation. The jack is then extended to give a predetermined load on the new foundation, thus pretesting the soil beneath.

This process is repeated along the entire underpinning length until the whole wall is being supported by the hydraulic jacks. Underpinning is then carried out using brickwork or concrete walling between the jacks which are later removed and replaced with underpinning to complete the whole operation.

The required jacking loads should be carefully calculated, due al-

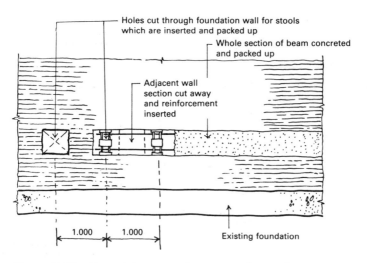

Holes cut through foundation wall for stools
which are inserted and packed up

Whole section of beam concreted
and packed up

Adjacent wall
section cut away
and reinforcement
inserted

1.000   1.000

Existing foundation

Figure 4.12   Proprietary stools system for underpinning

lowance being made for the number of sections which are open at any
one time. It may be necessary to adjust the jacking loads as the work
proceeds, and extensometers or strain gauges should be used as an
accurate means of controlling the jacking operations.

4.7.3 Pynford Stools Method

When the superstructure and its foundation are in a weak condition,
continuous beam support to the wall may be essential.

The procedure (see figure 4.12) is to cut away portions of brickwork
above the existing foundation to enable precast concrete or steel
stools to be inserted and pinned. The intervening brickwork can then
be removed, leaving the structure entirely supported on the stools.
Reinforcing bars are threaded between and around the stools and
caged to form the ring beam reinforcement. After the formwork has
been placed and the beam cast, final pinning can be carried out using a
well-rammed dry mortar mix.

This technique has the advantage of simplicity and economy in the
amount of work involved.

4.7.4 Jacked Pile Underpinning

When the load has to be transferred to a greater depth in order to
reach a suitable subsoil of adequate bearing capacity, the technique of
jacked pile underpinning may be used economically and effectively
(see figure 4.13). The technique is quiet, vibration-free and flexible

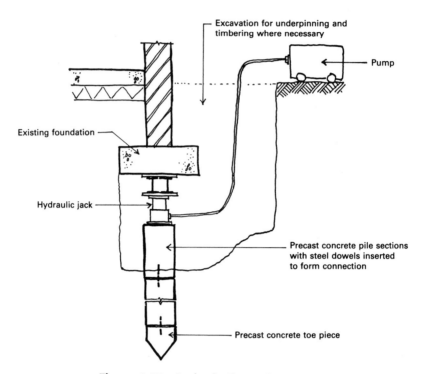

Figure 4.13   Jacked pile underpinning

because the pile depth can be adjusted to suit subsoil conditions encountered.

The method uses short precast concrete pile lengths jacked into the ground until a suitable subsoil is reached. When the pile has reached the required depth, the space between the top of the pile and the underside of the existing foundation is filled with a pinned concrete cap.

The existing foundation must be in a good condition because it has to act as a beam spanning over the piles when the whole work is completed.

In installing jacked piles, it is normal practice to work to a safety factor of 1.5, that is, the jacking force is equal to one and a half times the calculated working load.

4.7.5 Needle and Piles

The arrangement of needles (beams) and piles depends on many factors, including the state of the structure and the necessity or otherwise of avoiding disturbance to the use or contents of the building.

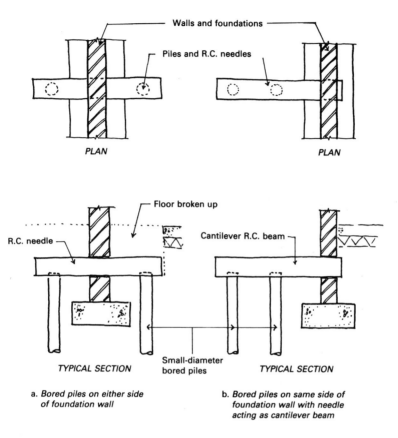

Figure 4.14 Needle and pile underpinning

The most straightforward method is probably to sink pairs of piles at intervals along the wall, one on either side, connected by a horizontal needle or beam passing through the wall just above or immediately below the foundation, whichever best suits the circumstances (see figure 4.14).

An alternative method which may sometimes be more suitable is to stagger the piles on each side of the wall. This has the effect of halving the number of piles required, although each will take a greater load, and of lengthening the beams.

These methods, because of the internal piles, necessitate work within the building being underpinned. Where this is not possible, groups of two or more piles along the outside of the building may be used to support the wall by means of cantilever capping beams projecting under the wall.

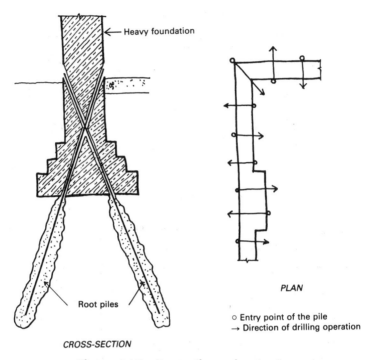

CROSS-SECTION

Figure 4.15   Root pile underpinning

4.7.6 Root Piles

The foundation reinforcement is formed by a double series of small-diameter piles, rotary drilled through existing masonry and taken to an adequate depth in the subsoil below (see figure 4.15).

When concreted, the piles are automatically bonded with the upper structure; there is no need for complementary connecting structures, risky cuts in the walls or disturbance to the building activities.

The construction of the piles, spaced along the foot of the walls, does not present any risk to the stability of the existing structures. No vibration is generated. The construction of the piles does not introduce any particular stress in the wall or soil: this is of vital importance in buildings, especially for ancient monuments, in which the conservation of the existing equilibrium is of paramount importance.

In principle, root piles can be considered practically inactive at the time of construction. If the building has a subsequent settlement, the piling responds immediately, absorbing part of the load and reducing at the same time the stress on the soil. If, despite this, the building continues to settle, the piles continue to take the load until, finally, the entire building load is supported by them.

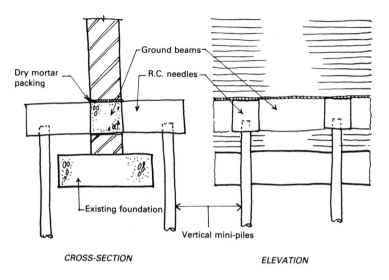

CROSS-SECTION   ELEVATION

Figure 4.16   Underpinning with vertical mini-piles and needle beams

4.7.7 Underpinning by Mini-piles

Mini-piles consist substantially of very heavy metal pipes which can bear considerably higher loads than root piles.

First, the drilling is carried out with any system suitable for the particular soil. Once the fixed depth is reached, a steel pipe and reinforcement are introduced. Cement and sand grout is then pumped in under pressure to fill the annular spaces as the pipe is extracted in order to form a bulb at the foot of the pile.

Where existing foundations are of adequate thickness and quality, walls can be underpinned by installing raking mini-piles through the footings. This is usually done by alternating the operation between the inside and outside of the building.

Raking piles should not be used if the foundations are too small or non-existent. It is better to install vertical piles on each side of the load-bearing walls and then to connect them by a reinforced concrete beam (see figure 4.16).

4.7.8 Ground Injection

Injection of the ground with cement or chemicals to fill voids or to permeate and strengthen the ground is sometimes used as a means of underpinning (see figure 4.17). Cement grouting is useful to fill voids in the ground beneath foundations which have been caused by erosion or by vibration effects in loose granular soils.

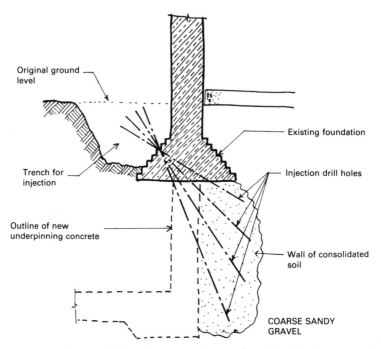

Figure 4.17   Ground injection to safeguard underpinning operation in coarse sandy gravel

Chemicals can be used for injection into coarse sands or sandy gravels to produce a wall or block of consolidated ground beneath the foundations to the desired level for underpinning. The process usually starts at ground level, thus avoiding the necessity of shoring, and the wall of the consolidated ground acts as a retaining wall when excavating is done close to the existing foundations.

4.8 Underpinning Pad Foundations or Column Bases

4.8.1 Temporary Support to Columns

In underpinning framed structures, the main problem is to provide satisfactory support to columns while they are being underpinned (see figure 4.18). Before underpinning, the columns must be relieved of their loads by dead shores erected under all beams bearing on them.

Reinforced concrete columns and brick piers can be supported by means of a horizontal yoke formed of two pairs of rolled steel beams positioned in chases on the sides of the columns. The lower pair should be strong enough to transfer the load to temporary support

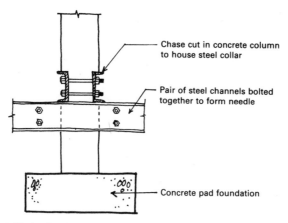

a. *Steel collars to concrete column*

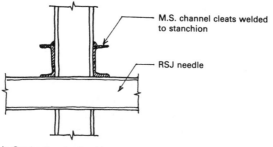

b. *Steel collars to stanchion*

Figure 4.18 Support to column prior to underpinning

while the upper pair are at right angles and bear on them. The pairs of beams are tied together by transverse tie rods or angles. Reinforced concrete collars may also be used in some cases instead of steel collars fabricated from channels.

Steel stanchions can be supported on steel needles by steel angle or channel cleats welded to the stanchion flanges and bearing on the needles.

4.8.2 Needle and Piles

The column loading is transferred from the collar to cross beams or needles which in turn transmit the loads to the ground at a safe distance from the proposed underpinning excavations. One end of the needle is usually made to rest on a concrete bearing pad on a firm

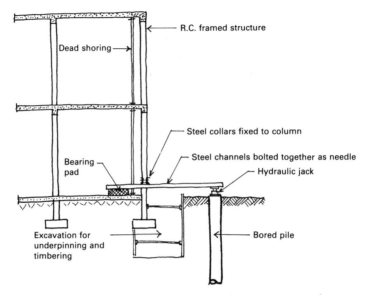

Figure 4.19   Pile and needle method of supporting column

support and the load is distributed to a safe bearing stratum with a hydraulic jack on a precast or bored pile (see figure 4.19).

Circumstances may make it impossible to provide support to the needles on two sides of a column or stanchion; in such cases a counterweighted cantilever support must then be used (see figure 4.20). This type of support is formed from a pair of long steel needles on a fulcrum support some distance away from the column. One end of the needles would be connected to the yoke, or cleats attached to the column, and the other would be held down by kentledge or tension piles. A hydraulic jack placed between the needles and the fulcrum support enables the latter to be precompressed and any settlement taken up to prevent movement of the column.

4.9 Underpinning Floors

Domestic floor slabs can settle owing to poorly compacted fill, or to the compression or shrinkage of natural soils. These settlements are shown by gaps between skirting boards and floor finishes and, in more severe cases, by cracks in internal partitions founded on the slab, damage to floor finishes or distortion of door frames. Therefore, circumstances may demand some treatment to the slab in order to stabilise the movements.

Before a settling floor slab is underpinned, any voids should be

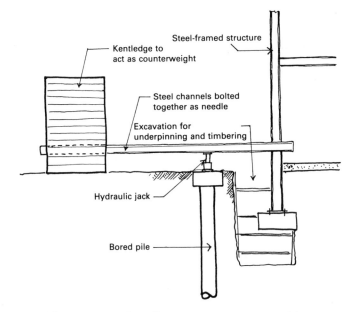

Steel-framed structure

Kentledge to
act as counterweight

Steel channels bolted
together as needle

Excavation for
underpinning and timbering

Hydraulic jack

Bored pile

Figure 4.20 Cantilever support to stanchions

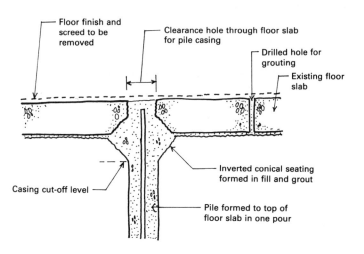

Floor finish and
screed to be
removed

Clearance hole through floor slab
for pile casing

Drilled hole for
grouting

Existing floor
slab

Casing cut-off level

Inverted conical seating
formed in fill and grout

Pile formed to top of
floor slab in one pour

Figure 4.21 Floor slab underpinning with mini-piles

grouted through holes at about 1.000 m spacing in the slab. Mini-piles
should normally be placed at centre-to-centre spacing not exceeding
1.500 m with maximum distances of 300 mm from slab edges. If pile
spacings are large or the slab thickness significantly less than 100 mm,

the permissible concrete stresses may be exceeded at slab–pile joints. In these cases, it may be necessary to break out the slab and replace it with a thicker one. Additional slab support should be provided by forming inverted conical cavities immediately beneath the slab at each pile position before the pile concrete is poured (see figure 4.21).

Related and Further Reading

Barnbrook, G. *House Foundations: for the Builder and Designer*. Cement and Concrete Association, UK (1981).

British Standards Institution. *CP 102: 1973 Protection of buildings against water from the ground*.

British Standards Institution. *BS 4027: 1980 Specification for sulphate-resisting Portland cement*.

British Standards Institution. *BS 8004: 1986 Code of Practice for foundations*.

Brown, R. W. *Design and Repair of Residential and Light Commercial Foundations*. McGraw-Hill, Maidenhead, UK (1990).

Building Research Establishment, UK. *Soils and Foundations: Part 2*. Digest 64 (1972).

Building Research Establishment, UK. *Soils and Foundations: Part 1*. Digest 63 (1979).

Building Research Establishment, UK. *Soils and Foundations: Part 3*. Digest 67 (1980).

Building Research Establishment, UK. *Low-rise Buildings on Shrinkable Clay Soils: Part 2*. Digest 241 (1980).

Building Research Establishment, UK. *Concrete in Sulphate-bearing Soils and Groundwaters*. Digest 250 (1984).

Building Research Establishment, UK. *The Influence of Trees on House Foundations in Clay Soils*. Digest 298 (1985).

Building Research Establishment, UK. *Mini-piling for Low-rise Buildings*. Digest 313 (1986).

Building Research Establishment, UK. *Simple Measuring and Monitoring of Movement in Low-rise Building Part 1: Cracks*. Digest 343 (April, 1989).

Building Research Establishment, UK. *Simple Measuring and Monitoring of Movement in Low-rise Building Part 2: Settlement, Heave and Out-of-plumb*. Digest 344 (May, 1989).

Building Research Establishment, UK. *Assessment of Damage in Low-rise Buildings*. Digest 251 (1990).

Building Research Establishment, UK. *Underpinning*. Digest 352 (June, 1990)

Chudley, R. *Construction Technology*, Volume 3. Longman, London (1988).

Grahame, K. G. Trees as a cause of foundation failure. *Building Technology and Management*, UK (August, 1973).

Hanna, T. H. Foundation failures: Causes, identification and prevention – an overview. *Proceedings of International Conference on Structural Failures*, Singapore (1987).

Harrison, D. The effect of soil shrinkage on buildings. *Construction Repair*, UK (September, 1980).

Hunt, R., Dyer, R. H. and Driscoll, R. *Foundation Movement and Remedial Underpinning in Low-rise Buildings*. Building Research Establishment, UK (1991).

Hutchinson, B. D., Barton, J. and Ellis, E. *Maintenance and Repair of Buildings and their Internal Environments*. Newnes-Butterworths, London (1975).

Hyde, S. A. Causes and effects of settlement. *Chartered Surveyor* (October, 1980).

Johnson, R. *Foundation Problems Associated with Low-rise Housing*. Technical Information Service No. 61, Chartered Institute of Building, UK (1986).

Mika, S. L. J. and Desch, S. C. *Structural Surveying*. Macmillan, London (1988).

Pryte, J. Underpinning. *Construction Repair*, UK (March, 1989).

Ransom, W. H. *Building Failures: Diagnosis and Avoidance*. Spon, London (1987).

Seeley, I. H. *Building Maintenance*, 2nd edn. Macmillan, London (1987).

Thorburn, S. and Hutchinson, J. F. *Underpinning*. Surrey University Press, London (1985).

Tomlinson, M. J. *Foundation Design and Construction*. Pitman, London (1980).

5 Concrete Defects

Traditionally, reinforced concrete has been considered as a highly durable structural material requiring little or no maintenance over many decades. In fact, it is this, together with its versatility, that makes concrete the most popular structural material in many parts of the world. But, like any other material, concrete is not completely inert to chemical action or immune from physical deterioration arising from climatic changes, abrasion, damage from high velocity water, fire, impact, explosion, foundation failure or overloading.

5.1 Durability of Concrete

A structure would be considered as durable if it fulfilled its intended duty for the whole of its design life with the least maintenance. It would be unrealistic to expect any structure to maintain its 'as new' condition without any maintenance.

All materials deteriorate: this is not a defect but rather an inherent characteristic. The total deterioration of a material can be expressed as a function of the environment, design, workmanship, material properties, and its use.

Concrete has the potential of an almost unlimited life, unless it is subjected to chemical attack by an aggressive environment or suffers some physical damage. Serious carbonation, chemical attack on the concrete, cracking and spalling due to poor-quality materials or workmanship, and/or corrosion of the reinforcement are all signs of distress that indicate a concrete of low durability (see figure 5.1).

Low durability may be caused either by the environment to which the concrete is exposed or by some internal causes within the concrete itself. The external causes can be physical, chemical or mechanical. For example, they may be due to weathering effects, occurrences of extreme temperatures, abrasion, electrolytic action, and attack by natural

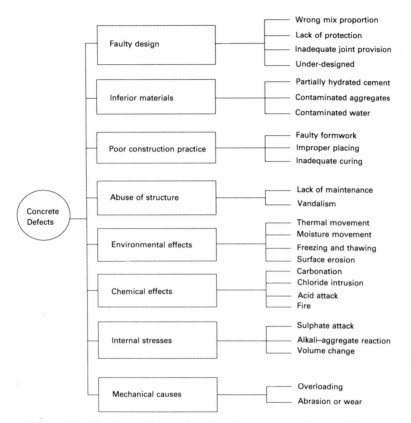

Figure 5.1 Factors adversely affecting concrete durability

or industrial liquids and gases. The extent of damage to the concrete produced by these agents depends largely on its quality.

The internal causes include alkali–aggregate reaction and volume changes, as well as the permeability of the concrete. The last cause determines the vulnerability of concrete to external agencies, so that in order to be durable, concrete must be relatively impervious.

5.2 Permeability of Concrete

Permeability determines the relative ease with which concrete can become saturated with water. A concrete of low permeability is generally more durable than one which is highly permeable.

The permeability of concrete is a function of its porosity as well as the size, distribution and continuity of the pores. Therefore, the cement gel has a low permeability because of the extremely fine texture of the hardened cement paste which contains numerous but very fine pores. In the case of rocks, the pores, though fewer in number, are much larger and lead to higher permeability.

Other factors contributing to the degree of permeability of concrete include the following:

- The quality of the cement: for the same water:cement ratio, coarse cement tends to produce a paste with a higher porosity than a finer cement.
- The permeability of the aggregate itself affects the behaviour of the concrete: if the aggregate has a low permeability, its presence reduces the effective area over which flow can take place.
- The quality and quantity of the cement paste: the quality of the cement paste depends on the amount of cement in the mix, the water:cement ratio and the degree of hydration of the cement. Permeability decreases rapidly with the progress of hydration and it is also lower if the cement content of the paste is increased.
- The degree of compaction of the concrete: a well-compacted concrete reduces the porosity and hence the permeability of the concrete.
- The standard of curing: permeability of steam-cured concrete is generally higher than that of wet-cured concrete.
- The characteristics of any admixtures used in the mix: air-entraining is expected to increase the permeability of concrete although it reduces segregation and bleeding, and improves workability.
- The presence of cracks allows direct entry of moisture.

5.3 Human Factors Causing Concrete Failures

5.3.1 Faulty Design

The effects of unsatisfactory design and/or detailing include poor appearance, inability to continue its function and catastrophic failure. These problems can be minimised only by a thorough understanding of structural behaviour in its broadest sense. Unfortunately, they often occur because of insufficient attention on the part of the designer.

Errors in design and detailing that may result in unacceptable cracking include improper selection and/or detailing of reinforcement, restraint of members subjected to volume changes caused by variations in temperature and moisture, lack of adequate contraction/expansion joints, and improper design of foundations, resulting in differential movement within the structure.

The use of inadequate reinforcement may result in excessive cracking of the concrete which may be unacceptable. On the other hand, honeycombing may occur because of the difficulty of compaction in an excessively reinforced structure.

The restraint of members subjected to volume changes results frequently in cracks. Stresses that occur in concrete due to restrained creep, temperature differentials and drying shrinkage can be many times more than those that occur due to loading. For example, a beam restrained against shortening, even if prestressed, can easily develop tensile stresses sufficient to cause cracking.

Poor foundation design may result in excessive differential movement within a structure. If the differential movement is relatively small, the cracking problems may be only visual. However, if there is a major differential settlement, the structure may not be able to redistribute the loads rapidly enough and a failure may occur.

5.3.2 Poor Construction Practices

A wide variety of poor construction practices can result in cracking in concrete structures. Foremost among these is the common practice of adding water to concrete to improve workability. Added water has the effect of reducing strength, increasing settlement and increasing ultimate shrinkage. When accompanied by a higher cement content to help offset the decrease in strength, an increase in water content will also mean an increase in the temperature differential between the interior and exterior portions of the structure, resulting in increased thermal stresses and possible cracking.

Other malpractices on the site include the following:

- Faulty formwork construction leading to grout leakage (see figure 5.2).
- Inadequate vibration, causing honeycombs.
- Misplacement of steel which reduces the specified concrete cover.
- Improper placing of concrete, such as dropping concrete from a great height to cause segregation.
- Lack of curing, causing incomplete hydration of cement.
- Poor construction joints.

All these malpractices can lead to a significant departure from the specification and hence considerable reduction in the durability of an otherwise well-designed structure.

It is essential, therefore, that site operatives are given clear unequivocal instructions concerning materials and standards of workmanship; adequate supplies of the correct materials are available on site when needed; and sufficient quality control is provided during the course of the construction.

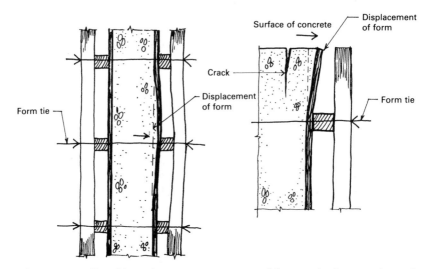

Figure 5.2   Cracking due to movement of forms during setting of concrete

5.3.3 Poor-quality Materials

The satisfactory functioning of a well-designed component can also be frustrated by the substitution of unsuitable materials when the specified materials are not immediately available (see table 5.1).

Reinforcement bars with loose rust and scale, rusty prestressing strands, aggregates with high salt or silt content, lumpy cement and polluted water used for mixing all result in poor quality concrete.

Even with good constituent materials, concrete mixed too long before use can cause difficulties in placing and compacting. Wrong proportioning of constituent materials, as for example, insufficient cement, high aggregate content or high water/cement ratio, could lead to inferior concrete.

5.3.4 Use of the Structure

Changes in the use of structures, such as buildings, warehouses and wharves, can lead to overloading. With the thrust on improved productivity and mechanisation involving the use of heavier equipment and cargo handling machinery, live and wheel loads have increased considerably over the years. These in turn contribute to greater impact and dynamic loading which are detrimental to the structures that were not designed and constructed for such purposes.

In particular, excessive loading beyond the elastic limit of concrete

Table 5.1   Causes of deterioration of concrete due to poor-quality materials

Component	Cause	Distress	Failure
Cement	Unsoundness	Volume expansion	Cracking
	Partially hydrated	Low strength	Premature failure
Aggregate	Alkali–silica reaction	Volume expansion	Cracking and disintegration
	High silt content	Poor bonding	Dusting of concrete surface
	Chloride salts	Corrosion of reinforcement	Spalling of concrete
Cement matrix	Plastic shrinkage	Bleeding of mix water	Surface cracking
	Drying shrinkage	Chemical and physical loss of water	Cracking
	Sulphate attack	Volume expansion	Cracking and disintegration
Steel reinforcement	Corrosion	Volume expansion	Spalling of concrete

may result in creep. For example, the development of micro-cracking and shortening of columns may create a chain-reaction effect that can spread to other structural members, causing ultimate collapse.

Other common defects in concrete as a result of overloading include spalling, cracking, flexural and shear fractures, and local disintegration.

5.4 Corrosion of Reinforcement

5.4.1 Mechanism of Attack

Corrosion of a metal is an electro-chemical process that requires an oxidising, moisture and electron flow within the metal. The attack

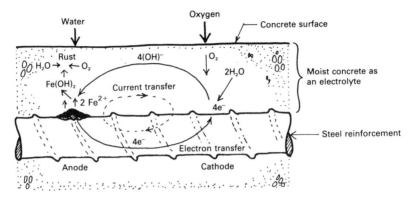

Figure 5.3   Simplified model of the corrosion process of steel
reinforcement in concrete

occurs with a series of chemical reactions taking place on and adjacent
to the surface of the metal (see figure 5.3).

At points on the surface (anodes), metal atoms lose electrons, forming ions that go into solution. At other points on the surface
(cathodes), oxygen and water combine with free electrons to form
hydroxyl ions. The hydroxyl ions move toward the anodes and combine with the metal ions to form hydrous metal oxides. In the case of
steel, iron oxide (rust) forms as a deposit at the anodes. On an individual piece of metal, there may be many anodes and cathodes, and
these sites may be adjacent or widely spread.

The electrical resistivity of concrete has the decisive influence on the
intensity of the corrosion current which is responsible for electro-
chemical action. For example, if the moisture content or chloride
content increases, the electrical resistivity of the concrete decreases
considerably.

5.4.2 Protection of Steel

When steel is embedded in concrete, the concrete cover provides a
mechanical barrier to the movement of water and oxygen to the steel.
This barrier is more or less effective depending on the quality of the
concrete, that is, its impermeability and the thickness of the cover.

When concrete sets, the calcium hydroxide or lime produced by
hydration goes into the pores of the set cement gel as a strong alkaline
solution with a high pH value between 12.5 and 13.5. This in turn forms
a very thin film of oxide on the surface of the reinforcing steel and
protects the latter against corrosion (see figure 5.4).

Reinforcement will not corrode so long as the high alkalinity in the
concrete is maintained. This phenomenon is generally known as pas-

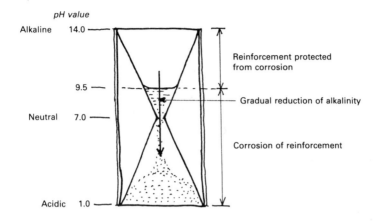

Figure 5.4 Relationship between risk of corrosion and alkalinity of concrete

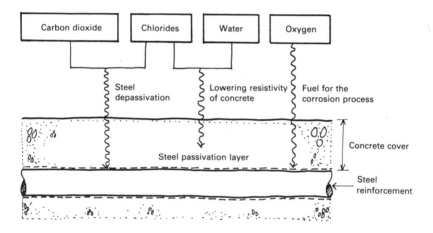

Figure 5.5 Critical environmental factors on corrosion of steel reinforcement

sivation of the steel by the alkaline concrete environment.

The corrosion reaction, however, can still proceed (see figure 5.5) when:

- Chloride or carbon dioxide penetrates through the concrete cover to the reinforcement and destroys the natural passivity provided by free lime in hydrated cement.
- Low concrete resistivity allows electrolytic cells to be established at the steel surface.
- Oxygen penetrates through the cover to fuel the corrosion process.

5.4.3 Carbonation

Carbonation is the effect of carbon dioxide in the air on cement products, mainly the hydroxides in the presence of moisture. The calcium hydroxide is converted to calcium carbonate by absorption of carbon dioxide; calcium carbonate is only slightly soluble in water and, therefore, when it is formed, it tends to seal the surface pores of the concrete.

As a result of the reaction, the layer of concrete close to the surface of the concrete becomes carbonated and this carbonated layer is not sufficiently alkaline (pH below 9) to protect reinforcing steel. Apart from the reaction between carbon dioxide and calcium hydroxide, the former also dissolves in any moisture present to form carbonic acid.

Carbonic acid is a weak electrolyte which allows the steel to be oxidised by the atmospheric oxygen and then reacts with water to form hydrated ferric oxide. The corrosion product occupies a much greater volume than the original metal from which it was formed and thus sets up bursting forces in the surrounding concrete (see figure 5.6).

The depth of carbonation is approximately proportional to the

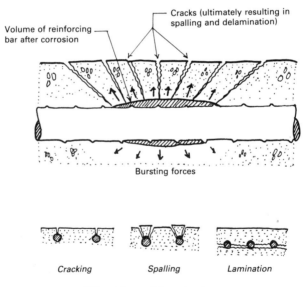

Different forms of Corrosion damage

Figure 5.6   Cracking and spalling of concrete caused by corrosion of the reinforcement

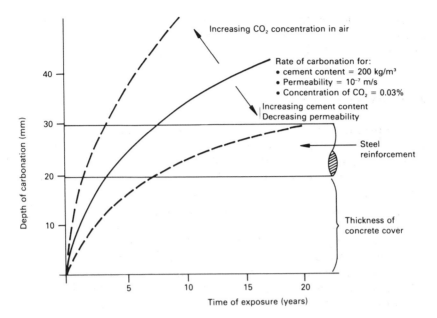

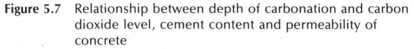

Figure 5.7 Relationship between depth of carbonation and carbon dioxide level, cement content and permeability of concrete

square root of time. The rate at which carbonation reaches the reinforcement is dependent on the following factors (see figure 5.7):

- Time: rate decreases with increasing time of exposure to air.
- Cover to reinforcement: the greater the cover, the better the protection afforded to the steel.
- Concentration of carbon dioxide in the atmosphere: rate increases with increasing carbon dioxide concentration in the air.
- Permeability of concrete: this depends on concrete quality; carbonation depth increases by four times when the water: cement ratio is increased from 0.4 to 0.8.
- Alkali content in the concrete: this depends on the cement content and the type of cement.
- Condition of concrete cover: any imperfections in the cover such as segregation, poor compaction or cracking enable carbonation to progress more rapidly.

Concrete of good quality usually carbonates very slowly; even after a period of 50 years, carbonation is unlikely to penetrate to a greater depth than 5–10 mm. On the other hand, a permeable concrete may carbonate to a depth of 25 mm in less than 10 years.

The best prevention against carbonation, therefore, is the use of good quality concrete which is impermeable with adequate cover to the reinforcing steel.

5.4.4 Chloride Intrusion

High concentrations of chloride ions in concrete (above 0.4 per cent by weight) can penetrate into and break down the protective film which forms on the reinforcement in an alkaline situation.

The consequent effects are to reduce the alkalinity of the concrete to pH 5, increase the flow of corrosion currents and penetrate the passivating iron oxide film on the steel surface. The surface of the steel then becomes activated locally and a small anode is formed, the passive surface providing the cathode. The anode is much smaller in area than the cathode and, as a result, the formation of the ferrous ions in the anode extends deeper and deeper, and a pit is formed (see figure 5.8).

The resultant expanded products cause cracking and spalling of the surrounding concrete which, in turn, promotes chloride intrusion and further corrosion.

Only soluble chlorides are involved in the corrosion process. They are, therefore, compounded where the concrete is porous and moist.

From the fresh concrete, the mix materials may be subjected to various degrees of contamination associated with chlorides derived from the aggregates, the water, de-icing salts in temperate countries or the use of calcium chloride as an accelerating agent in concrete. From external environments, the problem is aggravated in highly polluted areas. Also, the presence of cracks in the concrete structure will obviously increase the penetration of chlorides and hasten the corrosion of the reinforcement.

It should be noted that, in practice, it is possible to have both carbonation and chloride attack taking place simultaneously. The risk of corrosion in this case is very much dependent on the chloride ion content and the rate of carbonation (see figure 5.9).

5.5 Chemical Aggression

5.5.1 Sulphate Attack

Sulphates are present in soils, particularly in clays, sea-water, ground-water and industrial waste or from acid rain. Sulphate solution reacts with hydrated tricalcium aluminate to form calcium sulphoaluminate. The resulting crystallised products from the reaction cause an increase

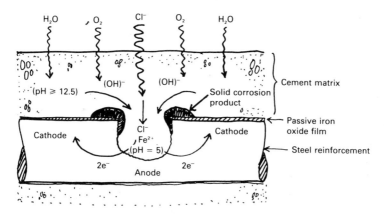

Figure 5.8 Pitting corrosion caused by chlorides

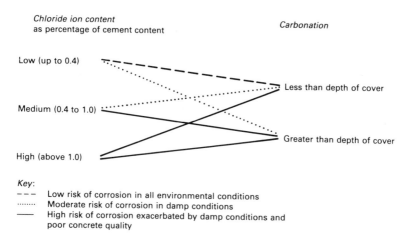

Figure 5.9 Risk of corrosion in relation to concrete analysis (Source: *The Durability of Steel in Concrete, Part 2: Diagnosis and Assessment of Corrosion-cracked Concrete*, BRE Digest 264, Building Research Establishment, UK, 1982)

in the volume of the hardened concrete and contribute to internal disruption or spalling of the surface. Concrete attacked by sulphates has a characteristic whitish appearance with progressive cracking and eventually the concrete may become soft and friable.

The intensity and rate of sulphate attack depend on a number of factors, the principal ones being:

- The percentage of tricalcium aluminate in the cement: rate of attack is faster when there is a higher amount of tricalcium aluminate.
- The permeability of the concrete: dense concrete with a low water: cement ratio increases the resistance of the concrete against sulphate attack.
- The solubility of the sulphates: sulphates of low solubility experience a slower rate of attack.
- Concentration of the solution: the rate of attack increases with an increase in the strength of the solution.
- The rate at which the sulphate removed by the reaction with cement can be replenished: concrete which is exposed to the pressure of sulphate-bearing water on one side experiences a higher rate of attack.

The vulnerability of concrete to sulphate attack can be reduced by the use of cement low in tricalcium aluminate, such as sulphate-resisting cement. Improved resistance is also obtained by replacing some of the cement with pozzolanas which tend to remove free calcium hydroxide and render the attack inactive. In addition, every effort must be made to produce an impermeable concrete. The number of construction joints should be minimised since these can be particularly prone to attack. For concrete structures in sulphate-bearing soils, protective coatings such as bitumens, tars and epoxy resins could be applied on exterior surfaces, although some of these coatings may be eroded away by groundwater flow.

5.5.2 Acid Attack

Concrete structures exposed to the atmosphere and swampy and peaty soils are often subject to acid attack, such as carbonic and sulphuric acids, and other acidic fumes by dissolving and removing part of the set cement, leaving behind a soft area.

In practice, acid attack occurs at values of pH below 6.5. For values of pH between 3 and 6, the attack progresses at a rate approximately proportional to the square root of time.

The severity of attack depends on a number of factors, the main ones being:

- The type and quantity of the acid present: peaty water with carbon dioxide with a pH as low as 4.5 is particularly aggressive.
- Whether the acids are likely to be continuously renewed.
- The pressure and velocity of flow of groundwater against the concrete: any increase in these two factors will also increase the attack.
- The cement content and impermeability of the concrete and type of aggregate.

Where severe attack is probable, a concrete made with an increased cement content and a reduced water:cement ratio should be used. In addition, there should be either a substantial sacrificial thickness of the same quality concrete or the concrete should be protected by a coating of inert material such as epoxies, polyurethanes, polyesters and bituminous compounds.

5.5.3 Alkali–aggregate Reaction

Alkali–aggregate reactivity is a particular mechanism of deterioration in concrete which may occur when alkaline solutions present in cement react with certain forms of silica in the aggregate to produce an alkali–silicate gel. The gel, being hygroscopic, absorbs water, and this results in an expansion of the volume that creates tensile stresses within the concrete and causes cracking.

The main external evidence for deterioration of concrete due to alkali–aggregate reactivity is the development of cracking. In unrestrained members this appears as characteristic randomly distributed cracks, but in concrete where the expansive forces are restrained by, for example, reinforcement, the pattern of cracking will be modified and cracks tend to run parallel to reinforcing bars (see figure 5.10). Other signs of the problem are weeping of the gel from cracks and the formation of 'pop-outs'.

Another form of alkali–aggregate reaction is that between some dolomitic limestone aggregates and the alkalis in the cement. The main effect is expansion of concrete similar to that occurring as a result of alkali–silica reaction. One distinction between the two types of alkali–aggregate reactions is that in the alkali-carbonate reaction, the alkali is regenerated.

The main factors influencing the progress of the alkali–aggregate reaction includes the presence of non-evaporable water in the paste, and the permeability of the paste. Moisture is necessary for initiating and supporting the reaction which is accelerated under conditions of alternating wetting and drying.

To obviate the problem it is necessary to reduce water ingress to the concrete so that although gelling will still be present, it cannot imbibe water and exert an expansive force.

5.5.4 Leaching of Lime

In the process of cement hydration, soluble calcium hydroxide is formed. This material is easily dissolved by water that is lime-free and that contains dissolved carbon dioxide.

Water which produces mild carbonic acid solution has a greater

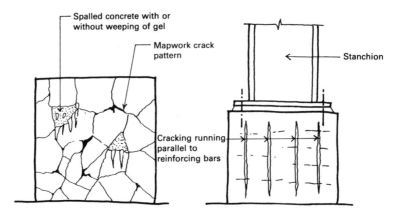

Figure 5.10   Physical appearance of deterioration caused by alkali–aggregate reaction

capacity for dissolving calcium hydroxide than pure water. As a result of this action, water will slowly leach out the lime from the concrete and in doing so will weaken the hydraulic bond and etch the surface. At the surface, reaction between the calcium hydroxide and carbon dioxide will cause precipitation of a white deposit of calcium carbonate.

Generally, this type of leaching does not result in any serious problem; the loss of strength is not substantial, but the porosity of the concrete is increased and its capacity for holding water is thus greater. The consequence is a possibility of corrosion of the reinforcement.

A homogeneous and dense concrete with a low permeability significantly reduces the effectiveness of the leaching action.

Early efflorescence can be removed with a brush and clean water. But heavy deposits of the salt may require acid treatment with dilute hydrochloric acid. Since lime is removed by the acid, the surface of the concrete becomes darker.

5.6 Cracking of Plastic Concrete

5.6.1 Plastic Shrinkage Cracks

Plastic shrinkage cracking in concrete occurs most commonly on the exposed surfaces of freshly placed floors and slabs (or other elements with large surface areas) when subjected to a very rapid loss of moisture caused by low humidity, wind and/or high temperature. Plastic shrinkage usually occurs within a few hours of placing concrete and prior to final finishing, before curing starts.

When moisture evaporates from the surface of freshly placed concrete faster than it is replaced by bleed water, the surface concrete shrinks. Because of the restraint provided by the concrete below the drying surface layer, tensile stresses develop in the weak, stiffening plastic concrete and resulting in shallow cracks that are usually short and fairly straight. These cracks are often fairly wide at the surface and are usually transverse in direction.

The rate of evaporation from the concrete surface depends on the following factors:

- Relative humidity.
- Wind velocity.
- Temperature of the fresh concrete.
- Air temperature.
- Degree of exposure of the concrete surface to the environment.

If cracks follow the pattern of the reinforcement, it may be difficult at first to determine whether they are due to plastic shrinkage or plastic settlement. If it can be shown that the cracks pass through the slab and follow the pattern of steel, then they are almost certainly plastic-shrinkage cracks which have been oriented by the steel.

Precautions to be taken to reduce the risk of plastic shrinkage cracking consist of the following measures:

- Maintaining a low initial concrete temperature.
- Reducing the time between placing and commencement of curing, that is, early curing is necessary.
- Minimising evaporation during the first few hours after casting by erecting wind barriers and sunshades.

In many instances, the simple operation of brushing cement grout into the cracks will satisfactorily solve the problem. But this should be done as soon as possible after the concrete has hardened.

5.6.2 Settlement Cracks

After initial placement, vibration and finishing, concrete has a tendency to consolidate. During this period the plastic concrete may be locally restrained by reinforcing steel. This local restraint may result in voids and/or cracks adjacent to the restraining steel (see figure 5.11). These cracks increase with increasing bar size, increasing slump and decreasing cover.

Settlement cracks are also caused by concrete arching or wedging

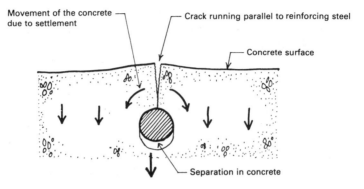

Figure 5.11   Cracking of concrete due to settlement of plastic concrete

across the top of a column form. This is very common below mushroom-heads. The reinforcement links can cause bridging or help to support the concrete in a plain column, and cracks will often coincide with the top links.

The cracks that are formed usually penetrate at least to the reinforcement and are usually wider inside the concrete than on the surface.

Anything which reduces bleeding will reduce the risk of plastic-settlement cracking. The most effective way of eliminating plastic settlement cracking is to re-vibrate the concrete after the cracks have formed, although the concrete must be sufficiently plastic if this operation is to be successful.

Air-entraining admixtures significantly reduce bleeding. Consequently, it is generally accepted that the incorporation of air-entraining admixtures or water-reducing admixtures is the most effective way of reducing bleeding and settlement cracks.

5.7 Cracking of Hardened Concrete

5.7.1 Drying Shrinkage Cracks

Drying shrinkage may be defined as the reduction in volume of concrete caused by the chemical and physical loss of water during the hardening process and subsequent exposure to unsaturated air.

If the shrinkage of concrete could take place without any restraint, the concrete would not crack. It is the combination of shrinkage and restraint (usually provided by another part of the structure or by the subgrade) that causes tensile stresses to develop. When the tensile strength of concrete is exceeded, it will crack.

In massive concrete elements, tensile stresses are caused by differential shrinkage between the surface and the interior concrete. The larger shrinkage at the surface causes cracks to develop that may, with time, penetrate deeper into the concrete.

The magnitude of tensile stresses is influenced by a combination of factors, including the amount of shrinkage, the degree of restraint, the modulus of elasticity and the amount of creep. The amount of drying shrinkage is influenced by the amount and type of aggregate, and the water content of the mix. The greater the amount of aggregate, the smaller the amount of shrinkage. The higher the stiffness of the aggregate, the more effective it is in reducing the shrinkage of the concrete. The higher the water content, the greater the amount of drying shrinkage.

Drying shrinkage can be reduced by using the maximum practical amount of aggregate in the mix. The lowest usable water content is also desirable. Shrinkage cracking can be controlled by using properly spaced contraction joints and proper steel detailing.

5.7.2 Thermal Stresses

Temperature differences within a concrete structure may be due to cement hydration or changes in ambient conditions, or both. These temperature differences result in differential volume changes. When the tensile strains due to the differential volume changes exceed their tensile strain capacity, concrete will crack. The effects of temperature differentials due to the hydration of cement are normally associated with mass concrete, while temperature differentials due to changes in the ambient temperature can affect any structure.

Considering thermal cracking in mass concrete, Portland cement liberates heat as it hydrates, causing the internal temperature of the concrete to rise during the initial curing stage. The concrete rapidly gains both strength and stiffness as cooling begins. Any restraint of the free contraction during cooling will result in tensile stress. Tensile stresses developed during the cooling stage are proportional to the temperature change, the coefficient of thermal expansion, the effective modulus of elasticity and the degree of restraint. The more massive the structure, the greater the potential for temperature differential and degree of restraint.

Thermal contraction cracks extend right through the member. While these cracks are seldom significant structurally, they do form permanent planes of weakness through the member unless they are properly repaired by injection.

Procedures for controlling thermally induced cracking include reducing the maximum internal temperature, delaying the onset of cooling, controlling the rate at which the concrete cools and increasing the tensile strain capacity of the concrete.

5.7.3 Crazing

Crazing is the cracking of the surface layer of concrete into small, irregularly-shaped contiguous areas. The cracks do not affect the structural integrity of the concrete. It is generally accepted as being the result of surface tensile stresses caused by shrinkage of the surface relative to the mass which is due to differential moisture movement.

The problem of crazing is particularly serious in large surface areas of concrete such as road slabs. In order to prevent crazing of the surface on drying out, loss of water must be prevented even prior to setting of the concrete.

If it is thought that there is a risk of crazing under certain circumstances, then this risk can be reduced by the application of a surface repellent. A crazed surface which is aesthetically unacceptable will either have to be covered or removed.

5.8 Physical Aggression

5.8.1 Abrasion

Concrete surfaces, particularly industrial floors, are subjected to wear. This may be due to attrition by sliding, scraping or percussion.

Resistance of concrete to abrasion is difficult to assess because the damaging effects depend on the exact cause of wear. But it has been established that the compression strength of concrete is the paramount factor in determining the abrasion resistance of the concrete surface. Therefore, it is obvious that lightweight concrete is unsuitable when surface wear is expected.

The aggregate properties also have some influence on abrasion resistance, but this is only significant if the aggregate quality is poor or especially good. For improved resistance, however, it is possible to treat the concrete surface with a suitable finish.

5.8.2 Damage Caused by High-velocity Water

In the case of hydraulic structures, the effects of fast-moving water and abrasive materials carried by the water can have adverse effects on the concrete and lead to erosion and cavitation.

1 Erosion

Erosion of concrete is another type of wear which occurs in concrete in contact with flowing water containing solid particles or grit.

The rate of erosion depends on a number of factors, of which the following are the more important:

- The quality of the concrete in terms of its compressive strength and cement content.
- The quality of the aggregate: concrete with large aggregates erodes less than mortar of equal strength, and hard aggregates improve the erosion resistance.
- The velocity of the flowing water.
- The quantity, shape, size and hardness of the solid particles carried by the flowing water.
- The flow characteristics, that is, whether the flow is continuous or intermittent.

2 Cavitation

The effect of a high-velocity jet of water striking a concrete surface is to erode the cement paste, resulting in the loosening of the fine and coarse aggregate. Repeated erosion of the concrete creates holes and pits.

Generally, damage by cavitation is found on the surface of aprons and tunnels carrying high-velocity water. Cavitation damage is easily distinguishable from normal erosion by its jagged appearance, in contrast to the smooth worn surface eroded by water-borne particles.

The best resistance to cavitation damage is obtained by the use of high-strength concrete. Good bonding between the aggregate and mortar is essential. In addition, it is necessary to provide smooth and well-aligned surfaces free from irregularities such as depressions, projection, joints and abrupt changes of profile, to ensure uninterrupted hydraulic flow.

5.8.3 Freezing and Thawing

Concrete structures which are located in very exposed areas in temperate countries may suffer damage by surface scaling of the concrete due to frost action. This disruption of the concrete surfaces is caused by penetration of the surface layers by moisture which subsequently freezes and expands when the temperature falls below zero.

Porous concrete which can become highly saturated with water is particularly liable to damage from frost attack. Use of de-icing salts containing chlorides greatly increases the chance of frost attack. For pavement-quality concrete, air is entrained into fresh concrete using an admixture which creates about 5 per cent of small (0.5 mm diameter) stable, evenly-distributed air bubbles. These provide voids into which the ice can expand without disrupting the concrete.

5.9 Dusting

The surface of concrete becomes soft and rubs off readily under abrasion or traffic as a fine powdery material. Dusting is most often encountered on floors where traffic and abrasion are heavy. Sometimes it is encountered on walls and can be so severe that it prevents the application of paint or coatings.

Excessive bleeding can be a cause of dusting. Increased water at the surface of the slab will raise the water:cement ratio and reduce the strength of that portion of the concrete that will be subjected to abrasion if finishing operations are carried out while the water is present. High slump mixes will often result in dusting of floors because of segregation. Excessive silt content in fine aggregate can also result in dusting.

5.10 Honeycombs

Honeycombing results when the concrete mortar does not completely fill the voids between the coarse aggregate particles. The result is a rough surface with cavities up to hundreds of millimetres deep. Occasionally, honeycombing will extend completely through the member and make it structurally unsound. It is more common in vertical surfaces than in horizontal ones.

Like so many other types of defects that can arise from human factors, honeycombing can stem from either improper mix design or poor site practices. If the workability of the mix is too low for the condition in which it is to be placed, honeycombing may occur. Poor aggregate grading with a high proportion of one or two grades, together with a shortage of fines will also contribute to this defect. Insufficient fine aggregate is also one of the most common causes of the problem.

Another common cause is excessive mixing by poor scheduling of ready-mix trucks in hot, dry weather. The workability of the concrete in the mixer is reduced and the concrete becomes too stiff to be properly consolidated.

Honeycombing can also be caused by leaking formwork that retains the coarse aggregate but allows the cement grout to escape (see figure 5.12).

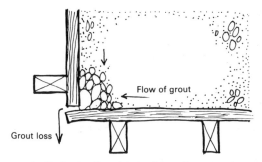

a. *Ineffective detailing of timber forms allows grout loss*

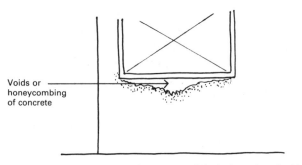

b. *Poor detailing technique may result in the formation of voids under opening*

Figure 5.12   Typical examples of poor construction practices which lead to honeycombing of concrete

To avoid honeycombs:

- Use a satisfactory mix and proper sand/aggregate ratio, well-graded aggregates, air entrainment and appropriate workability.
- Choose a maximum size aggregate in keeping with formwork and reinforcement clearances.
- Ensure that all form joints are tight.
- Use vibrations and other recommended placing practices.

If honeycombing does occur, repair is usually expensive, depending on the extent of structural damage. If appearance is important, then even if the member is structurally sound, the surface will need extensive and expensive patching. If the member is structurally weakened, it may need to be replaced completely.

5.11 Weathering

Weathering may be defined as changes in the characteristics of the material, particularly in its surface appearance, brought about by the weather. In Singapore, this takes the form of surface deterioration due to rainwater, surface staining and the growth of dark algae. The causes of weathering include:

• Dirt in the atmosphere deposited on the surface of the concrete by wind-driven rain.
• Deposits washed on to the surface from adjoining surfaces.
• Chemical attack from aggressive compounds in the atmosphere.
• Fungal and algal growths on the surface.

Most problems arise from initial surface deterioration caused by dissolved carbon dioxide in rainwater forming carbonic acid. This etches the surface of the concrete, causing a slight colour change in which the colour of the fine aggregate may dominate. When the surface of the concrete has been slightly etched and the surface alkalinity is reduced, this forms an ideal place for algae and other organisms to flourish.

Many problems can be overcome by using a dense concrete with a low water:cement ratio, and hence low permeability, as well as by detailing structures to provide means for rainwater to be removed from the surface without causing streaking, water runs or staining.

The application of waterproofing liquids such as silicones and orthosilicates may improve the appearance due to weathering, but these measures are often short-lived.

5.12 Colour Variations

It is practically impossible to produce a concrete surface that is completely uniform in colour. There will always be some variations, the acceptability of which is a matter of subjective judgement. Variation in a supposedly uniform surface is bound to be conspicuous, but the same degree of variation in a profiled or textured surface will be far less noticeable.

Colour variations may result from a number of factors, including concrete mix design, formwork surface texture and variations in curing conditions, formwork absorbency or stiffness, vibration and release agent. Leaking of water through joints in formwork usually causes a dark discoloration in the immediate vicinity.

If colour variations are judged to be unacceptable when formwork is struck, the probable pattern of weathering should be considered before anything is done to the surface, because weather staining may eventually mask the inherent colour variation. If some remedial treatment is considered to be necessary, however, the only practical course, short of demolition and rebuilding, is to apply some form of paint or surface coating which must be suitable for application to an alkaline surface. Treatment to expose the aggregate, such as bush-hammering or abrasive blasting, may produce a more uniform colour because the colour of the aggregate will predominate over the colour of the matrix, but it will completely change the nature of the surface.

Related and Further Reading

American Concrete Institute. *Cracking and Fracture of Concrete and Cement Paste*. Publication SP-20 (1968).

American Concrete Institute. *Durability of Concrete*. Publication SP-47 (1975).

American Concrete Institute. *Corrosion of Metals in Concrete*. Publication SP-49 (1975).

American Concrete Institute. *Hot-weather Concreting*. ACI Committee 305 (1977).

American Concrete Institute. *Erosion Resistance of Concrete in Hydraulic Structures*. ACI Committee 210 (1979).

American Concrete Institute. *Sulphate Resistance of Concrete*. Publication SP-77 (1982).

American Concrete Institute. *Guide to Durable Concrete*. ACI Committee 201 (1982).

American Concrete Institute. *Control of Cracking in Concrete Structures*. ACI Committee 224 (1982).

Beeby, A. W. *Structural Cracking of Concrete*. Building Technical File No. 8 (January, 1985).

British Standards Institution. *BS 8110: Parts 1 and 2: 1985. The structural use of concrete.*

Browne, R. D. Practical considerations in producing durable concrete. *Proceedings of Conference on 'Improvement of Concrete Durability'*. Telford, London (1985).

Building Research Establishment, UK. *The Durability of Steel in Concrete, Part 1*. Digest 263 (1982).

Building Research Establishment, UK. *The Durability of Steel in Concrete, Part 2*. Digest 264 (1982).

Building Research Establishment, UK. *The Durability of Steel in Concrete, Part 3*. Digest 265 (1982).

Building Research Establishment, UK. *Alkali–aggregate Reactions in Concrete*. Digest 330 (1988).

Building Research Establishment, UK. *Sulphate and Acid Resistance of Concrete in the Ground*. Digest 363 (July, 1991).

Concrete Society, UK. *Non-structural Cracks in Concrete*. Technical Report No. 22 (1982).

Everett, L. H. and Treadaway, K. W. J. *Deterioration due to Corrosion in Reinforced Concrete*. Information Paper 12/80, Building Research Establishment, UK (1980).

Figg, J. W. *Chemical Attack on Hardened Concrete: Effects of Sulphates and Chlorides*. Bulletin of the Institution of Corrosion Science and Technology No. 75 (July, 1979).

Gutt, W. H. and Harrison, W. H. *Chemical Resistance of Concrete*. Current Paper 23/77, Building Research Establishment, UK (1977).

Hobbs, D. W. *Influence of Mix Proportions and Cement Alkali Content upon Expansion due to Alkali–silica Reaction*. Technical Report 534, Cement and Concrete Association, London (1980).

Kenn, M. J. *Factors Influencing the Erosion of Concrete by Cavitation*. CIRIA Technical Note 1, CIRIA, London (1968).

Lea, F. M. and Davey, N. The deterioration of concrete in structures. *Journal of Institution of Civil Engineers*, London, No. 7 (May, 1949).

Neville, A. M. *Properties of Concrete*. Pitman, London (1983).

Papworth, F. Design and construction for durability. *Proceedings of Conference on 'Deterioration and Repair of Concrete Structures'*. Singapore Concrete Institute (1986).

Powers, T. C. *Resistance to Weathering – Freezing and Thawing*. Special Technical Publication No. 169, American Society for Testing and Materials (1956).

Roberts, M. H. *Carbonation of Concrete made with Dense Natural Aggregates*. Paper IP 6/81, Building Research Establishment Information, UK (1981).

Schiessl, P. CEB – Working guide for durable concrete structures, Part I: Protection of reinforcement (First version). *CEB–RILEM International Workshop on 'Durability of Concrete Structures'*, Copenhagen (May, 1983).

Shaw, J. D. N. Concrete decay – causes and remedies. *Proceedings of Conference on 'Our World in Concrete and Structures'*, Singapore (1986).

Smith, F. L. *Effect of Aggregate Quality on Resistance of Concrete to Abrasion*. Special Technical Publication No. 205, American Society for Testing and Materials (1958).

Sommerville, G. The design life of concrete structures. *The CIDB Review, Jan.–Mar. 1988*. Construction Industry Development Board, Singapore (1988).

Turton, C. D. *Plastic Cracking of Concrete*. Construction Guide Publication 45.038, Cement and Concrete Association, UK (1981).

Tuthill, L. H. *Resistance to Chemical Attack*. Special Technical Publication No. 169, American Society for Testing and Materials (1956).

Wellman, R. J. Reasons for concrete failures. *Proceedings of Conference on 'Structural Failures'*, Singapore (1987).

6 Concrete Defects – Inspection and Diagnosis

Concrete, by nature, is a non-uniform, non-isotropic structural material consisting of aggregate particles, air voids and moisture distributed heterogeneously in a hardened matrix. Variations in its production and subsequent attack by the environment mean that concrete is not totally immune to defects although it is generally a durable and maintenance-free material.

There is, therefore, a need for a regular system of inspection of all reinforced concrete structures so that any deterioration can be detected and recorded at its early stages, and a decision then taken on what remedial works, if any, should be carried out. However, it must be noted that the object of periodic inspections is to arrest deterioration at its early stages and it in no way implies that such structures are specially vulnerable to structural failure.

6.1 The Survey

The objectives of a structural survey are obviously dictated by the client's requirements. Whether the survey is to satisfy a mandatory requirement or to assess the strength of the structural members after a fire, the underlyihg requirement is for the following to be identified.

- What is the present state of deterioration and condition of the member?
- What will be the future rate of deterioration?
- Are repairs required urgently?

In order that the objectives are achieved, a systematic approach to structural survey of the building is necessary (see figure 6.1).

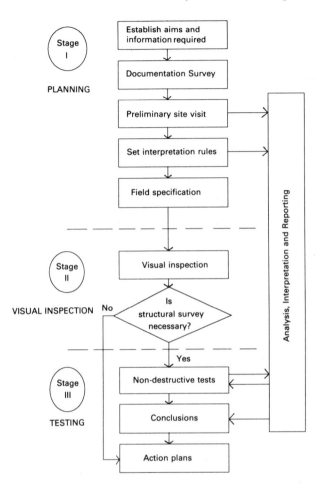

Figure 6.1   Flowchart to illustrate the inspection process

6.1.1 Planning

Careful planning is essential. Ideally, a programme should be evolved to obtain as much information as possible at the minimum cost and in the shortest time. Testing should only proceed as far as is necessary to get conclusions with a satisfactory degree of confidence and accuracy to meet the objectives of the survey.

The engineer responsible for the survey should obtain as much information as possible about the structure. The type of information which would be useful to collect during the documentation survey includes the following:

- Date of construction of structure.
- Details of construction, including architectural, structural and 'as-built' drawings.
- Present use of the structure.
- Previous changes of use (if any).
- Records of previous deterioration and repairs.
- Reports of previous surveys (if any).

The importance of the documentation survey should not be under-estimated. The above information will often indicate possible underlying causes of deterioration and assist in formulating proposals for detailed investigation, sampling and testing.

At this stage it may also be necessary to make a site visit in order to assess practical restrictions such as access and safety requirements.

Finally, there must be agreement between all parties in connection with the interpretation of test results before commencement of any testing. This practice will reduce possible disputes that may arise later on and prevent litigation from any party.

6.1.2 Field Specification

The 'field specification' is a planning document advising both the client and the engineers of the survey objectives, methods and scope. It contains all the client's information pertinent to the survey, including previous survey results, maintenance and repair records. It should also contain *pro forma* sheets designed to record all the information and data gathered on the site in a logical manner. These papers contain a plan of each element to be covered by the engineer, a drawing to locate the element in the overall structure and a reference grid system of the element to relate all the test data.

The field specification also provides the engineer with a list of each task that is required to be done, together with a work schedule. If carefully planned out, unproductive time will be reduced to a minimum.

6.1.3 Visual Inspection

The visual inspection is meant to give a quick scan of the structure to assess its general state of health. The information obtained from the inspection will determine whether there is a need for further comprehensive investigation using more sophisticated testing techniques.

Binoculars, telescope, magnifying glass, cover meter, rebound hammer, instrument for measuring crack widths and other simple tools are usually needed for the visual survey. In addition, a reliable camera is essential to record all defects detected during the inspection.

Beside classifying the defects, their size and extent should also be recorded. In many instances, it is necessary to go beyond the surface manifestation of deterioration and investigate the condition of the underlying concrete and reinforcement.

Some important conclusions that may be obtained from a well-executed visual inspection of the structure include the following:

- Spalling of concrete indicates corrosion of steel reinforcement; if spalling occurs in spite of adequate cover, the concrete is likely to be porous and weak.
- When spalling occurs in flat roofs and bathrooms and is accompanied by damp and wet patches, it is likely that water penetration is the cause of the problem.
- Vertical and diagonal cracks in beams indicate that the beams may be overstressed in flexure or shear respectively; either the beams are under-designed or the applied loads are higher than those assumed in design.
- Vertical cracks in columns indicate a high level of compressive stress in the members which tend to split vertically under the lateral bursting pressure and weaken the confining links.
- Random cracking in floors indicates shrinkage of concrete and lack of movement joints.
- Diagonal cracks along walls and at beam ends indicate differential settlement of foundations; in the case of beams, the diagonal cracks are concentrated towards one end of the beam.

In order to speed up the survey process and to obtain conformity between different engineers' interpretations of visual defects, a classification system can be devised (see table 6.1).

The main difficulty in carrying out visual inspection is the presence of finishes which hide the structure. Though the structural defects often propagate through the finishes, visual inspection may not reveal anything if the structural defect has been patched up and a new finish has recently been applied. Such information should be made available by the client to the engineer during the documentation survey.

If the visual inspection does not reveal any signs of deterioration or distress, it is safe to assume that the structure is not potentially dangerous. In case of doubt, a check of the structural analysis, design and details by a competent engineer is necessary.

Table 6.1   Diagnosis and summary of defects
(Source: Higgins, D. D., Diagnosing the causes of defects or
deterioration in concrete structures, *Concrete*, October 1981,
pp. 33–34)

| | *Symptom* | | | *Likely to be noted in a new construction* | *May appear after some time* |
Cause	*Cracking*	*Spalling*	*Erosion of surface*		
(1) Structural deficiency	yes	yes	—	yes	yes
(2) Corrosion of reinforcement	yes	yes	—	—	yes
(3) Chemical attack	yes	yes	yes	—	yes
(4) Frost damage	yes	yes	yes	yes	yes
(5) Fire damage	yes	yes	—	—	—
(6) Internal reaction in the concrete	yes	yes	—	—	yes
(7) Restrained thermal contraction and expansion	yes	yes	—	yes	yes
(8) Restrained shrinkage	yes	—	—	yes	yes
(9) Creep	yes	yes	—	—	yes
(10) Rapid early evaporation	yes	—	—	—	—
(11) Plastic settlement	yes	—	—	—	—
(12) Mechanical damage	yes	yes	—	yes	yes
(13) Miscellaneous inadequate construction		various			

6.1.4 Assessment of Reinforcement Condition

In a number of cases, strength is not the most critical parameter to be
investigated. Instead, information is needed to determine the risk of
corrosion of reinforcement, to delineate cracks and discontinuities,
and to locate areas of poor compaction, voids and honeycombing.

Density, permeability, cement content and strength tests are carried
out to determine the quality of the concrete. They help to identify the
basic cause of the corrosion. Strength of concrete can be determined
by a combination of destructive and non-destructive tests as discussed
in section 6.2.

Where signs of corrosion are visible, it is likely that there is corrosion
in other parts of the concrete, but the extent of corrosion is not serious
enough to cause spalling or cracking. Hidden corrosion can be detected by electropotential mapping. However, the degree of corrosion
and the rate of corrosion are still unknown and must be determined by
other means, such as concrete resistivity tests.

While a small number of tests are adequate to understand the cause of corrosion, a large number of tests are necessary to understand the extent of the area affected by corrosion.

In order to find out whether corrosion has been caused by chlorides or carbonation, tests on a few samples, probably about five, would be sufficient. The purpose is to establish the cause of corrosion which is not likely to vary from one part of the structure to the other.

Depth of carbonation can be determined by spraying phenolphthalein indicator solution on freshly fractured concrete surfaces. While the uncarbonated concrete turns purplish red when the indicator is sprayed on it, carbonated concrete remains unaffected.

The major problem is in deciding on the extent of repair. If the visual inspection shows widespread corrosion damage in all the elements of a structure, no further tests may be required and complete repair may be started. But if the corrosion damage is localised, further inspection of the concrete surfaces is necessary to estimate the full extent of the repair. Locating the steel bars with a cover meter and hammering to sound out the concrete condition at the location of the steel bars will identify surfaces which are about to spall.

In areas where there are no symptoms, the presence of corrosion can be detected by electropotential mapping. But, since the extent and rate of corrosion cannot be detected, the problem of deciding on whether to repair, or simply to apply a protective coating still remains.

The loss of reinforcement section due to general rusting is not generally severe. This is particularly so when the symptoms have just appeared.

Even if electropotential mapping indicates corrosion activity in some areas which appear sound otherwise, it is preferable not to remove the concrete cover completely over the whole area. However, cover may be removed in a few locations to examine the condition of the steel.

6.1.5 Assessment of Concrete Strength

When structural malfunction is detected, a structural check and a material check are the main items for investigation. A structural check involves the checking of the original calculations and drawings based on the original specifications for the properties of materials. After a material check has been done, the structure has to be assessed once again to ascertain its strength and stability based on the actual properties of the materials in the structure.

1 Initial Structural Check

The initial check is for the original calculations, drawings and specifications. If these are available, the task of carrying out a structural check is simpler. The problem is that the original information is not always available, in whole or in part. If this is the case, the engineer has to determine the dimensional configurations and structural arrangements. He then has to open it up not only to ascertain the quality of materials, but also to determine the reinforcement details. The foundations will have to be exposed to determine their size and type.

Even when original drawings are available, it has been found on occasions that the 'as-constructed' details are different from 'as-drawn' details. Selective opening up is still necessary to ascertain that the structure has been constructed according to approved drawings.

2 Material Check

Regarding quality of materials, the problem is mainly with the concrete. Conventional steel is seldom found to be deficient in material properties unless it has been damaged by fire, overstress or improper welding.

Testing core samples is the best way to determine the compressive strength of concrete. This may be possible while assessing a small structure. However, in a large structure, it is seldom feasible to take a number of samples large enough for statistical validity. The engineer has to resort to indirect methods such as ultrasonic pulse velocity measurements and Windsor probes.

6.2 *In situ* Testing

The type of non-destructive tests which are used for *in situ* testing of concrete offers significant advantages in speed, cost and minimum damage in comparison with other tests involving the removal of a sample for subsequent examination. These distinct advantages allow more extensive testing to give better results than would otherwise be possible.

The range of properties that can be determined using *in situ* testing techniques is large and includes concrete density, strength, surface hardness, surface absorption, reinforcement location and condition, and cover measurements. Some of these tests have been briefly mentioned in the previous section.

6.2.1 *Non-destructive Tests to Assess Reinforcement Condition*

There is available a number of non-destructive tests devised to determine the risk of reinforcement corrosion, location and size of steel bars, cover measurements and other defects caused by poor workmanship such as voids and honeycombs. These techniques vary from

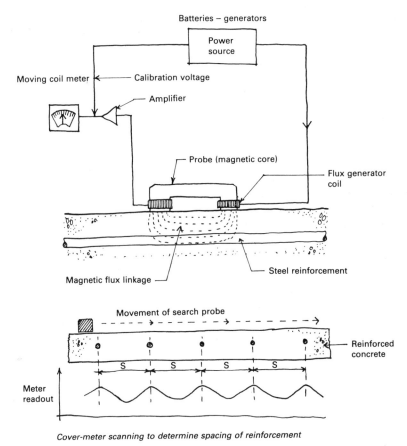

Cover-meter scanning to determine spacing of reinforcement

Figure 6.2   Principle of operation of the cover meter

simple magnetic devices to highly advanced infra-red thermographic methods.

1 Cover Measurement

The principle of the test is that the presence of steel affects a magnetic field (see figure 6.2). As the electromagnetic probe is swept over the concrete surface, any reinforcement within the range of the instrument will cause the indicator to deflect. If the probe is moved until the maximum deflection is obtained, the bar in question is then assumed to be parallel to the probe and directly beneath it.

Direct readings of the cover or bar size can be obtained very quickly. The equipment is easy to use, although some training is needed to interpret the results.

The method is most appropriate for lightly reinforced members and may be used for the following:

- Quality control checking of reinforcement bars and concrete cover.
- Location of reinforcement as a preliminary step to some other tests in which reinforcement should be avoided, such as coring and ultrasonic pulse velocity measurements.
- Examination of concrete members of which records are not available.

The presence of closely spaced reinforcement bars, laps, transverse steel, metal ties or aggregates with magnetic properties can present difficulties. This test does not give any indication of the concrete quality.

2 Half-cell Potential Measurement

In this test, the electric potential of steel reinforcement is measured relative to a reference electrode called the half-cell (see figure 6.3). The half-cell is usually a copper/copper sulphate or silver/silver nitrate cell with the concrete as the electrolyte. The risk of corrosion of the reinforcement in the region around the test location may be related empirically to the measured potential difference.

The half-cell provides a relatively fast method of assessing reinforcement corrosion over a wide area without having to remove the concrete cover. Because it is portable equipment, field measurements can be readily taken and results plotted in the form of equi-potential contour diagrams which indicate zones of varying degrees of corrosion.

This method, however, does not provide information on the rate of corrosion. It is also important that the results should be interpreted carefully to take into account the effects of protective or decorative coatings on the concrete surface.

3 Resistivity Measurement

Resistivity of concrete is related to its moisture content, water-cement ratio and chloride content. Hence, a measurement of concrete resistivity will give an indication of the rate of corrosion which may occur if oxygen and moisture are present at the reinforcement.

The Wenner technique is usually used to obtain *in situ* measurements (see figure 6.4). In this technique, four electrodes are placed in a straight line on or just below the surface at equal spacings apart. An electrical current is then passed through the outer electrodes while the voltage drop between the inner electrodes is measured. The apparent resistivity of the concrete may be calculated from the known current,

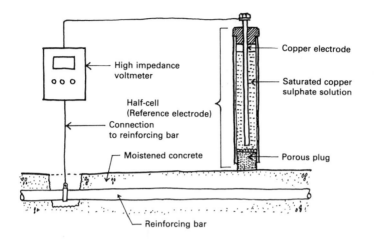

Half-cell potential (mV) relative to copper/copper sulphate reference electrode	Percentage of active corrosion
< − 350	95
−200 to −350	50
> −200	5

Interpretation of test measurement

Figure 6.3   Reinforcement potential measurement

voltage drop and electrodes spacing. The higher the resistance, the slower will be the corrosion process.

The equipment is relatively cheap, simple to operate and many measurements can be quickly made. It is very useful when used in conjunction with other methods of testing, for example, the half-cell potential test. However, if the moisture content is high, the equipment may not be reliable. In addition, adjacent bars may affect the results.

4 Permeation Characteristics Test
The initial surface absorption test involves measurement of the rate of water movement per unit area into a concrete surface subjected to a constant applied head (see figure 6.5). The equipment consists of a cap which is clamped and sealed to the concrete surface, with an inlet connected to a reservoir and an outlet connected to a horizontal calibrated capillary tube and scale. Measurements are made of the movement of water in the capillary tube over a fixed period of time following closure of a tap between the cap and reservoir.

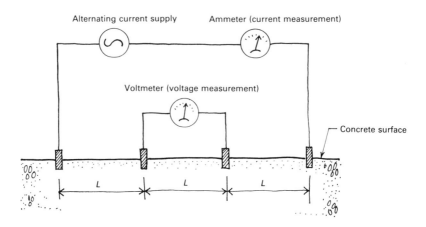

Resistivity (ohm-cm)	Likely corrosion rate (non-saturated concrete)
< 5000	Very high
5000–10 000	High
10 000–20 000	Low/moderate
> 20 000	Low

Interpretation of test measurement

Figure 6.4   Concrete resistivity measurement by the four-probe method

The absorption of water by a dry surface is initially high, but decreases as the water-filled length of capillaries increases, thus permitting measurements to be taken at specified time intervals from the start of the test.

This method provides *in situ* measurement of the rate of water penetration of a concrete surface.

Results are affected by variations in moisture content of the concrete. It is virtually impossible to obtain comparable conditions with *in situ* concrete and hence will reduce the reliability of quantitative results in this application.

6.2.2 Chemical Tests

Chemical testing of hardened concrete is mainly used to identify the causes of deterioration due to chlorides or sulphates, or to check specification compliance involving cement content and aggregate-cement ratio. Most of the chemical tests are very costly and they are,

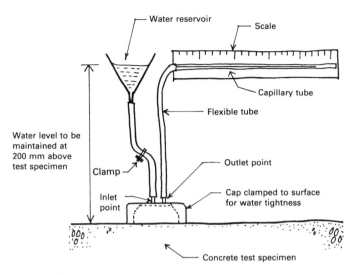

Figure 6.5   Initial surface absorption test

therefore, confined to resolving disputes rather than as a means of quality control.

1 Test for Chloride Ions

It is necessary to clean the concrete surface to remove all deposits of salts, particularly if the concrete has been subjected to sea sprays. Dust samples are then collected by drilling holes in the concrete. The samples are usually obtained at different depths of the concrete in order to determine how the chloride content varies with the depth (see figure 6.6). The results so obtained will provide important information as to whether the chlorides were present in the concrete at the time of construction or whether the chlorides entered from the environment.

There are available several methods of analysis of chloride ions. Simple site tests such as the 'Quantab' and 'Hach' techniques are well documented and provide useful preliminary information before more elaborate laboratory analysis is carried out.

The recommended laboratory method is the 'Volhard' method which is relatively straightforward and reliable. The test involves treating the concrete samples with acid to dissolve the cement, and the chloride content is then determined by titration against silver nitrate.

2 Cement Content

A common method of determining the cement content is based on the fact that the silicates in Portland cement are more readily decomposed

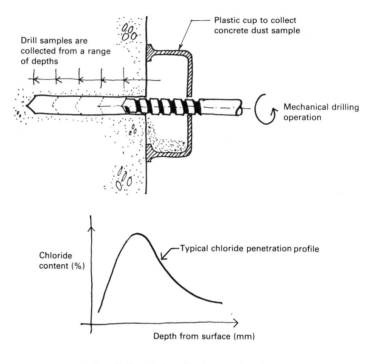

Typical profile for chloride which has penetrated the
hardened concrete

Figure 6.6   Determination of chloride content of hardened concrete

and soluble in dilute hydrochloric acid than are the silica compounds
contained in aggregates.

Briefly, the procedure is to crush a representative sample and then
to dehydrate it at 550°C for about 3 hours. Small portions of the
sample are treated with a 1:3 hydrochloric acid. The quantity of soluble
silica is determined by simple analytical procedures and, if the composition of the cement is known, the cement content of the original
volume of the sample can be calculated.

The accuracy of the test is lowest for mixes with low cement contents
and it is usually in this type of mix that the exact value of cement
content is required.

3 Water:Cement Ratio
The most popularly used method involves determining the volume of
the capillary pores and the weight of cement and combined water.

In this method, a sample of the concrete is oven-dried at 105°C and the air is then removed from the pores under vacuum. The pores are refilled with carbon tetrachloride whose weight is measured. Hence, the weight of the water which originally occupied the pores can be calculated.

The sample is now broken up. The carbon tetrachloride having been allowed to evaporate, the aggregate is separated out and weighed. The loss in weight and the carbon dioxide content of the remaining fine material are found. From these two quantities, the weight of combined water can be calculated. Note that the sum of the combined water and the pore water gives the original mixing water.

This method has been further developed into a standard method in BS 1881: Part 6: 1971.

6.2.3 Non-destructive Tests to Assess Strength

Current practice uses methods of evaluating the quality of concrete which rely on simulated tests on cast specimens in compression and flexure. The disadvantages of this approach are:

- Delay in obtaining test results.
- Test specimens may not truly represent the material in the structure for various reasons, including different conditions of placing, compacting and curing.
- The question of necessity for testing the specimens to failure is often raised.
- The high cost incurred in carrying out the tests.

Since non-destructive tests cannot be expected to yield absolute results, the use of such tests must depend on some other properties of concrete from which an estimate of its strength may be obtained. Such properties include its hardness, resistance to penetration by projectiles, rebound characteristics and pulse velocity through the concrete mass. Each of these techniques has its merits and limitations in terms of cost, speed, accuracy and damage to the structure (see table 6.2).

1 Ultrasonic Pulse Velocity Test
The principle of the test depends on the fact that the velocity of a wave passing through an elastic medium is a function of the modulus of elasticity of the material and its density (see figure 6.7). The technique consists of measuring the time of travel of an ultrasonic wave generated through the concrete. The time taken for the pulse to travel between the initial onset and its reception is measured electronically. The average velocity of wave propagation, or pulse velocity, is determined by dividing the known path length between the transducers by the time taken.

Table 6.2   *Strength tests: relative merits and limitations*
(Source: Bungey, J. H., *The Testing of Concrete in Structures*,
Surrey University Press, London, 1987)

Test method	Cost	Speed of test	Damage to concrete	Representativeness	Reliability of strength calibrations
Collapse load test	High	Slow	Total	Good	Good
Overload test	High	Slow	Variable	Good	Good
Cores	High	Slow	Moderate	Moderate	Good
Penetration resistance	Moderate	Fast	Minor	Near surface only	Moderate
Pull-out/ Internal fracture	Moderate	Fast	Minor	Near surface only	Moderate
Ultrasonics	Low	Fast	None	Good	Moderate
Rebound hammer	Very low	Fast	Unlikely	Surface only	Poor

The main advantages of this method are that it is totally non-destructive, quick to operate and reflects the quality of the interior of the concrete member. It is particularly useful in obtaining a considerable number of readings in a relatively short time for the assessment of uniformity of hardened concrete.

The technique causes some surface staining from the use of some couplants. Surface preparation is necessary. Skill is needed to interpret the results because such factors as moisture variations and metal reinforcement can affect the readings.

2 Surface Hardness Test
This test is based on the principle that the rebound of an elastic mass depends on the hardness of the surface on which the mass impinges.

The apparatus consists of a metal plunger, one end of which is held against the concrete surface while the free end is struck by a spring-loaded mass which rebounds to a point on a graduated scale (see figure 6.8). The magnitude of the rebound is registered by an index rider.

The amount of rebound increases in concrete strength for a particular concrete mix. The test is sensitive to the presence of aggregate and of voids immediately below the plunger, so that it is necessary to have at least 10–12 readings over the area to be tested in order for it to be representative of the member.

The main advantages are the speed and low cost, as well as the fact that the apparatus can be used horizontally, vertically and inclined.

The results obtained relate only to a surface zone of up to 30 mm depth and may be affected by localised hardening due to carbonation. Finishes obviously must be removed before testing since they tend to

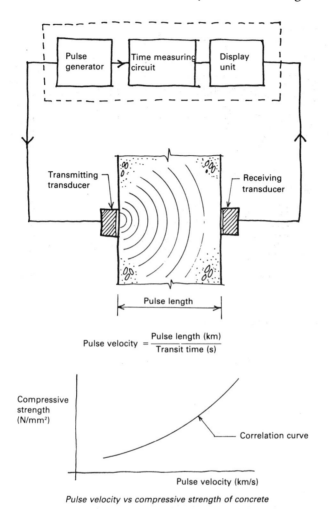

$$\text{Pulse velocity} = \frac{\text{Pulse length (km)}}{\text{Transit time (s)}}$$

Pulse velocity vs compressive strength of concrete

Figure 6.7   Ultrasonic pulse velocity measurement

affect the results. The test results are also influenced by the surface texture of the concrete, moisture, cement type, mix proportions and rigidity of the structure.

3 Penetration Resistance Test

The test consists of firing a standard probe into the concrete with a standard cartridge. The depth of penetration, which will usually lie between 20 and 40 mm, is measured and the mean of three readings is related empirically to compressive strength by calibration charts (see figure 6.9). The strength is assessed by the length of probe which

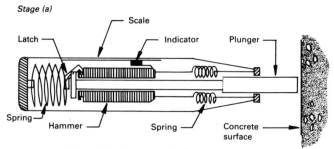

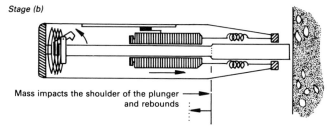

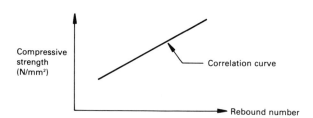

Rebound number vs compressive strength of concrete

Figure 6.8   Diagrammatic presentation of operation of rebound hammer

remains upstanding on the concrete surface.

The equipment is easy to use and does not require surface preparation. The results are not influenced by surface conditions, moisture content or ambient temperature but by the hardness of aggregate used.

Some damage in the form of cracking may be caused. Reinforcements must be avoided and simple safety precautions should be taken.

4 Pull-out Tests

Pull-out tests involve measurement of the force required to extract a

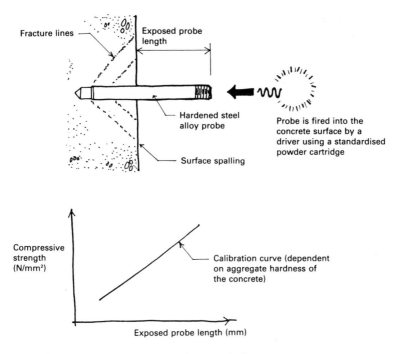

Exposed probe length vs compressive strength of concrete

Figure 6.9   Penetration resistance test

metal insert from within the concrete against a reaction ring. Because of its shape, the steel rod is pulled out with a cone of the concrete. The concrete is simultaneously in tension and in shear, the generated lines of the cones running at about 45° to the direction of pull. The pull-out force is then related to the compressive strength of the concrete.

Two versions of the test are commercially available: the LOK test which uses a 25 mm diameter insert cast into the concrete at a depth of 25 mm; and the CAPO test in which a steel ring is expanded into a groove undercut from an 18 mm diameter drilled hole to provide a similar configuration (see figure 6.10). In both cases, a hand-operated jack is used with a 55 mm reaction ring. An average of six readings should be taken for correlation with the compression strength.

This method of testing is quick and requires only one exposed surface. But a minimum edge distance of at least 100 mm is required and reinforcement has to be avoided. Pre-planning is required or drilling and under-reaming are necessary. Both methods will cause some damage to the concrete surface.

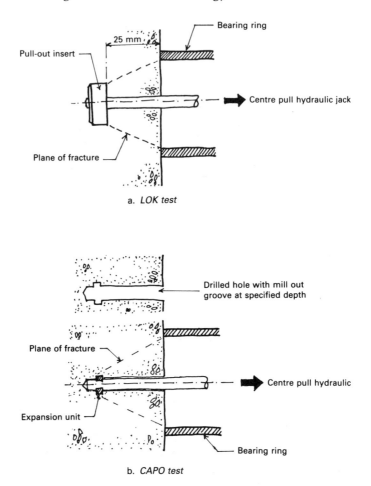

Figure 6.10   Pull-out tests

5 Cores

The most reliable method of obtaining an estimate of the strength of concrete in a structural member is the cutting of cores for subsequent preparation and crushing in a laboratory.

Drilled cores of 50 to 200 mm diameters and various lengths are obtained by using a diamond-tipped cutter which is clamped to the concrete surface and normally requires a water supply. However, to achieve a worthwhile accuracy, the cores should be at least 100 mm in both diameter and length and at least three cores are required from the given location.

After trimming and capping to provide parallel end faces, cores should be stored under water for at least 48 hours prior to testing to standardise moisture conditions. It is vital that all cores should be properly marked and identified.

The basic testing list includes the following:

- Visual inspection for surface conditions, depth of deterioration, fractures, unusual deposits, colouring or staining, voids, construction joints and other features.
- Compressive and tensile strength.
- Transverse, longitudinal and torsional frequencies.
- Static modulus of elasticity.
- Chemical tests on mix proportions, chloride content and other properties.

The process of drilling and analysing concrete cores is expensive and takes a relatively long time. This test is partially destructive and some caution is essential so that the integrity of the member is not affected by the coring.

6.3 Tests of Internal Condition and Integrity

The determination of delamination can be reliably detected with the human ear in conjunction with surface tapping. This approach, however, depends very much upon the experience and subjective assessment by the investigator in differentiating sound from unsound regions. Furthermore, the results obtained from such investigation cannot be readily quantified. But equipment is now available commercially to give comparative results.

In practice, from a plot of surface temperature contours derived from an infra-red thermographic survey it is possible to identify sound and delaminated regions as well as voids. The principle makes use of surface temperature differentials that exist during heating and cooling due to internal heat variations. Unfortunately, these differences are very small and extraneous effects must be carefully considered.

Subsurface scanning by radar for delamination, voids and reinforcing bars may find increasing use when this technique is fully developed.

Another technique depends on the dynamic response of a structural member to imposed impulse or vibration applied at another part of the member. This method is useful in detecting cracks and deterioration.

6.4 Selection of Test Methods

Test selection is based on a combination of factors such as:

- The availability and reliability of calibrations.
- The effects and acceptability of surface damage.
- Practical limitations such as member size and type, surface condition, depth of test zone required, location of reinforcement and accessibility.
- The degree of accuracy required.
- Economic consideration of the value of work under investigation and the cost of delays in relation to the cost of the test programme.

Generally, the complexity of calibration tends to be greatest for those tests which cause the least damage. For example, while surface hardness and pulse velocity tests cause no damage, are cheap and quick, and are ideal for comparative and uniformity assessments, their calibration for absolute strength estimates poses many problems. Core tests, on the other hand, provide the most reliable information, but also cause the most damage and are slow and expensive.

When comparison with concrete of similar quality is all that is necessary, the choice of test method is governed primarily by practical limitations. For example, the surface hardness test may be used for new concrete, while ultrasonics is selected where two opposite faces of the member are accessible.

The test programme is also influenced by the costs of the tests in relation to the value of the project involved, the costs of delays to construction and of possible remedial works.

6.5 Interpretation of Results

It is essential that there is agreement on the way that results should be interpreted in order to avoid disputes. Interpretation should take into account the capabilities and accuracies possible from the tests, as well as environmental effects and practical difficulties.

Examples of environmental factors include differential rates of weathering and chemical attack between parts of existing structures, as well as the influence of moisture conditions. The last factor is particularly important for permeability, integrity and strength tests, because the calibrations prepared under laboratory conditions may not be the same as those for site conditions.

Assessment of moisture conditions internally within concrete is often beset with difficulties such as variations of in-place concrete strength and mix proportions, and the influence of reinforcing steel on test results. These factors will affect the locations and the number of individual tests to be carried out, which is very often a compromise between accuracy and cost.

Having established and agreed on the procedures to be adopted, interpretation should be on-going throughout testing by an experienced engineer. In this way, the programme may be modified as necessary.

6.6 Recommendations for Action

If a visual inspection has not shown any signs of distress or deterioration, the structure may be assumed to be safe, and non-destructive testing is unnecessary. At best, it is only necessary to check all the structural calculations and details, and construction records. If the check reveals deficiencies in design or construction, doubts arise as to why there are no symptoms. A thorough structural check may be required in this case.

If there are signs of distress, deterioration or structural malfunction, the engineer has to make the crucial recommendation as to whether the building should be demolished, or its structure repaired and strengthened.

If there are signs of severe distress in a structure, it may be better to evacuate the building, particularly if monitoring indicates that the cracks are widening and the deformations are increasing.

Related and Further Reading

American Concrete Institute. *Corrosion of Metal in Concrete.* ACI Report 222R–85 (1985).

American Society for Testing and Materials. *Penetration Resistance of Hardened Concrete.* ASTM C803-79 (1979).

American Society for Testing and Materials. *Standard Test Method for Rebound Number of Hardness of Concrete.* ASTM C805–79 (1979).

American Society for Testing and Materials. *Standard Test Method for Half-cell Potentials of Reinforcing Steel in Concrete.* ASTM C876–80 (1980).

American Society for Testing and Materials. *Standard Test Method for Pulse Velocity through Concrete.* ASTM C803–82 (1982).

American Society for Testing and Materials. *Standard Test Method for Pull-out Strength of Hardened Concrete.* ASTM C900–87 (1987).

British Standards Institution. *BS 4408: Part 1: 1969 Non-destructive methods of test for concrete – electromagnetic cover measuring devices.*

British Standards Institution. *BS 4408: Part 2: 1969 Recommendations for non-destructive methods of test for concrete – strain gauges for concrete investigations.*

British Standards Institution. *BS 1881: Part 5: 1970 Methods of testing hardened concrete for other than strength.*

British Standards Institution. *BS 4408: Part 3: 1970 Non-destructive methods of test for concrete – gamma radiography of concrete.*

British Standards Institution. *BS 4408: Part 4: 1970 Non-destructive methods of test for concrete – surface hardness methods.*

British Standards Institution. *BS 4408: Part 5: 1970 Non-destructive methods of test for concrete – measurement of the velocity of ultrasonic pulses in concrete.*

British Standards Institution. *BS 6089: 1981 Guide to assessment of concrete strength in existing structures.*

British Standards Institution. *BS 1881: Part 114: 1983 Methods for determination of density of hardened concrete.*

British Standards Institution. *BS 1881: Part 120: 1983 Method for determination of the compressive strength of concrete cores.*

British Standards Institution. *BS 1881: Part 122: 1983 Method for determination of water absorption.*

British Standards Institution. *BS 1881: Part 201: 1986 Guide to the use of non-destructive methods of test for hardened concrete.*

British Standards Institution. BS 1881: Part 202: 1986 Recommendations for surface hardness testing by rebound hammer.

British Standards Institution. *BS 1881: Part 203: 1986 Recommendations for measurement of velocity of ultrasonic pulses in concrete.*

British Standards Institution. *BS 1881: Part 124: 1988 Methods for analysis of hardened concrete.*

Building Research Establishment, UK. *Simplified method for the detection and determination of chloride in hardened concrete.* Information Sheet 12/77 (1977).

Building Research Establishment, UK. *Determination of chloride and cement content in hardened Portland cement concrete.* Information Sheet 13/77 (1977).

Bungey, J. H. *The Testing of Concrete in Structures.* Surrey University Press, London (1987).

Chabowski, A. J. and Bryden-Smith, D. W. *Internal Fracture Testing of insitu Concrete: A Method of Assessing Compressive Strength.* Information Paper IP 22/80, Building Research Establishment, UK (October, 1980).

Child, C. A. Checking carbonation and chlorides on site. *Concrete* (May, 1988).

Concrete Society, UK. *Concrete Core Testing for Strength.* Technical Report No. 11 (1976).

Construction Industry Development Board. *Building Diagnosis – A Guide to Non-destructive Testing Methods on Concrete.* Construction Industry Development Board, Singapore (1988).

Crane, A. P, *Corrosion of Reinforcement in Concrete Structures*. Ellis Horwood, Chichester, UK (1983).

Higgins, D. D. Diagnosing the causes of defects or deterioration in concrete structures. *Concrete* (October, 1981).

Institution of Structural Engineers. *Appraisal of Existing Structures*. Institution of Structural Engineers, London (July, 1980).

Jones, R. *Non-destructive Testing of Concrete*. Cambridge University Press, London (1962).

Khoo, L. M. *Pull-out Technique – An Additional Tool for insitu Concrete Strength Determination*. Publication SP 82, American Concrete Institute, Detroit (1984).

Langford, P. and Broomfield, J. Monitoring the corrosion of reinforcing steel. *Construction Repair*, UK (May, 1987).

Malhotra, V. M. *Testing Hardened Concrete: Non-destructive Methods*. Monograph No. 9, American Concrete Institute, Detroit (1976).

Malhotra, V. M. *Insitu/non-destructive Testing of Concrete*. Publication SP 82, American Concrete Institute, Detroit (1984).

Malhotra, V. M. and Carino, N. J. (ed.). *CRC Handbook on Nondestructive Testing of Concrete*. CRC Press, Florida, USA (1991).

Munday, G. L. and Dhir, R. K. *Assessment of insitu Concrete Quality by Core Testing*. Publication SP 82, American Concrete Institute, Detroit (1984).

Neville, A. M. *Properties of Concrete*. Longman, London (1988).

Pullar-Strecker, P. *Corrosion Damaged Concrete: Assessment and Repair*. Butterworths, London (1987).

Schupack, M. Fast field test for chloride ions. *Concrete Construction* (July, 1989).

Snell, L. M. *et al*, Locating reinforcement in concrete. *Concrete International* (April, 1986).

7 Repair of Concrete Structures

Reinforced concrete is generally a very durable structural material and very little repair work is usually needed. However, its durability can be affected by a variety of causes, including those of design and construction faults, use of inferior materials and exposure to aggressive environments. The need for a repair is primarily dictated by the severity of the deterioration as determined from the diagnosis. Good workmanship is essential if anything more than just a cosmetic treatment to the concrete is required.

7.1 Performance Requirements of Repair System

Having established the causes of the defect by carefully diagnosing the distress, the next step should be to consider the requirements of the repair method that will offer an effective solution to the problem (see figure 7.1).

1 Durability
It is important to select repair materials that provide adequate durability. Materials used for the repair job should be at least as durable as the substrate concrete to which it is applied.

2 Protection of Steel
The mechanism of protection provided to the reinforcing steel depends on the type of repair materials used. For example, cementitious materials can protect the steel from further corrosion by their inhibitive effect of increasing the alkalinity of the concrete, whereas epoxy resin mortars can give protection against the ingress of oxygen, moisture and other harmful agents.

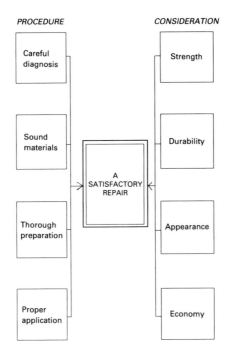

PROCEDURE   CONSIDERATION

Figure 7.1   Essential requirement of a satisfactory repair

3 Bond with Substrate
The bond with the substrate must produce an integral repair to prevent entry of moisture and atmospheric gases at the interface. With most repair materials, the bond is greatly enhanced with the use of a suitable bonding aid such as an unfilled époxy primer for epoxy resin systems and a slurry of Portland cement, plus any latex additives for a Portland cement-based repair system. Precautions should also be taken to re-move all loose and friable materials from the surfaces to be bonded.

4 Dimensional Stability
Shrinkage of materials during curing should be kept to a minimum. Subsequent dimensional changes should be very close to those in the substrate in order to prevent failure.

5 Initial Resistance to Environmentally Induced Damage
Some initial exposure conditions may lead to premature damage to repairs. For example, partially cured Portland cement repairs can de-teriorate from hot weather preventing full hydration of the cement. To prevent this from happening, extra protection during curing time may be necessary.

6 Ease of Application
Materials should be easily mixed and applied so that they can be worked readily into small crevices and voids. Ideally, the material should not stick to tools, and should not shear while being trowelled nor slump after placement.

7 Appearance
The degree to which the repair material should match the existing concrete will depend on the use of the structure and the client's requirements. A surface coating may be required when appearance is important or when cover to reinforcement is small.

7.2 Selection of Repair Method

A suitable repair counteracts all the deficiencies which are relevant to the use of the structure. The selection of the correct method and material for a particular application requires careful consideration, whether to meet special requirements for placing, strength, durability or other short- or long-term properties. These considerations include:

1 Nature of the Distress
If a live crack is filled with a rigid material, then either the repair material will eventually fail or some new cracking will occur adjacent to the original crack. Repairs to live cracks must either use flexible materials to accommodate movements or else steps must be taken prior to the repair to eliminate the movement (see table 7.1).

2 Position of the Crack
Techniques which rely on gravity to introduce the material into the crack are more successfully carried out on horizontal surfaces but are rarely effective on vertical ones.

3 Environment
If moisture, water or contaminants are found in the crack, then it is necessary to rectify the leaks. Repairs to stop leaks may be further complicated by the need to make the repairs while the structure is in service and the environment is damp.

4 Workmanship
The skill of the operatives available to carry out the repairs is another relevant factor. Sometimes this can mean the difference between a permanent repair and premature failure of the repair material.

Table 7.1 Selection of an appropriate method of crack repair
(Source: Little, D., Resin based repair methods, *Proceedings of Seminar on Deterioration and Repair of Concrete Structures*, Singapore, June 1986)

	Restore structural strength	Prevent ingress of moisture to reinforcement	Restore watertightness	Improve appearance [1]	Allow for subsequent movement
Resin injection	√	√	√	X	X
Vacuum impregnation	√	√	√	X	X
Polymer emulsions	X	√ [2]	?	X	X
Cement-based materials	?	√	?	√	X
Stitching	√	?	?	X	X
Movement joints	X	√	√	?	√
Bandaging	X	√	X	X	√
Surface coatings	X	√ [3]	√ [3]	√	√ [3]

√ indicates good chance of success; X indicates poor chance of success; ? indicates success depends very much on individual circumstances.

Notes: (1) As will be appreciated, this depends very much on individual opinions and circumstances.
(2) Effective when material fully fills the crack.
(3) With appropriate coatings.

5 Cost

The cost of repair materials is usually small compared with the costs of providing access, preparation and actual labour (see figure 7.2).

6 Appearance

The repaired surface may be unsightly, particularly when it appears on a prominent part of the building. In this case, the repair system will include some form of treatment over the entire surface.

7.3 Materials for Repair

There is available a wide range of materials differing in cost and performance for concrete repairs, both for making good spalled areas as

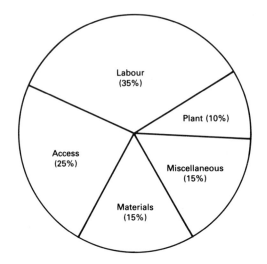

Figure 7.2   Cost components of a typical concrete repair

well as for overall protection by surface coating. Many manufacturers promote their materials proportioned in pre-weighed packages together with accompanying instructions on mixing, pot life and application.

7.3.1 Cement/Sand Mortars

Unmodified cement/sand mortars, often with special waterproofing admixtures added, are the most cost-effective repair materials available for damaged areas where the cover exceeds 25 mm. These materials have mechanical properties that resemble more closely those of the substrate. They are also fire-resistant and less sensitive to variation in temperature.

However, unmodified cement/sand mortars have poor strength in compression, tension and flexure and high surface permeability. Other disadvantages include poor adherence to the substrate, high shrinkage after setting and bond failure.

7.3.2 Polymer Latex

Polymer latex emulsions of various types are used in conjunction with Portland cement to obtain certain advantages: reduced permeability, stronger bond to existing concrete; increase in tensile strength of the repair; improved workability; and better chemical resistance.

There are a number of different types of polymer-modified latex available, including polyvinyl acetate (PVA), styrene butadiene rubber (SBR), polyvinylidene chloride (PVDC), acrylics and modified acrylics. The polymer latex acts in several ways:

- It functions as a water-reducing plasticiser to give better workability and reduce shrinkage.
- It improves the bond between the repair mortar and the substrate.
- It reduces the permeability of the repair material to water, carbon dioxide and oils.
- It increases the resistance of the repair material to chemical attack.
- It acts, to some degree, as an integral curing aid.

Styrene butadiene and acrylics are most widely used in concrete repair. When they are properly formulated, they are durable and perform well. On the other hand, polyvinyl dichloride is not recommended for reinforced concrete because of the possibility that free chlorides may be released in the long term. Polyvinyl acetate is also unsuitable for external applications or in damp environments because of the danger of the polymer breaking down under wet alkaline conditions.

7.3.3 Epoxy Resins

Most epoxy resins compounds used in concrete repairs are solvent-free and cure by chemical reaction between the resin and a hardener. Various formulations can be obtained by adjusting the proportions of resin, hardener and fillers to suit the conditions of use.

Factors that must be taken into account when choosing a formulation include the nature and condition of the substrate, the properties required from the cured material, the ambient temperature during application, the required viscosity of the fresh material, the rate of dissipation of heat from the compound while it cures, and the time available for placing it.

The basic characteristics of epoxy resins include the following:

- Outstanding adhesive qualities to concrete as well as steel.
- Resistance to most acids and alkalis and other chemicals.
- Rather vulnerable to organic solvents.
- Low shrinkage when the compound cures and changes from the liquid to the solid state.
- High compressive, tensile and flexural strength.
- Poor resistance to fire.

It is good practice to apply primer coats to both concrete substrate and steel to ensure good bonding. It is important to ensure that adequate cleaning of the steel is done and there is sufficient resin to fill up the voids between the aggregate particles, or else the materials may not form an impermeable barrier.

Epoxy resin systems develop high strength and have a shorter curing time than cementitious materials; they also have low shrinkage during and after curing. Special precautions need to be taken in handling the materials to prevent skin contact.

7.3.4 Polyester Resins

Polyester resins are slightly cheaper than epoxies but are still considerably more expensive than cementitious mortars. These compounds cure by action of a catalyst and are less sensitive to inaccuracies in proportioning than epoxies. They possess a number of desirable qualities such as good resistance to a wide range of chemicals, high resistance to abrasion and water penetration, and high bond strength with most building materials.

They are also used with glass fibres to form linings to liquid-retaining structures.

The amount of heat evolved during curing is greater than with epoxies. Shrinkage may continue over a longer time. Most polyesters do not bond well to damp surfaces. Like epoxies, they have little resistance to fire.

See table 7.2 for a comparison of the physical properties of various products used to repair concrete, and table 7.3 for a selection of repair materials.

7.4 Repairs to Spalled Concrete

7.4.1 Preparation

The first step in the repair process (see figure 7.3) is to cut away all loose or deteriorated concrete until the sound alkaline concrete core is reached, preferably behind corroding reinforcement. Cutting back should be approximately at right angles to external surfaces to avoid feather edging.

All exposed reinforcement must be thoroughly cleaned and loose rust, scale or any contamination removed by abrasive blast cleaning. Wire brushing by hand is not usually effective.

Sometimes the steel may be so seriously corroded as to require replacement. This is achieved by cutting away the corroded portions and replacing with new bars of the same type and size, either welded or tied to existing bars.

Table 7.2   Comparison of physical properties of typical products used in concrete repairs (Source: Shaw, J. D. N., Concrete decays, causes and remedies, *Proceedings of the 11th Conference on 'Our World in Concrete and Structures'*, Singapore, August 1986)

	Epoxy resin grouts, mortars and concretes	Polyester resin grouts, mortars and concretes	Cementitious grouts, mortars and concretes	Polymer modified cementitious systems
Compressive strength (N/mm^2)	55–110	55–110	20–70	10– 80
Compressive modulus *E*-value (kN/mm^2)	0.5– 20	2– 10	20–30	1– 30
Flexural strength (N/mm^2)	25– 50	25– 30	2– 5	6– 15
Tensile strength (N/mm^2)	9– 20	8– 17	1.5–3.5	2– 8
Elongation at break (%)	0– 15	0– 2	0	0– 5
Linear coefficient of thermal expansion per °C	$25-30\times10^{-6}$	$25-35\times10^{-6}$	$7-12\times10^{-6}$	$8-20\times10^{-6}$
Water absorption, 7 days at 25°C (%)	0– 1	0.2–0.5	5–15	0.1–0.5
Maximum service temperature under load (°C)	40– 80	50– 80	In excess of of 300° dependent upon mix design	100–300
Rate of development of strength at 20°C	6–48 hours	2–6 hours	1–4 weeks	1–7 days

In many instances, it is beneficial to apply a protective primer to the prepared steel immediately after cleaning. The primer should have a passivating effect, be impermeable and have good adhesive strength and good adhesion to subsequent repairs.

7.4.2 Cement-based Repairs

If the repair surrounds some reinforcement, it is usually unnecessary to provide additional mechanical anchorage but, in other cases,

Table 7.3   Selection of concrete repair materials (Source: Taylor, G., *Maintenance and Repair of Structural Concrete*, Maintenance Information Service Paper No. 87, CIOB, UK, 1981)

Applications Materials	Large spalls cover (mm)			Small spalls cover (mm)		Crack sealing	Structural crack repair
	>25	12–25	6–12	12–25	6–12		
Sand/aggregate/cement compositions including gunite	√						
SBR, acrylic and co-polymer lattices						√	
Latex-modified cementitious mortars		√		√			
Polyester resins, low viscosity						√	
Polyester resin mortars					√		
Epoxy resins, low viscosity							√
Epoxy resin mortars			√		√		
Universal bonding aids, PVA						√	
DRY SERVICE CONDITIONS ONLY							
PVA-modified mortars		√	√				

anchorage has to be provided by fixing in the concrete.

With hand-applied repair, it is advisable to use a resin or latex as a surface bonding agent. The most frequently used bonding agent consists of a slurry of polymer latex and Portland cement mixed on site in the proportions recommended by the manufacturer. Some polymers are used alone, without cement, as bonding coats.

The slurry is applied to all concrete and steel surfaces to which a bond is required, and the patching mortar must be applied while the slurry is still tacky. The concrete should be wetted before the material

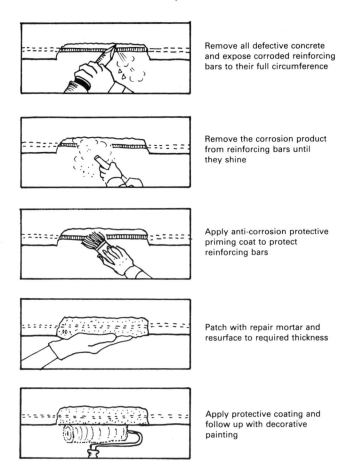

Remove all defective concrete and expose corroded reinforcing bars to their full circumference

Remove the corrosion product from reinforcing bars until they shine

Apply anti-corrosion protective priming coat to protect reinforcing bars

Patch with repair mortar and resurface to required thickness

Apply protective coating and follow up with decorative painting

Figure 7.3   Typical repair procedure for corrosion-damaged concrete

is applied, but there must be no standing water on the surfaces.

Epoxy resin formulations can also be used as bonding agents as alternatives to polymer latexes. The resin is applied on to the prepared surfaces of concrete and steel and, while it is still tacky, the patching mortar or concrete is applied. Epoxy resins adhere very strongly to clean, sound concrete or steel surfaces, and bonding agents based on them are formulated so that they bond well with freshly placed concrete or mortar.

After the prepared surfaces have been coated with bonding agent or a coating of neat cement slurry, the repair material consisting of 1:3 cement and sand, often with a polymer admixture, is applied in layers not exceeding 20 mm thick. Each layer should be keyed to receive the succeeding layers. The outer layers should not be richer in cement or thicker than the inner layers to prevent failure due to shrinkage stresses. The mortar should only contain just enough water to make it workable. It should be pressed or rammed into the spalled areas as firmly as possible.

It is necessary to ensure that cement-based materials used in repairs do not dry out too quickly. The method of curing will depend on local conditions; water-soaked covers and curing membranes are common ways of protection.

7.4.3 Resin-based Repairs

Epoxy resin mortars can be used for small jobs where rapid curing and chemical resistance are required. The normal practice is to apply a priming coat to the prepared surfaces and then build up to the desired profile with resin mortar.

As usual, the priming coat is applied soon after the preparation has been done in order to protect the surfaces. The interval between coats should not be too long, otherwise there will be bond failure.

Resins include a wide range of materials and careful selection of the correct type for the job is necessary. Selection considerations include the ambient temperature ranges during application; the time that will be available for application; the time between coats; the viscosity; the rate of curing; and the surface condition.

Resin-based materials cure by exothermic chemical reaction immediately the constituents are mixed. It is essential that the materials should be well-compacted and impermeable. Since they do not protect the reinforcement by alkalinity, they must, therefore, protect it by excluding oxygen, moisture and any other corrosive substances.

7.5 Sprayed Concrete

Gunite (see figure 7.4) is a general term for sprayed concrete in which the maximum aggregate size is less than 10 mm; that containing aggregate of 10 mm or greater in size is known as shotcrete.

Basically two systems exist: the wet process and the dry process. In the wet process, all the mix constituents and water are premixed and conveyed to the gun via compressed air; in the dry method, the dry constituents are conveyed to the ejection nozzle where the water is injected.

Normally low water contents are used and compaction is achieved by the velocity of the mix. But control of the water content depends entirely on the operator and his skill is particularly important.

Surfaces to which the sprayed concrete is to be applied must be

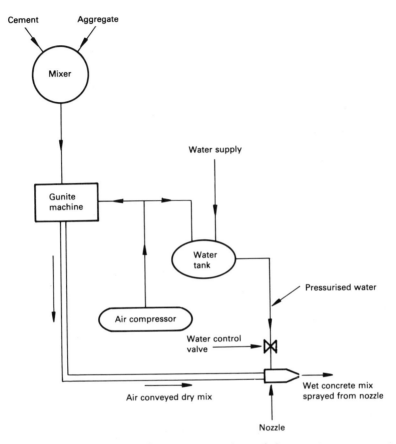

Figure 7.4   Diagrammatic representation of the gunite process

similarly prepared as with other methods of repair. In most cases, it is advisable to provide fabric mesh reinforcement in order to restrain and distribute shrinkage.

The thickness of the cover will depend on the severity of exposure and it is usually between 40 and 50 mm. Additional bar reinforcement can be fixed in structural repairs but congestion of reinforcement should be avoided.

The finished surface of gunite will not be as smooth as the surface obtained with the use of formwork. A certain amount of trowelling is permissible. In order to set the dimensions of the members to be repaired, timber batten guides may be fixed along the edges. Gunite is applied in two coats to the total thickness. The edges of the first coat must be roughened before the second coat is applied (see figure 7.5).

Damp curing is necessary and any conventional method of curing may be used.

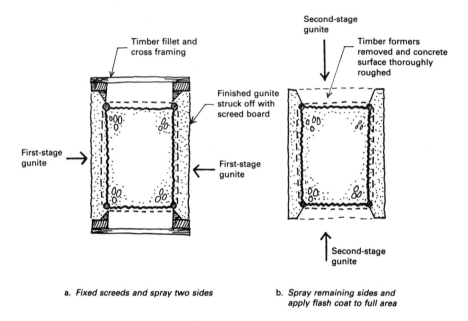

a. *Fixed screeds and spray two sides*   b. *Spray remaining sides and apply flash coat to full area*

Figure 7.5   Typical two-stage column repair by guniting

7.6 Large Volume Repair

With structures that have been extensively damaged, or where a large volume of repair material is needed, it becomes necessary to fix some kind of formwork and fill it with concrete or grout. The concrete is placed by conventional ways or it may be formed by injecting grout into a mass of dry aggregate.

7.6.1 Poured Concrete

Defective concrete is first removed and loose concrete is chipped away from the face and around the reinforcement. Additional reinforcement can be added by securely fastening it to existing bars.

It may be necessary to apply a protective coating to the steel in the form of a corrosion-inhibiting paint, a cement and polymer slurry or a resin-based slurry.

The formwork must be designed so that the concrete will fill it completely without creating any air-pockets (see figure 7.6). There must be adequate access for compaction purposes. All joints must be sealed to prevent leakage.

For pours where there is easy access for placing and compacting the

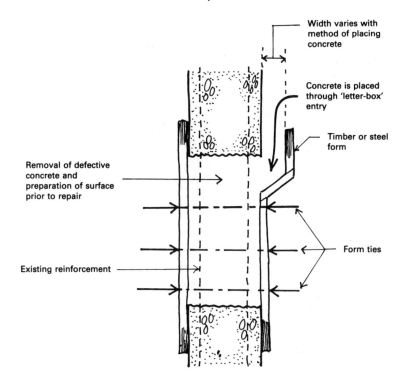

Figure 7.6   Letter-box formwork for wall or column repairs

concrete or where the thickness is 100 mm or more, a mix containing
20 mm aggregate in the normal proportions can be used. But for
thinner sections and more difficult access, a 10 mm maximum-sized
aggregate is preferred. Concrete mixes must also be designed to minimise bleeding and shrinkage.

The methods used to place the concrete are usually similar to those
used in new work, except that the quantities are smaller. Hand work,
therefore, is likely to be used instead of mechanical means.

Care must be taken to make sure that the repair concrete completely
fills up confined spaces without trapping any air. If access is available,
compaction can be done by internal vibration. Some external vibration
can be applied by using a mechanical hammer on the formwork.

7.6.2 Preplaced Concrete

The use of preplaced or prepacked concrete is well suited for certain
types of repair, particularly in underwater work.

In this method (see figure 7.7) formwork is erected in the normal
way, but it is filled with clean coarse aggregate, usually 20 mm or larger

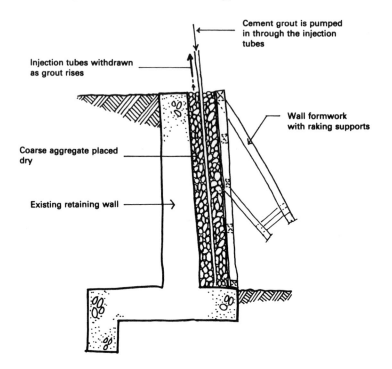

Cement grout is pumped
in through the injection
tubes

Injection tubes withdrawn
as grout rises

Wall formwork
with raking supports

Coarse aggregate placed
dry

Existing retaining wall

Figure 7.7   Prepacked aggregate/concrete repair to retaining wall

in size. Cement grout is then pumped into the forms from the bottom until all the voids are filled as the air or water is vented at the top.

It is essential that the forms must be watertight and designed to withstand the full hydrostatic head of grout.

Prepacked concrete has the advantage that the coarse aggregate is in inter-particle contact, thereby eliminating segregation and settlement and minimising drying shrinkage. The main disadvantage is that the injected cement paste is prone to bleeding.

7.7 Drypacking

Drypacking or plugging is the hand placement of a low water content mortar followed by tamping or ramming of the mortar into place, producing an intimate contact between the new and existing work. With this method there is little shrinkage and the patch remains tight and is of good quality with respect to durability, strength and water-tightness.

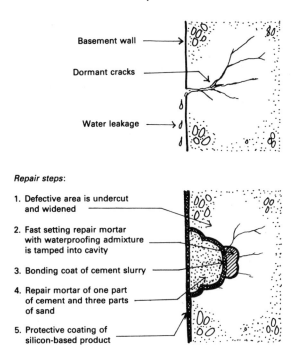

Basement wall

Dormant cracks

Water leakage

Repair steps:

1. Defective area is undercut and widened

2. Fast setting repair mortar with waterproofing admixture is tamped into cavity

3. Bonding coat of cement slurry

4. Repair mortar of one part of cement and three parts of sand

5. Protective coating of silicon-based product

Figure 7.8   Repair of a crack in a basement wall

This method of repair (see figure 7.8) is used for filling small, relatively deep areas, including those caused by dormant cracks. But it is not suitable for repairing large shallow areas or active cracks.

Before a crack may be repaired by drypacking, the adjacent surface must be widened and undercut with a saw. After the hole has been thoroughly cleaned and dried, a bonding coat of cement slurry should be applied. Placing of the dry pack mortar should then start immediately.

The mortar consists of one part of cement and three parts of fine sand with just sufficient water added so that the mix can be moulded into a ball by slight pressure of the hands without any extrusion of water.

The repair should be built up in thin layers. The surface of each layer should be scratched to facilitate bonding with the next. The last layer is finished with a wooden float. Curing is effected by using either water or a curing compound.

The repair may produce an unsightly patchy appearance. It may be necessary, therefore, to clean down and treat the whole surface with a rendering or to apply a coat of paint when the surface has dried out.

7.8 Sealing of Cracks

Before a crack is repaired it is necessary to determine its cause so that the correct method of repair can be decided. If the cause of the crack is unlikely to recur, it may be filled with a rigid material. But if it is caused by, say, some movement that is likely to continue, then any attempt to seal the crack against further movement may cause a new crack to appear alongside the old one.

7.8.1 No Further Movement Expected

Sometimes it may be sufficient to seal a narrow crack against moisture penetration by simply brushing dry cement or neat cement grout over it. Another way is to seal it with latex emulsion of low viscosity.

If it is necessary to fill a crack with a more rigid material, the most common method is to inject an epoxy resin of low viscosity into it (see figure 7.9).

This is done by first cleaning the crack thoroughly. A superficial seal is then applied over the crack at the surface by using a fast-setting polyester resin or a thermoplastic material into which injection nipples are fixed at intervals. Many of the materials used for sealing the crack between injection points can be peeled off easily on completion of the repair work.

For vertical surfaces, for example, a thixotropic resin is usually used, so that it will not drain out before it has cured. The injection starts at the lowest point and when the resin flows out of the next point, the injection gun is moved up to the next and the lower point is sealed. The process is repeated until the whole crack is sealed. The pressure used for injection must be carefully controlled to avoid a bursting action on the concrete. For small-scale work, special cartridges of resin can be used in a sealant gun.

7.8.2 Further Movement Expected

When a crack is subjected to continuing movement it is necessary to reduce the strain in it to a reasonable amount. This can be achieved by widening the whole crack at the surface and sealing it with an elastic material such as polysulphide rubber or a preformed neoprene strip (see figure 7.10). Alternatively, a 'bandage' can be applied by fixing a flexible sealant strip over the crack with only the edges of the strip bonded to the concrete.

In both cases, it is best to apply the seal when the crack is at its widest so that there will be less tendency for failure due to subsequent

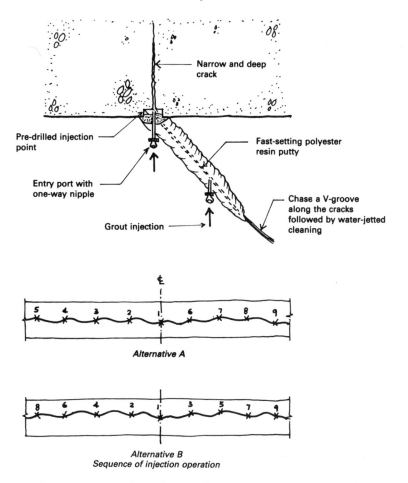

Figure 7.9   Crack sealing with resin injection technique

movements. It is also important that bonding is done in such a way that
the sealant is subjected to direct stress only.

7.9 Surface Coatings

After completion of any repair work it is desirable to treat both the
repaired areas and the rest of the structure with some coatings, principally to reduce the permeability of concrete to moisture, carbon dioxide and other aggressive agents. At the same time, the coatings can
also obliterate surface irregularities such as patchiness, discoloration
and stains, and match colours and textures.

a. *For vertical members (e.g. walls)*

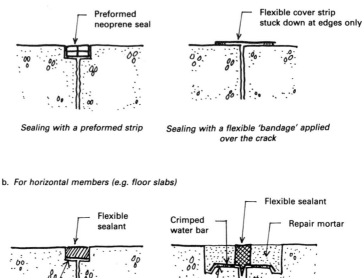

Sealing with a preformed strip   Sealing with a flexible 'bandage' applied
                                                  over the crack

b. *For horizontal members (e.g. floor slabs)*

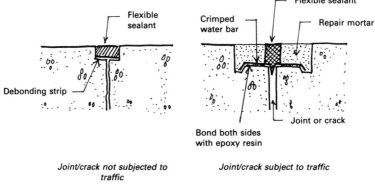

Joint/crack not subjected to   Joint/crack subject to traffic
        traffic

Figure 7.10   Treatment to cracks where further movement is
                         expected

7.9.1 Types of Coatings

Coatings comprise a blend of ingredients which cure to form a cohesive film. The behaviour of the paint as a liquid, and of the cured coating, depend largely on the relative quantities and types of raw materials used. The raw materials include binders, diluents, fillers, pigments and solvents, some or all of which may be used as the main constituents of a coating.

The various types of coatings available for concrete include:

1 Solvent-based Coatings

Solvent-based coatings are widely used because of their versatility and the wide range available. They are easily applied with the use of airless sprays and rollers.

Careful control of film thickness is necessary during application, otherwise the cured film is likely to blister. Ventilation is essential to ensure that all of the solvent evaporates before the film cures.

2 Solvent-free Coatings

A number of solvent-free coatings are available to overcome some of the drawbacks with solvents. Solvent-free coatings are most often specified because of the reduced risk of toxicity and fire hazard during application. Another advantage is their relative ease of achieving self-levelling properties.

The major disadvantage with solvent-free coatings is that they are relatively difficult to apply in comparison with the solvent-based type; this is due primarily to their higher viscosity.

3 Water-borne Coatings

Another approach to overcome the problems associated with solvents is to suspend or emulsify the uncured material in water. For example, in emulsion paints, water is added as a vehicle for the paint system.

Water-borne coatings are easily applied using conventional methods. The major disadvantage is that they will not cure properly in humid conditions which do not allow sufficient water evaporation.

4 Reinforced Coatings

These are typically solvent-free materials reinforced by fibres made from glass, rayon or polycarbonate.

The fibre-reinforced systems are normally used for repairing liquid-retaining structures which are badly cracked. The reinforcement permits the coating to bridge cracks and the typically high film thickness (3–5 mm) ensures that there is no passage of water under normal conditions. In addition, the high tensile strength of the material makes it resistant to cracking due to thermal effects.

Fibre-reinforced coatings are usually applied in layers by hard-rolling the fibre into the resin with a ribbed roller. The process can be accelerated by using a spraying machine but the laminate must still be thoroughly rolled to wet out the fibres.

7.9.2 Choice of Coating

The coating should be compatible with both the original and repaired concrete surfaces in respect of flow, penetration, film formation, adhesion and flexibility.

Ideally, surface coatings should:

• Possess excellent bond to the substrate.
• Be durable, with a useful life exceeding 20 years.

- Experience minimum colour change and little chalking.
- Have maximum permeability to the passing of water vapour from the concrete substrate.
- Have permeability coefficient to the passage of oxygen and carbon dioxide from the air to the concrete.
- Be available in a reasonable range of attractive colours.

The choice of protective coating systems is quite wide and various compositions have been used to coat concrete, including bituminous compounds, chlorinated rubber, polyvinyl copolymers, acrylics, polyurethanes and epoxy resins (see table 7.4). Long-term durability depends upon a number of factors such as chemical composition of the binder, formulation of the coating material, film thickness and application techniques.

With the more specialised polymer repair materials, appropriate coatings that can be used with the repair have been developed by the manufacturers. It is, therefore, necessary to obtain them from the same source. On the other hand, coatings that go well with cementitious materials are readily available. However, high-performance coating systems that provide good chemical and water resistance can be chosen from polyurethanes, epoxies, chlorinated rubbers or bitumens.

Where the natural appearance of masonry must be retained, colourless penetrating resin solutions, mainly of acrylic compositions, can be used to seal and waterproof the surface.

7.9.3 Preparation

It is essential that concrete surfaces are thoroughly clean and sound. All dirt, especially any contamination by oil or grease and loose debris, should be removed. Sometimes fungicidal treatments may also be required.

Coating systems can only be expected to form continuous effective films if they are applied to sound concrete surfaces. Small voids or blowholes must be filled prior to application of the selected coating.

Differences in porosity, suction rates and alkalinity of fresh cement, and the presence of laitance and mould oil, can all affect the effectiveness of the coating. The dryness of the original concrete and the repair at the time of application is also very important, especially when solvent-based coatings are used.

7.9.4 Performance

Normally, some chalking and surface erosion of the finishes are expected. In addition, other types of premature failure can also occur as a result of substrate or application faults.

Table 7.4 Types of coating for protection and redecoration of repaired reinforced concrete (Source: The Durability of Steel in Concrete, Part 3: The Repair of Reinforced Concrete, BRE Digest 265, HMSO, London, 1982)

Type	Thickness (mm)	Vapour permeance of typical films	Resistance to			Application, characteristics, comments	Durability outside (years)	Repainting
			Water	Alkalis, chemicals	Solvents, oils			
Water-thinned, vinyl and acrylic polymer emulsion paints								
Smooth, matt or fine textured	0.05–0.20	Medium to high	Moderate to high	Moderate to high (depending on formulation)	Low to moderate	Easy application; tolerant of damp surfaces, allow substrate drying; film formation a problem in cold, damp conditions or if rewet before properly dried; frost susceptible; fairly flexible films; good adhesion	3–10; depending on formulation and thickness	Same type or textured
Thick, smooth, 'plastic' coatings	0.20–0.50	Low	High (after fully dry)	Moderate	Low to moderate	Poor drying conditions, trapped moisture or early rewetting can cause swelling, blistering, loss of adhesion; very flexible; easy brush or spraying; harden and chalk later	5–10	Same or smooth, matt or textured emulsion
Medium to heavy textured	0.50–3.0	Medium (depending on thickness and uniformity)	Moderate to high	High	Moderate	Best rolled or sprayed for uniform coverage and texture to give reproducible permeability and protection; some flexibility but splitting or 'mud-cracking' can occur by drying shrinkage or movement; good adhesion to sound substrate	10, soiling in polluted areas	Emulsion, matt or fine textured

continued on p. 146

Table 7.4 continued

Type	Thickness (mm)	Vapour permeance of typical films	Resistance to			Application, characteristics, comments	Durability outside (years)	Repainting
			Water	Alkalis, chemicals	Solvents, oils			
Bituminous emulsions	0.25–1.0	Low to very low	High	High	Low	Easy application; require surface free from loose powdery material for good adhesion; soft yielding film; surface weathers but can be overcoated with specific decorative or protective emulsion with light-colours to reduce heat absorbance	Up to 10; depending on thickness and formulation (or over-coating)	Bituminous emulsions (compatible emulsion top coats)
Solvent-thinned, clear acrylic or resin co-polymer solutions	(0.015–0.040 residual film)	Medium to high	High	Moderate to high	Low to moderate	Thin, penetrating; usually fairly rapid drying; surface film may be 'glossy' and darken; susceptible to UV radiation, embrittlement crazing and erosion outside; possible patchiness	3	Same type or opaque masonry paints
Acrylic solution paints	0.10–0.15	Low to medium	High	High	Low to moderate	Good application and drying; good adhesion, smooth sheen; not very flexible; good colour stability	5+ (experience limited)	Same type
Sprayed or rolled resin-based textured coatings	0.6–1.2	Low to medium (depending on thickness and formulation)	High	Low	Moderate	Require alkali-resistant sealer on fresh concrete; fairly flexible initially but hardens; require sound base for good adhesion; good appearance, can hold soiling but some self-cleaning by chalking	10–15	Same type (thinner) or emulsion and other masonry paints (except chlorinated rubber)

Type								
High-build chlorinated rubber paints	0.10–0.20	Low to very low	Very high	High	Low	Sticky brushing but good uniformity by spraying; slow through drying; soft and flexible initially but harden; smooth moderate gloss but usually chalk later	7+	Chlorinated rubber paints (possible solvent 'pick-up' problem)
Chemically-cured epoxy or epoxy/polyurethane systems (PU)	0.10–0.20	Low to very low	Very high	High	High	Two-component, mixed just before applying; sticky to apply especially on rough surfaces; good curing at normal temperature with low shrinkage; good adhesion and abrasion resistance; may be time limits between successive coats; not flexible unless especially formulated. Epoxy paints chalk strongly on weathering. Polyurethane top coats which chalk less give protection. Aliphatic PU gives best colour stability	7+; best types 10+	Same type; possible adhesion problems unless old paint has adequate 'key', e.g. well abraded
Bitumen paints	0.10–0.25+	Low to very low (depending on thickness and uniformity)	High	High	Low	Easy application; porous surfaces may need bitumen primer; soft film surface rapidly weathers in sunlight and can craze or crack; good choice for below ground; adhesion good	4–5; better if top coat pigmented with aluminium	Same type

Solvent-based coatings are generally less tolerant of dampness. The film formation is more dependent on temperature for water-thinned paints. In both cases, however, the temperature of the air and the concrete mass affect the rates of drying and curing of the coating. Chemically cured coatings are difficult to apply to porous or rough surfaces.

Two-coat systems are usually recommended when brushing is adopted; spraying can give more coverage and uniform films; and rollers give good texture with some acceptable variability of permeability unless the material is uniformly spread.

7.10 External Reinforcing

7.10.1 Stitching

This method involves drilling holes on both sides of the crack and grouting in 'dogs' that span across the crack (see figure 7.11). Stitching may be used when tensile strength must be re-established across major cracks.

Stitching a crack tends to stiffen the whole structure; and the stiffening may increase the overall structural restraint, causing the concrete to crack elsewhere. Therefore, it may be necessary to strengthen the adjacent section using external reinforcement embedded in a suitable overlay.

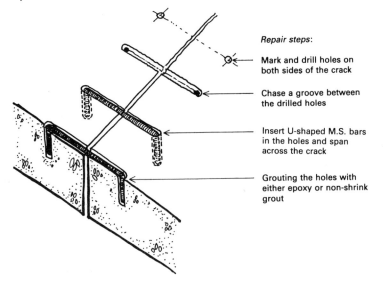

Repair steps:

Mark and drill holes on both sides of the crack

Chase a groove between the drilled holes

Insert U-shaped M.S. bars in the holes and span across the crack

Grouting the holes with either epoxy or non-shrink grout

Figure 7.11   Stitching method of repairing wall/slab cracks

Pairs of holes are first drilled on opposite sides of a crack. A chased groove is then made and cleaned. The mild steel 'dogs' are then inserted and anchored in the holes with either a non-shrink grout or an epoxy resin-based bonding system.

The stitching 'dogs' are usually fixed in various lengths and orientation, and should be so located that the tension transmitted across the crack is not applied to a single plane within the section but is spread over an area.

Spacing of the 'dogs' should be reduced at the end of the cracks. Where possible, stitching should be done on both sides of the concrete section so that further movement will not bend the 'dogs'.

Stitching will not close up a crack but can prevent it from propagating further. Where there is a water problem, the crack should be made watertight as well as stitched to protect the 'dogs' from corrosion. This repair should be completed before stitching begins.

7.10.2 Prestressing Steel

Post-tensioning is often the desirable solution when a major portion of a member must be strengthened or when the cracks that have formed must be closed.

This technique depends on prestressing strands or bars to apply a compressive force (see figure 7.12). Adequate anchorage must be provided for the prestressing steel.

The effects of the tensioning force and eccentricity on the stress within the structure should be carefully analysed before commencement of repair work using this method.

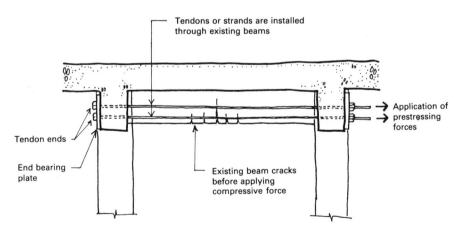

Figure 7.12 Application of external prestressing for tensile cracks

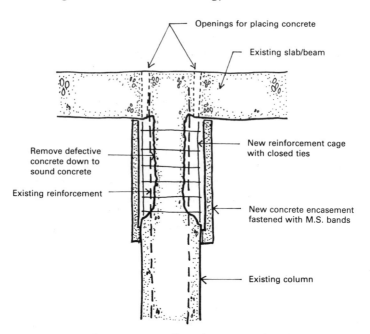

Figure 7.13 Use of concrete collars for strengthening compression concrete member

7.10.3 Jacketing

Concrete members which are cracked through the cross-section may be restored either by constructing a new reinforced concrete collar or by installing a series of tensioned steel straps around the existing members. Concrete jackets are commonly used for compression members such as columns and piles (see figure 7.13).

A cage of steel reinforcement is fixed around the damaged section and new shotcrete or formed concrete overlay is then applied. The new reinforced concrete collar will effectively restore the compressive strength, shear strength or flexural strength to the column. The concrete collar is only effective, however, within the confined area of the cage for shear and flexural forces. It is, therefore, important to check the strength of the existing connection between pile and pile cap or beam and column.

An alternative method of collaring is to install steel plates to act as compression members around the cracked column sections. But this method is suitable only for in-door conditions where exposure is not so severe.

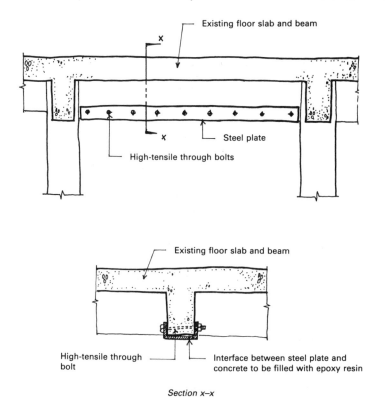

Figure 7.14 Beam strengthening with steel plates

7.10.4 Steel Plate Bonding

The use of mild steel plates over reinforced concrete members for greater shear and flexural strength has been found to be economical and effective for underdesigned structures (see figure 7.14).

In this technique, mild steel plates of calculated cross-sectional area are fixed on to the weak members by bolts and bonded with a suitable epoxy resin by injection. An epoxy with high bonding characteristics is usually used between two different materials, such as steel and concrete, to transfer stresses from the concrete to the steel plates. After installation and grouting, anti-corrosion protection is applied on the exposed surfaces of the steel plates.

One distinct advantage of the method is that the size of the member is not increased significantly. Therefore the technique can be used to its full advantage in areas which do not have sufficient headroom or

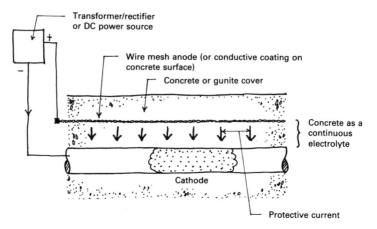

Figure 7.15   Typical cathodic protection system

working space. Other merits include the speed of repair without having to vacate the premises.

7.11 Cathodic Protection

When an electrical current flows from one area (anode) of a reinforcing bar to another (cathode), the anodic area will corrode in preference to the cathodic area. In practice, there can be thousands of these corrosion cells being set up in a single slab.

The main application of cathodic protection (see figure 7.15) is found in buried reinforced concrete water pipelines. In this process, an external durable anode is introduced into or on the concrete which is then connected to a DC power source. The electric current is forced through the anode into the concrete and to the reinforcing steel. A wire connected to the steel bar brings the current back to the source. When sufficient protection current flows on to the steel to balance or nullify the corrosion current, the corrosion process will stop.

7.12 Repairs to Fire-damaged Structures

The need to assess the residual strength of fire-damaged structural members is an important prerequisite for any structural repair.

The residual strength of normal quality concrete is not much reduced by temperatures up to 300°C, but is affected by higher temperatures, particularly if the temperature rises above 500°C. In respect of reinforcing steel, the effect is more complex. Significant loss of

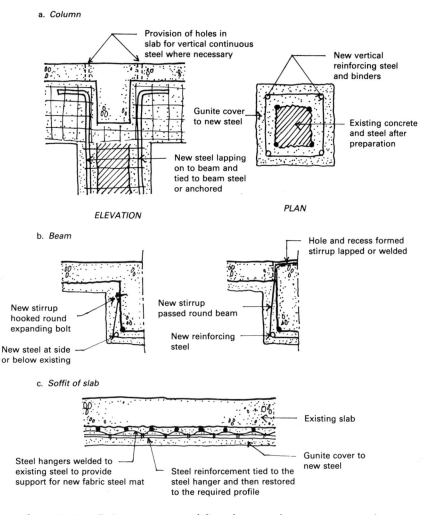

a. *Column*

Provision of holes in slab for vertical continuous steel where necessary

New vertical reinforcing steel and binders

Gunite cover to new steel

Existing concrete and steel after preparation

New steel lapping on to beam and tied to beam steel or anchored

ELEVATION

PLAN

b. *Beam*

Hole and recess formed stirrup lapped or welded

New stirrup hooked round expanding bolt

New stirrup passed round beam

New steel at side or below existing

New reinforcing steel

c. *Soffit of slab*

Existing slab

Gunite cover to new steel

Steel hangers welded to existing steel to provide support for new fabric steel mat

Steel reinforcement tied to the steel hanger and then restored to the required profile

Figure 7.16   Reinstatement of fire-damaged concrete members

strength may occur while the steel is at high temperatures, and this usually results in excessive deflections. However, recovery of yield strength after cooling is generally complete for temperatures below 450°C for mild steel and 600°C for high yield steel. For prestressing tendons, the effect is much more critical.

The sprayed concrete repair technique (see figure 7.16) is the most common method of repairing fire-damaged structures. Hand-applied mortars or patching method will be most suitable for repairs to smaller areas. In some cases where damage is beyond normal repair, recasting the affected area is normally recommended.

The engineer, in drawing up the repair specification, will have to examine the extent of damage in the structure. Some non-destructive tests may be used for this purpose. In every case, preparation of repair will involve cutting away deteriorated concrete back to sound concrete which is not affected by the fire. This is done usually by hand-held tools. A light welded steel mesh is typically incorporated in the repair when substantial areas or thickness of work is necessary.

Related and Further Reading

Allen, R. T. L. *The Repair of Concrete Structures*. Cement and Concrete Association, UK (1985).

Allen, R. T. L. and Edwards, S. C. *Repair of Concrete Structures*. Blackie, London (1987).

American Concrete Institute. *Specification for Materials, Proportioning and Application of Shotcrete*. ACI Report 506.2 (1977, revised 1983).

American Concrete Institute. *Control of Cracking in Concrete Structures*. ACI Report 224R-80 (1980).

American Concrete Institute. *Use of Epoxy Compounds with Concrete*. ACI Report 503R-80 (1980).

American Concrete Institute. *Guide to Joint Sealants for Concrete Structures*. ACI Report 504R-80 (1980).

American Concrete Institute. *Concrete Repair and Restoration*. ACI Report Compilation No. 5 (1980).

American Concrete Institute. *Causes, Evaluation and Repair of Cracks in Concrete Structures*. ACI Report 224.1R.84 (1984).

Ashworth, V. and Googan, C. G. Cathodic protection of concrete reinforcement. *Proceedings of Seminar on 'Corrosion in Concrete: Monitoring, Surveying and Control by Cathodic Protection'*, London (May, 1986).

Berkeley, K. G. C. and Pathmanaban, S. *Cathodic Protection of Reinforcement Steel in Concrete*. Butterworths, London (1990).

British Standards Institution. *BS 8007: 1987 Code of Practice for design of concrete structures for retaining aqueous liquids*.

Building Research Establishment, UK. *The Durability of Steel in Concrete Part 3: The Repair of Reinforced Concrete*. Digest 265 (1982).

Building Research Establishment, UK. *Sulphate and Acid Resistance of Concrete in the Ground*. Digest 363 (1991).

Cement and Concrete Association, UK. *Repairs to Concrete Structures, Diagnosis of the Causes of Defects and Deterioration*. Advisory Sheet No. 60 (1982).

Concrete Society, UK. *Underwater Concreting*. Technical Report No. 3 (1971).

Concrete Society, UK. *Assessment of Fire-damaged Concrete and Repair by Gunite*. Technical Report No. 15 (1978).

Concrete Society, UK. *Specification for Sprayed Concrete*. Publication 53.029 (1979).

Concrete Society, UK. *Code of Practice for Sprayed Concrete*. Publication 53.030 (1980).

Concrete Society, UK. *Non-structural Cracks in Concrete*. Technical Report No. 22 (1982).

Concrete Society, UK. *The Repair of Concrete Damaged by Reinforcement Corrosion*. Technical Report No. 26 (Oct., 1984).

Davies, H. and Rothwell, G. W. *The Effectiveness of Surface Coatings in Reducing Carbonation of Reinforced Concrete*. Information Paper IP 7/89, Building Research Establishment, UK (1989).

Fargeot, B. and Jartoux, P. External prestressing in the maintenance of structures. *Concrete Repairs*, Volume 2, pp. 73–76. Palladian, London (1985).

Greve, H. G. Restoring strength to damaged or deteriorated structural concrete. *Concrete Construction* (November, 1987).

Gunning, J. G. Concrete repair techniques. *Building Technology and Management*, UK (March, 1980).

Higgins, D. *Construction Guide: Repairs to Concrete Affected by Reinforcement Corrosion*. Publication No. 45.040, Cement and Concrete Association, UK (1984).

Higgins, D. Repairs to cracks in concrete. *Concrete Repairs*, pp. 23–26. CONCRETE publication, UK (1984).

Johnson, S. M. *Deterioration, Maintenance and Repair of Structures*. McGraw-Hill, New York (1965).

Leeming, M. Surface coatings for concrete. *Construction Repair*, UK (Feb., 1987).

Little, D. Resin based repair materials. *Proceedings of Seminar on 'Deterioration and Repair of Concrete Structures'*, Singapore (June, 1986).

Littlejohn, G. S. *Grouted preplaced aggregate concrete. Proceedings of Concrete Society Conference on 'Concrete in the Ground'*, London (1984).

Papworth, F. Inspection and repair, including cathodic protection. *Proceedings of Seminar on 'Deterioration and Repair of Concrete Structures'*, Singapore (June, 1986).

Perkins, P. H. *Concrete Structures: Repair, Waterproofing and Protection*. Applied Science Publishers, London (1977).

Shaw, J. D. N. The use of epoxy resins for the repair of deteriorated concrete structures. *Proceedings of Concrete Society Symposium on 'Advances in Concrete'*, Birmingham (1971).

Shaw, J. D. N. Polymers for concrete repair. *Civil Engineering*, pp. 63–65 (June, 1983).

Shaw, J. D. N. Materials for concrete repair. *Proceedings of 1st International Conference on 'Deterioration and Repair of Reinforced Concrete*, The Arabian Gulf (Oct., 1985).

Shaw, J. D. N. Concrete decay: causes and remedies. *Proceedings of 11th Conference on 'Our World in Concrete and Structures'*, Singapore (August, 1986).

Shaw, J. D. N. Adhesives in the construction industry: materials and case histories. *Construction and Building Materials*, UK, Vol. 4, No. 2 (June, 1990).

Tabor, L. J. *Effective Use of Epoxy and Polyester Resins in Civil Engineering Structures*. CIRIA Report No. 69, CIRIA, London (1978).

Taylor, G. *Maintenance and Repair of Structural Concrete*. Maintenance Information Service Paper No. 87, Chartered Institute of Building, UK (1981).

Williams, J. T. and Parker, A. J. Reinforced concrete: structural considerations and choice of products for repair. In Dhir, R. K. and Green, J. W. (eds), *Protection of Concrete*. Spon, London (1990).

8 Timber and Timber Components

Timbers used commercially are divided into softwoods and hardwoods. Softwoods are obtained from cone-bearing trees with needle-like leaves, for example, pine, fir or kauri. Hardwoods such as birch, teak or meranti are obtained from broad-leaved trees.

Timber does not deteriorate spontaneously and could last indefinitely if it were not attacked by certain external forces. The causes of timber failures, whether structural or non-structural, are numerous. But if preventive measures had been taken at the design, construction and post-construction stages, enormous sums of money could have been saved in its repair and replacement.

8.1 Structure of Timber

Each part of a tree contributes distinctly to its growth pattern, but the combined contribution affects the quality of the tree as a whole, which in turn directly influences the quality of the marketable timber.

8.1.1 Heartwood and Sapwood

A cross-section through a fully developed tree will, as a rule, show a comparatively dark coloured central portion or heartwood surrounded by a lighter coloured zone called sapwood (see figure 8.1).

The heartwood content of a tree increases with age. Thus, the log of an immature tree is chiefly composed of sapwood, the cells of which conduct mineral salt solutions from the soil to the leaves and the sap manufactured from them. Later on, this function is performed by the more recently formed growth rings, and the cells in the inner core become inactive and contribute to the heartwood which provides mechanical support of the tree only.

157

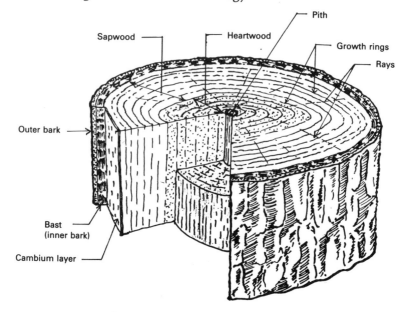

Figure 8.1   Section of tree trunk

Heartwood cells contain deposits of gum, resin and tannin which influence the colour and increase the durability. There is no appreciable difference in strength between sapwood and heartwood. But sapwood is more vulnerable to rot.

8.1.2 Cellular Structure

Approximately nine-tenths of the wood in softwoods consists of comparatively long, vertical tubular cells called tracheids. Tracheids fulfil the functions of conduction and mechanical support. The springwood with large cell cavities and thin walls readily provides conduction, while the summerwood with small cell cavities and thick walls gives mechanical support.

Cells called vessels perform the function of conduction in hardwoods, and in cross-section these appear as pores (see figure 8.2). Mechanical support is provided by cells called fibres which have thick walls.

The cellular structure of timber mainly accounts for the anisotropic nature of wood, particularly with regard to differences in strength, shrinkage movement and permeability along the grain and across the grain; as well as radially and tangentially to the growth rings.

In addition, the cellular structure also explains many aspects of the use of timber: for example, timber holds glue better than other non-

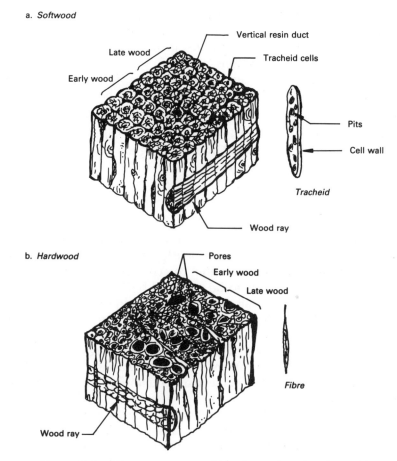

a. *Softwood*

Vertical resin duct

Late wood

Tracheid cells

Early wood

Pits

Cell wall

Tracheid

Wood ray

b. *Hardwood*

Pores

Early wood

Late wood

Fibre

Wood ray

Figure 8.2 Microstructure of hardwood and softwood

porous materials because the glue is able to form a 'key' by penetrating the cell cavities; the preservation of wood is easily achieved by forcing a liquid into the cellular structure; and timbers with thick cell walls and small cell cavities are hard and difficult to work, whereas those with thin cell walls and large cell cavities are easy to work.

8.1.3 Grain

The term grain is used to describe the general direction or arrangement of the fibres relative to the main axis. There are several types of grain, for example

- Straight grain, where the fibres are parallel.
- Irregular grain, where the fibres are inclined.

- Wavy grain, where the fibres frequently change direction.
- Spiral grain, where the fibres are arranged spirally.
- Interlocking grain, where the fibres in successive growth rings are inclined in opposite directions.
- Diagonal grain, where straight-grained timber has been improperly converted so that the fibres are inclined to the horizontal edges.

Marked local deviations from straight grain, as around knots, cause a reduction in most strength properties. Wavy and spiral grain can result in distortion during drying, and interlocked grain can make it difficult to obtain good machined surfaces.

8.2 Moisture Content

The moisture content of timber is the quantity of moisture contained by it, expressed as a percentage of the dry weight. When the timber is 'green', moisture is contained within the cells and the cellular walls.

Most of this moisture has to be removed before the timber can be used. The condition when all the cells are devoid of moisture but the cell walls are still saturated is referred to as the fibre saturation point, usually between 25 and 30 per cent moisture content. Any further reduction in moisture content will result in shrinkage of the timber which should be carefully controlled to avoid wastage. Timber, being hygroscopic, will attempt to achieve an equilibrium moisture content with its environment.

The various forms of distortion which may develop in timber during drying below fibre saturation point are caused by differential shrinkage. Timber is not homogeneous and the shrinkage takes place in all the three dimensions, being greatest across the grain in the direction tangential to the growth rings, and about half in the radial direction (see figure 8.3).

8.3 Mechanical Strength

Strength of timber is affected by factors such as density, moisture content and grain structure as well as by the various defects. Denser timber is stronger because it has thicker cellular walls which contribute to the strength. Generally, hardwoods are denser and thus stronger than softwoods because the growth rings are closer together.

An increase in moisture content will give rise to a reduction in strength (see figure 8.4). In addition, high moisture content supports fungal and insect attacks which, in both cases, also result in an indirect reduction in strength of the timber.

Grain structure and continuity influence the strength of timber to

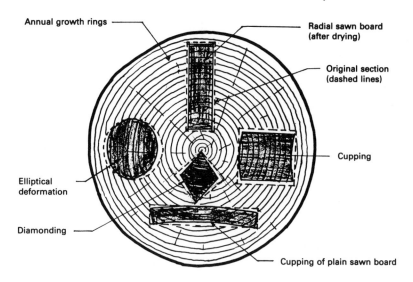

Figure 8.3   Characteristic shrinkage patterns caused by direction of the growth rings

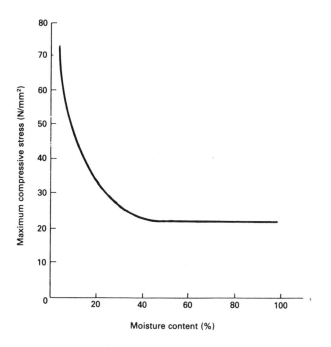

Figure 8.4   Relationship between moisture content and longitudinal compressive strength of timber

the extent that any disruption due to growth defects or conversion and seasoning defects will induce a reduction in strength from that of normal timber. For example, a slope of 1 in 25 in the grain can reduce the strength to 96 per cent of that of a normal specimen, while a slope of 1 in 15 can reduce the strength to 89 per cent.

Mechanical stress grading tests applied on timber specimens parallel to the grain and perpendicular to the grain will yield significant variations in strength.

See figures 8.5 and 8.6

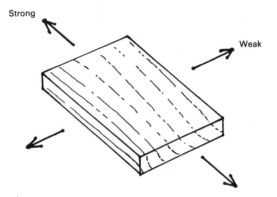

Figure 8.5   Anisotropic property of wood

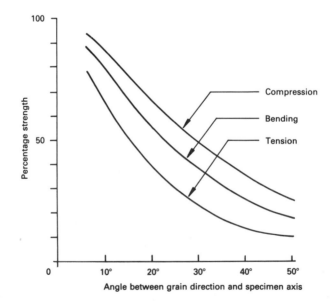

Figure 8.6   Effect of grain angle on the tensile, bending and compressive strength of timber

8.4 Factors Affecting Durability

Timber and timber-based products are organic substances and hence will be affected by climatic, biological and physical factors in the built environment. The relative importance of each factor depends upon circumstances. For example, heat, radiation and insect attack are of greater significance in the tropics than elsewhere.

1 Moisture
Atmospheric moisture, whether in liquid or vapour form, has the greatest effect on the durability of timber in external situations. Timber absorbs moisture, becomes saturated and swells. This is followed by surface drying, which causes shrinkage, and eventual opening up of the timber grain during the dry periods will enable moisture to penetrate to greater depths. This results in the slow disintegration of the unprotected timber surfaces and decay of the wet inner parts.

2 Heat
Dry heat greatly reduces moisture content and causes shrinkage. This often leads to splitting and cracking near the ends of boards.

Timber is a reasonably good insulator against heat because of its porosity and lightness. Although fire is a major hazard, the charred layer can protect the underlying wood against rapid burning.

3 Ultra-violet Radiation
Ultra-violet radiation, which is particularly intense in the tropics, causes colour changes and a gradual degradation of exposed timber surfaces. Depending upon the species, exposed timber will gradually assume a silver to brownish-grey colour.

4 Mechanical Wear
The most common form of mechanical wear is abrasion caused either by pedestrians or equipment continually passing over timber floors. The degree of abrasion depends on the type and hardness of the timber as well as the direction of the abrasive force.

8.5 Defects in Timber

Defects occur in timber at various stages, mainly during its growth and during the conversion and seasoning process. Any of these defects can affect timber either by reducing its strength or marring its appearance.

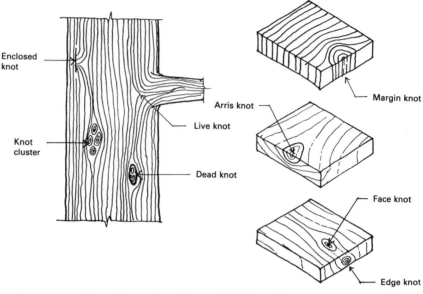

Figure 8.7   Natural defects: knots

8.5.1 Natural Defects

Natural defects occur during the growth of the tree and include the following:

1 Knots
A knot is the part of a branch which becomes enclosed within the growing trunk (see figure 8.7). Knots affect the strength of the timber because they cause a deviation of the grain. This is of particular import-ance where they occur in critical parts of structural timbers subject to high tension.

With a live knot there is complete continuity between the fibres of the branch and the tree. A dead knot has less than 25 per cent of the cross-section of the knot perimeter fibres continuous with those of the tree.

BS 1186 and CP 112 contain limitations on use regarding both strength and appearance.

2 Shakes
Shakes refer to a separation of fibres along the grain principally owing to stresses developing in the tree (see figure 8.8). They affect the strength of timber by reducing the cross-sectional area of the complete fibrous section.

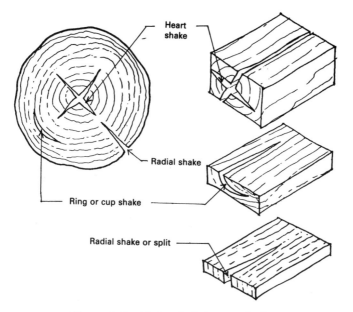

Figure 8.8 Natural defects: shakes

A heart shake is a radial shake originating at the heart; a ring or cup shake follows a growth ring; and a star shake consists of a number of heart shakes resembling a star.

8.5.2 Conversion Defects

Conversion is the term used to describe the process whereby the felled tree is converted into marketable sizes of timber (see figure 8.9). As the trunk is not of a constant girth throughout its entire length, it is not possible to obtain the same amount of marketable timber over the whole length of the trunk. There will be, therefore, varying lengths of different cross-section, and in these lengths there may be a number of growth defects which will limit the marketable lengths or size of section, or both.

The main methods of conversion are by radial or quarter sawing, tangential or plain sawing, and slab sawing.

While plain sawing may be the most economical, it produces sections in which the angle of grain or the axis of the annual growth rings is not optimum. This condition can result in distortion of the boards during seasoning.

Conversion defects are due basically to unsound practice in milling or attempts to economise during conversion of the timber (see figure 8.10). For example, a wane occurs in timber which contains, on one or

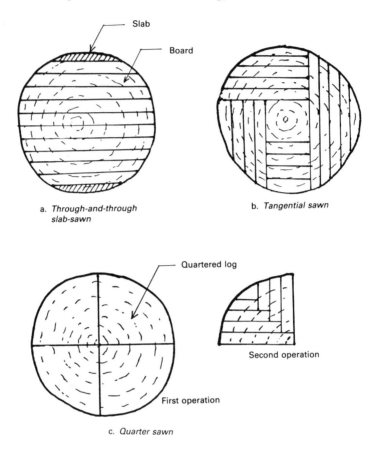

a. *Through-and-through slab-sawn*

b. *Tangential sawn*

c. *Quarter sawn*

Figure 8.9   Methods of timber conversion

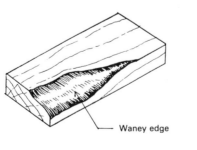

a. *Wane*

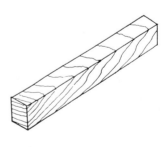

b. *Slope of grain*

Figure 8.10   Conversion defects

more faces, part of the bark or the rounded periphery of the trunk. This reduces the cross-sectional area, with consequent reduction in the strength. Slope of grain may be pronounced enough to amount to a defect.

8.5.3 Seasoning Defects

These defects are directly caused by the movement which occurs in timber due to changes in moisture content. Excessive or uneven drying, exposure to wind and rain, and poor stacking during seasoning can all produce distortions in timber. These defects are mostly irreversible and obviously result in high wastage. The common types of seasoning defects are:

1 Checks
Checking is the longitudinal separation of the fibres which does not extend throughout the whole cross-section of the wood. As the moisture evaporates more rapidly from the surfaces, they tend to shrink before the inner layers, and splitting occurs.

Splitting is the separation of the fibres which extends through a piece of timber from one face to another.

See figure 8.11.

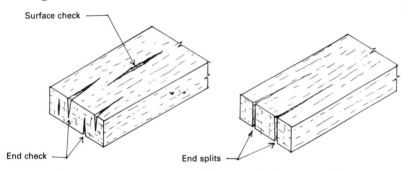

Figure 8.11 Seasoning defects: checks and splits

2 Warping
A warp is a distortion in converted timber which causes a departure from its original plane (see figure 8.12).

Cupping occurs when a sawn board curves in section away from the heart of the tree.

Twisting occurs in the piece of timber owing to differential drying out of distorted grain.

Springing and bowing are caused by improper placing of spacers between planks of timber during seasoning, resulting in uneven loading.

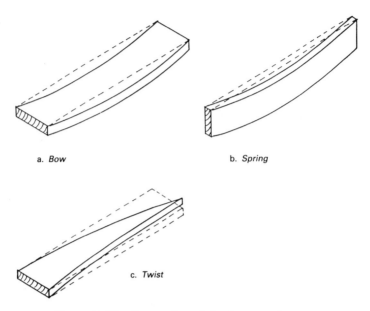

a. *Bow*   b. *Spring*

c. *Twist*

Figure 8.12   Seasoning defects: warping

3 Collapse
This is a condition which may occur during the early stages of seasoning very wet timber which may shrink unevenly and/or excessively. The
cells are flattened as a result of the partial vacuum created by the
evaporation of the water and its retarded replacement by air. Collapse
can be prevented if the timber is dried at low temperatures in the early
stages.

8.6 Fungal Attack

Fungi are the chief cause of decay of timber. The development of fungus
is dependent on moisture, oxygen and cellulose in the timber, and the
absence of any one of these prevents decay. A suitable temperature is
also essential for fungoid growth. Fungal attack can be caused by either
dry rot or wet rot.

8.6.1 Dry Rot

The fungus-producing dry rot is known as the *Serpula lacrymans*. The
conditions ideal for its growth include a moisture content of 30–40 per
cent and a temperature of 23°C. Partially seasoned wood fixed in a
warm, damp and poorly ventilated position is therefore susceptible to
dry rot attack.

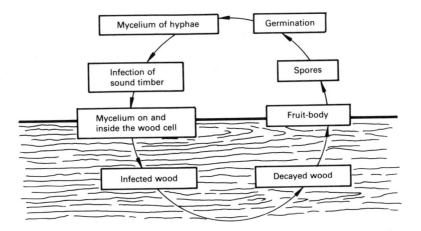

Figure 8.13 Life cycle of a wood-destroying fungus

The spores of the fungus develop under favourable conditions and minute, silky, hollow, thread-like hyphae rapidly spread over the surface of wood, across brickwork and concrete, and along steelwork. Dry rot is the most serious of all wood-rotting fungi because the parent fruit-body can produce millions of red dust-like spores which are readily distributed by air currents, insects, vermin and other animals (see figure 8.13).

During the development of the fungus, the hyphae attack the fibres of the wood and feed upon the substance of the cell walls which are gradually broken down. The decayed wood becomes friable and falls to powder under pressure by the fingers; it is dry; the surface becomes uneven; and cracks extend both with and across the grain, dividing it into cubical pieces. The colour is brown, the wood has a musty smell, it is reduced in weight and has very little strength.

Prevention
The following are some precautions that should be taken to prevent timber from being attacked by dry rot.

- All timber used for building purposes should be sound and well-seasoned with a moisture content not exceeding 20 per cent.
- The timber must be kept dry while it is in use. It is for this reason that dampness in buildings must be avoided. For example, dampness due to defective eaves gutters, roof coverings, drains and damp-proof courses may cause decay of timber.
- Adequate circulation of fresh air around all timbers must be provided, as stagnant moist air is particularly favourable to the growth of dry rot. Provision must therefore be made for sufficient cross ventilation under all timber floors, especially ground and basement floors.

Remedial Measures

The curative measures necessary to eradicate the problem depend upon its extent. Drastic steps must be taken in serious cases of attack. For example, the following would be the sequence of operations if an examination of a ground floor disclosed extensive decay:

1 The whole of the affected timber and 300–450 mm beyond is removed, including skirtings, floor boards, joists, wall plates and grounds, and immediately burnt, preferably on site. Any plaster behind which the fungus may have spread must also be removed.
2 The faces of the walls below the floor and the surface of the site concrete are well cleaned down with a wire brush.
3 Sterilising the surfaces of the walls and site concrete now follows. To ensure complete success, it is advisable to apply a reliable insecticide solution liberally in two coats. A suitable insecticide is a 4 per cent solution of sodium fluoride.
4 Necessary structural work, such as the insertion of a horizontal damp-proof course, the provision of air bricks, the construction of sleeper walls and the laying of site concrete, is carried out.
5 Finally, new floor timbers, skirtings, etc. are fixed. The timber must be sound and well seasoned, and treated with suitable preservative.

The whole process of replacement is costly but cannot be avoided if a permanent cure to the problem is desired.

8.6.2 Wet Rot

Wet rot may occur in timber which is excessively wet, whether located in the interior or exterior of the building. The cellar fungus, *Coniophora puteana*, is perhaps the most widely encountered wet rot fungus. It appears on timber as a very dark brown, vein-like pattern and destroys the cell structure of timber by consuming only the cellulose. The decay and growth is almost completely internal with very little external evidence apart from a dark discoloration and longitudinal cracking on the surface. In the final stages of attack, the wood becomes very brittle and is readily powdered.

Remedial Measures

Eradication of wet rot is very similar to that for dry rot. It is first necessary to eliminate all sources of moisture that support the growth of the fungus. Next, both the timber and the building should be dried out, either naturally or with the aid of dehumidifiers. All visibly affected woodwork should be cut out and burnt. Then sterilise non-combustible elements adjacent to infected timber by treating with a solution of 50 g sodium pentachlorophenate per litre of water. The

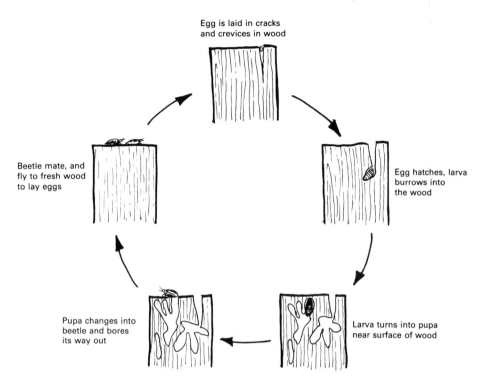

Egg is laid in cracks
and crevices in wood

Beetle mate, and
fly to fresh wood
to lay eggs

Egg hatches, larva
burrows into
the wood

Pupa changes into
beetle and bores
its way out

Larva turns into pupa
near surface of wood

Figure 8.14   Life cycle of a typical wood-destroying insect

remaining timber should be treated with at least two coats of suitable preservative. All new timber should be completely and thoroughly treated with preservative, preferably using one of the vacuum pressure methods.

8.7 Insect Attack

Beetles of one kind or another infest timber because the organic nature of the material is favourable to the grub's life cycle of hatching, growing and emerging (see figure 8.14).

The effect is to reduce the cross-sectional area of the timber and so reduce its strength. Eggs are laid in cracks and crevices in timber, hatching out as larvae or grubs which tunnel through the timber for the whole of their growth period; the larvae develop into pupae and then into beetles which emerge through flight holes to fly off and perpetuate the cycle. Common beetles include the following types:

- Death-watch beetles (*Xestobium ruforillosum*) which attack well-matured hardwoods in old buildings; softwoods and recently seasoned timber are spared.
- Common furniture beetles (*Anobium punctatum*) attack both hardwoods and softwoods, and especially old unpolished furniture and panelling.
- Powder-post beetles (*Lyctus*) infest sapwood of newly seasoned hardwoods; softwoods are immune and well-matured hardwoods in old buildings are not affected.
- Longhorn beetles (*Hylotupes bajulus*) can cause serious damage to sapwood of seasoned hardwoods.

8.8 Termite Attack

Termites are commonly but erroneously called 'white ants'. There are about 2000 known species of this pest, found mainly in the tropics. They are broadly classified as drywood termites and subterranean termites.

Drywood termites confine themselves entirely within the timber and need no contact with the ground, so in this respect they are similar to wood-boring beetles and the protective measures are similar. They may fly into buildings or be carried there in previously infested timber.

Subterranean or soil termites are more widespread and need to maintain contact with the ground. They cause destruction by constructing tubes or covered galleries in the soil over intervening plaster or concrete. They can therefore be physically excluded from buildings by taking precautions during the construction and by vigilance on the part of the occupier or maintenance personnel.

8.8.1 Protection of New Buildings

1 Site Preparation
The site should be well drained because high moisture conditions favour termites and decay. It is also advisable to clear the site of all wood, leaves and debris that could provide sources of food for termites. The remains of trees, shrubs and large plants should be removed from the site before construction work is started. Care should also be taken to remove all the temporary timber used in construction. Any termite mounds on the site should be levelled or removed, and the soil replaced and well compacted before soil poisoning is carried out.

2 Soil Poisoning
Poisoning the soil produces a barrier through which it is difficult for

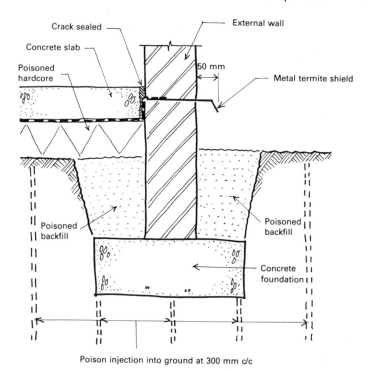

Figure 8.15 Precautions against subterranean termites

the termites to penetrate. The common poisons used for this purpose include dieldrin, aldrin and chlordane which are reasonably reliable to offer protection up to 10 years.

3 Physical Barriers

As an additional safeguard, metal shields can be incorporated. These shields, properly designed and installed, will give a high degree of protection but they need regular inspection as some termites may build substantial soil workings to their edges and so bypass them (see figure 8.15).

8.8.2 Protection of Existing Buildings

1 Survey and Inspection

At least two rigorous inspections should be carried out each year.

The equipment required is simple: a torchlight, a bradawl to probe the timber, a light hammer and some plastic bags to hold the specimens.

First an overall examination from the outside is done, taking note of the location of windows, gables, extensions and so on. This will reduce the possibility of overlooking part of the building.

The outside should then be closely examined for signs of attack such as wall stains, accretions of soil, debris, unfamiliar deposits and so on.

The final step in the inspection process involves the internal part of the building. It is probably best to start from the top down. All timber, whether structural or not, should be carefully inspected for possible damage, special attention being paid to locations which are not prominent such as roof spaces, underside of stairs, built-in fitments and other vulnerable features.

2 In situ Treatments
Extensively damaged timber should be cut out and replaced with sound timber pre-treated with preservative.

In the case of drywood termites, fumigation is the only reliable method, methyl bromide being the common agent. Fumigation, however, will only arrest the existing infestation but will not offer immunity against recurrence.

If fumigation is not possible, then after the removal of infested timber and replacement by pre-treated material, the woodwork can be brushed or sprayed at frequent intervals with a preservative such as lindane or dieldrin.

In the case of subterranean termites, it is essential in the first place to destroy all termites within the building. The treatment includes some measure of soil poisoning, the provision of barriers where possible, and surface treatment of all timber and wood-based products.

The extent to which the foundations and ground floors can be treated will obviously depend on the type of construction.

8.9 Preservation of Timber

In order to attack timber, both fungi and insects need favourable conditions of moisture, temperature, air and also suitable food. Many timbers have a natural resistance to attack owing not so much to high density and strength but often to the presence of natural oils or resins. Such timbers include cedar, oak and teak.

Other timbers may be rendered immune from attack by controlling any one of the conditions. Preservation is the process of treating the wood with substances that are poisonous to fungi and insects, the aim being to increase its durability. It is normally not necessary for the preservative to penetrate the wood completely, but only to form a continuous outer layer through which the destructive agents cannot penetrate. This layer must, of course, be sufficiently thick so that any slight cracks or mechanical damage to the surface of the timber do not expose the core of the untreated wood.

8.9.1 Properties of Preservatives

The most important properties desirable in a preservative are that it should be:

- Toxic to fungi and insects, but not to human beings and domestic animals.
- Permanent, not liable to leach out and chemically stable for a long period of time.
- Cheap and plentiful.
- Easy to apply.
- Non-corrosive to metals.
- Safe to handle.
- Capable of good penetration.
- Fire-resistant, or at least not increase the flammability of wood.
- Capable of subsequent painting or finishing.
- Colourless and odourless.

8.9.2 Types of Preservatives

There are three main types of wood preservatives available for upgrading the durability of timber, each with preferred methods of application.

1 Tar Oils
This type of preservative consists of various distillates from coal tar and is usually referred to as creosote. In the early life of creosote-treated timber, the odour and sticky surface can be objectionable. Creosote, therefore, is used mainly on timbers which are located on the exterior of buildings.

2 Water-soluble Preservatives
These preservatives are generally odourless and non-staining, and do not impose restrictions on finishing. The most commonly used formulations are copper–chrome–arsenic salts which are mixtures of copper sulphate, sodium or potassium dichromate, and arsenic pentoxide. However, treatment with these aqueous solutions, and the subsequent redrying, causes the timber to swell and then to shrink. This can result in a raising of the grain and sometimes distortion which is not entirely suited to the requirements of components machined to fine tolerances, such as doors and windows.

3 Organic Solvent Preservatives
These consist of fungicides, sometimes accompanied by an insecticide, dissolved in a petroleum distillate solvent. Their application to

timber components does not cause swelling or distortion; they are therefore particularly suitable for windows and doors. Such preservatives evaporate relatively quickly, leaving behind a surface generally compatible with paint, glue, putty and mastic.

8.9.3 Methods of Application

These vary from a surface treatment of notional protective value to full pressure impregnation. The following methods are arranged in ascending order of effectiveness.

1 Brush Application
This is the most common method of treating existing exposed timber with creosote or other preservative. The liquid should be applied liberally with a brush and any cracks in the timber should have special attention. At least two coats should be given, the first coat being allowed to dry before the second is applied. Where accessible, the treatment should be renewed every three years.

2 Deluging, Dipping or Steeping
These methods cannot be used for timber already fixed in position. The timber is simply immersed in a receptacle containing the preservative; the longer the immersion, the better the result. Depending on the preservative used, some pre-heating may assist penetration.

3 Open Tank Method
This method can be extremely efficient in ensuring penetration in permeable timbers. The application takes place in a large metal tank in which the preservative can be heated. The timber is fully immersed in the preservative, which is brought to a temperature of about 80°C at which it is maintained for several hours. The heat is then turned off, and the tank and preservative allowed to cool. During this cooling process, the air which has been expelled from the timber during heating is replaced by the preservative, thus giving a good penetration.

4 Pressure Application
Pressure application is by far the most effective method.
In the full cell method, the timber is placed in a large enclosed pressure vessel and is subjected to a vacuum for about an hour. While the vacuum is maintained, the preservative, usually preheated, is introduced into the vessel until it is filled. Pressure is then gradually increased until the required amount of preservative has been introduced into the timber, after which the pressure is reduced and the vessel is emptied. A further vacuum is applied briefly to clean the timber. The

empty cell process differs only from the full cell method by the absence of a preliminary vacuum stage. One method subjects the timber in the pressure vessel to an initial pressure, which is maintained while the cylinder is filled with preservative, after which pressure is increased to force the preservative into the timber. The pressure is subsequently released, allowing air which has been compressed to escape and in the process to expel excess preservative. A vacuum is then applied to assist the escape of air further.

8.9.4 In situ Injection Techniques

In situ injection of preservatives into timbers is a relatively recent development. This technique is used where fungal or insect attack in timber components is not sufficiently advanced to have caused a significant loss in their strength. One method uses specially designed plastic nozzles inserted into the timber to inject the preservatives under pressure. The technique has the distinct advantage of deeper penetration than could be achieved with surface application methods (see figure 8.16).

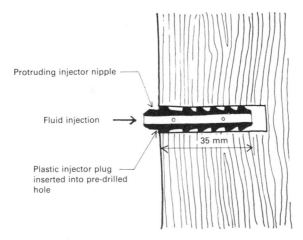

Figure 8.16   *In situ* injection technique for the preservation of timber component

In the Wykamol system, for example, hollow polypropylene injectors are inserted into pre-drilled holes in timber. The injector holes must penetrate to within 12 mm of the far face of the component and be at least 40 mm deep for the larger injectors and 30 mm for the smaller types.

The outer end of each injector has a nipple containing a non-return valve which is left protruding from the face of the timber component and to which the injection line and pump are attached. The organic preservative fluid is then injected under pressure for at least two minutes, or until the timber is seen to be saturated. After the injection procedure has been completed, the injection nipples can be cut off flush with the surface and the holes then sealed with putty and matching paint.

8.10 Repair of Timber Components

8.10.1 Compression Members

In the repair of a compression member, it may be necessary to cut out a decayed section and then insert new wood in order to build up the necessary cross-sectional area of the member. In this case, care must be taken to ensure that the cuts are made in a direction normal to the grain and that the line of grain in the inserted wood corresponds to that on either side (see figure 8.17).

An accurate fit is important as the joint is load-bearing and complete contact must be made. This may be easier to achieve if a stepped joint is used. This joint should be grouted with water-resistant glue. Pins may also be used to locate the insertion but should not be relied upon to transmit any loads.

8.10.2 Tension Members

In the repair of a tension member a different approach is necessary, although the criterion must still be the adequacy of the unaffected cross-sectional area of the member.

Timber has a high tensile strength which depends on the continuity of its grain structure. A wide shake or split along the grain, for instance, will not materially reduce the tensile strength of the timber, whereas a cut or knot or a drilled hole will do so.

The most satisfactory joint for a pure timber repair, if the member is not capable of taking the stress, is to splice an additional timber member together with the original member by means of bolt connections. This form of joint may be able to transmit the required moment close to a support, but it rarely develops the full flexural capacity of the members.

Where splitting of a member has occurred close to its support, it may be possible to retain the integrity of the member to shear by using bolts through, or straps around, the section (see figure 8.18).

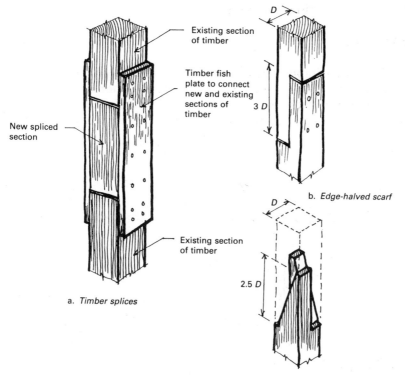

Existing section
of timber

Timber fish
plate to connect
new and existing
sections of
timber

New spliced
section

3 *D*

D

b. *Edge-halved scarf*

D

Existing section
of timber

2.5 *D*

a. *Timber splices*

c. *Scissor scarf*

Figure 8.17   Repair of timber compression members

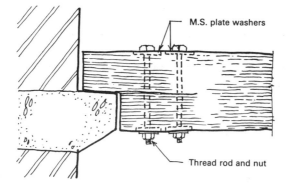

M.S. plate washers

Thread rod and nut

Figure 8.18   Strengthening of split timber

8.11 Use of Substitute Materials

8.11.1 Steel

While it is desirable that timber should be repaired with timber for compatibility, there are bound to be instances where it is expedient to compromise with the use of steel. The steel must, however, be placed so as to be concealed when the work is completed (see figure 8.19).

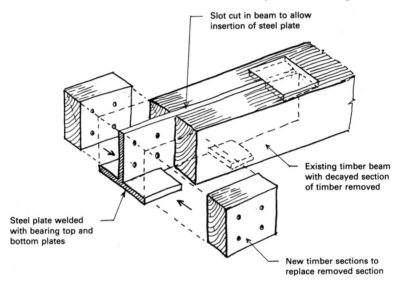

Slot cut in beam to allow insertion of steel plate

Existing timber beam with decayed section of timber removed

Steel plate welded with bearing top and bottom plates

New timber sections to replace removed section

Figure 8.19   Repair of timber beam end with steel plate

In this type of repair, the decayed or damaged portion of the timber is first removed and subsequently replaced by new timber which is butted to the old and joined by a vertical plate housed in a central slot and carried back at least three times its own depth on either side of the junction. The plate is secured by a series of staggered bolts whose heads are sunk below the surface.

8.11.2 Resins and Reinforcement

The major structural uses of epoxy resins are in the *in situ* repair of beam ends, the grouting and filling of timber sections affected by fungal and insect attack, and the *in situ* strengthening of floor beams which have become overstressed owing to cutting or overloading (see figure 8.20).

Typical beam end repairs consist of providing temporary support, cutting away the decayed end, placing permanent wood formers to match the original wood, and drilling through sound wood from the

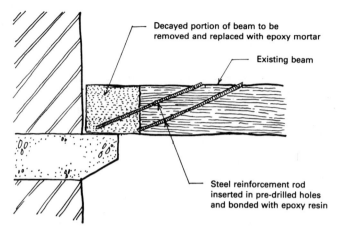

Figure 8.20 Repair of decayed beam end using epoxy mortar and steel reinforcing bars

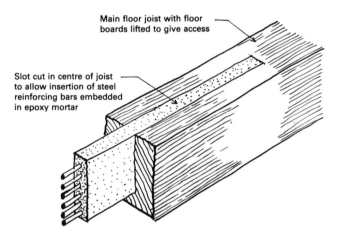

Figure 8.21 Strengthening of existing timber joists by the insertion of resin-bonded stiffening reinforcement

top of the beam at an angle into the bearing zone. Reinforcement rods are placed in the drillings, followed by a pour of an epoxy resin polymer grout to fill the voids. The grout is allowed to permeate the semi-decayed area between the bearing and the sound wood.

Floor beam strengthening techniques may involve cutting a slot along the beam length and inserting stainless steel rods bonded with epoxy resin (see figure 8.21). These systems are to be preferred to unsightly plates mounted on the surface, and are much more efficient in providing up to 50 per cent increase in the load-bearing capacity.

Related and Further Reading

Ashurst, J. and Ashurst, N. *Practical Building Conservation*, Volume 5. Gower, Aldershot, UK (1988).

Berry, R. W. Timber: Stopping the rot. *Building Trades Journal*, UK (December, 1986).

Building Research Establishment, UK. *Timber in Tropical Buildings*. Overseas Building Notes 146 (1972).

Building Research Establishment, UK. *Flooring and Joinery in New Buildings: How to Minimise Dimensional Changes*. Timber Research Laboratory Technical Note 12 (August, 1975).

Building Research Establishment, UK. *Termites and Tropical Building*. Overseas Building Notes 170 (1976).

Building Research Establishment, UK. *Decay in Buildings – Recognition, Prevention and Cure*. Timber Research Laboratory Technical Note 44 (September, 1977).

Building Research Establishment, UK. *Fungus Growths in Buildings following Wetting from Burst Pipes*. Timber Research Laboratory Technical Note 15 (November, 1977).

Building Research Establishment, UK. *Preservation of Timber for Tropical Building*. Overseas Building Notes 183 (1979).

Building Research Establishment, UK. *Preservative Treatments for External Softwood Joinery Timber*. Timber Research Laboratory Technical Note 24 (December, 1979).

Building Research Establishment, UK. *Avoiding Joinery Decay by Design*. Information Paper 10/80 (1980).

Building Research Establishment, UK. *Timber Decay and its Control*. Timber Research Laboratory Technical Note 53 (September, 1980).

Building Research Establishment, UK. *The Moisture Content of Timber in Use*. Timber Research Laboratory Technical Note 46 (September, 1982).

Building Research Establishment, UK. *Wood Preservatives: Application Methods*. Digest 201 (1984).

Building Research Establishment, UK. *Timbers: their Natural Durability and Resistance to Preservative Treatment*. Digest 296 (1985).

Building Research Establishment, UK. *Dry Rot: its Recognition and Control*. Digest 299 (1985).

Building Research Establishment, UK. *Preventing Decay in External Joinery*. Digest 304 (1985).

Building Research Establishment, UK. *Identifying Damage by Wood-boring Insects*. Digest 307 (1986).

Building Research Establishment, UK. *Timber for Joinery*. Digest 321 (1987).

Building Research Establishment, UK. *Wood Floors: Reducing Risk of*

Recurrent Dry Rot. Defect Action Sheet (Design) DAS 103 (June, 1987).

Building Research Establishment, UK. *Insecticidal Treatments against Wood-boring Insects*. Digest 327 (December, 1987).

Building Research Establishment, UK. *Wet Rots: Recognition and Control*. Digest 345 (1989).

Building Research Establishment, UK. *Blue Staining of Timber in Service: its Cause, Prevention and Treatment*. Information Paper 9/91 (May, 1991).

Building Research Establishment, UK. *In-situ Treatment of Exterior Joinery using Boron-based Implants*. Information Paper 14/91 (August, 1991).

Coggins, C. R. *Decay of Timber in Buildings*. Rentokil Library (1980).

Desch, H. E. (revised by Dinwoodie, J. M.) *Timber, its Structure and Properties*. Macmillan, London (1981).

Purslow, D. F. *Methods of Applying Wood Preservatives*. HMSO, London (1974).

Richardson, B. A. *Remedial Treatment of Buildings*. Construction Press, London (1980).

Seeley, I. H. *Building Maintenance*, 2nd edn. Macmillan, London (1987).

Singh, J. The ecology and environmental control of timber decay in building. *Construction Repair*, UK (April, 1989).

Timber Research and Development Association (TRADA). *Timber Pests and their Control*. TRADA, UK (1984).

9 Brickwork and Stonework

Brickwork and stonework are used primarily in the construction of walls, by bedding and jointing small brick units or stones into established bonding arrangements.

Brick types vary from hard durable engineering bricks to less durable lightweight bricks. They may be made of clay, sand or concrete. The natural stones used in building, classified according to their origin, are igneous, sedimentary and metamorphic. Mortars, used as the bonding material, vary in mix and react to conditions differently, depending on consistency.

The defects that occur in brickwork or stonework may be the result of inherent faults, deficiencies in production, design, materials or workmanship, and attack by environmental agents.

9.1 Bricks

9.1.1 Production Defects

The drying and burning of clay to produce bricks has been practised traditionally in many parts of the world. Modern research into the chemistry and physical properties of clays and kilning techniques have increased the speed of production and improved the quality of the bricks. However, many brickworks exist, particularly in the developing countries, which have not taken full advantage of modern developments, and consequently, there is often considerable variability in the quality of bricks.

The production process involves preparation of the earth, moulding, drying and burning. In general, good clay bricks have a compact texture, are reasonably free from cracks, lime, stones and pebbles, and the harder varieties give a metallic ring when struck with a trowel. Good bricks are well and uniformly burnt.

The common defects arising from the production process can be summarised as follows:

1 Defects of Size
Oversized bricks are caused by poor material selection and preparation and/or underfiring.

Undersized bricks are caused mainly by poor material preparation, faulty moulds and/or overfiring.

2 Defects of Shape
The causes of mishapened bricks are many, including poor preparation of moulds or moulding techniques, faults in stacking, rough handling and uneven drying. If the bricks are considerably overburnt, incipient fusion takes place and the bricks, called burrs, come out of the kiln or clamp stuck together. Burrs are suitable only for hardcore purposes.

3 Defects of Body
Faults in the raw material body can give rise to defects such as cracking, bloating and laminations.

Cracking and warping of bricks, causing incipient weakness, may be due to exposure of green bricks to direct sunlight or rapid drying winds. Similar effects will be produced by putting green bricks into the kiln too soon.

Large cracks may be caused by rain getting on to hot bricks.

4 Defects of Appearance
These defects are caused primarily by faulty wires in the case of wire-cut bricks. Dark spots are caused by the presence of unevenly distributed iron sulphide in the clay.

Figure 9.1 summarises the production defects of bricks.

9.1.2 Selection of Bricks

The choice of bricks is often influenced by price, but the quality required must also be carefully considered in order to avoid defects developing during the service life of the material. Therefore, the selection of suitable bricks for any particular purpose has often to be a trade-off between appearance and durability requirements on the one hand, and cost on the other.

According to BS 3921 clay bricks or blocks are broadly classified into three qualities, as follows:

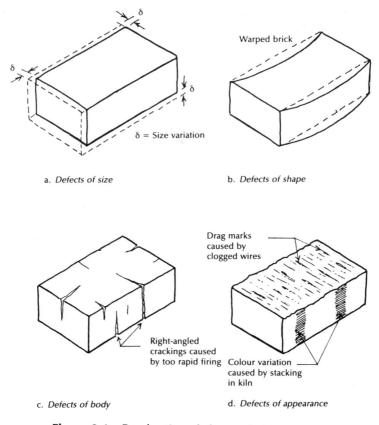

a. *Defects of size*

b. *Defects of shape*

c. *Defects of body*

d. *Defects of appearance*

Figure 9.1 Production defects of clay bricks

- Internal quality: Suitable only for internal use.
- Ordinary quality: Deterioration of brickwork is unlikely to occur if these bricks are used in accordance with sound building practice.
- Special quality: These bricks are extremely durable even when used in situations of extreme exposure.

Generally, the selection of bricks for internal use does not need to be as stringent as that for facing bricks. Nevertheless, care should also be exercised in their selection since soluble clays and lime nodules can be troublesome.

Ordinary quality bricks have to be well fired; be of reasonably uniform texture; and be reasonably free from deep extensive cracks, from damage to edges and corners, from pebbles and from expansive particles of lime.

The soluble-salt content of special quality units is determined by a specified test, and methods are given for assessing whether the frost resistance is adequate.

Bricks for use below damp-proof course level are not always given the attention they deserve, probably because of the misconception that any defects arising from such bricks are not always so apparent as in the case of facing bricks. This is, however, a dangerous practice and can result ultimately in expensive remedial measures.

Although it is not always possible to assess the quality of bricks by their colour, variability of colour of bricks of the same source and method of production can often be an indication of strength and durability variations.

9.1.3 Storage of Bricks

Bricks on the site are rarely kept under adequate cover. Defects in the bricks resulting from the lack of adequate protection on the site are rarely apparent before use. However, bad weather conditions can be detrimental to bricks in that saturation by rain can be responsible for both subsequent efflorescence and decoration defects.

9.1.4 Soluble Salts in Bricks

Underburnt bricks contain a high salt content. The salts come from the raw clay from which the bricks are made, or are formed in the burning process.

Most clay bricks contain some soluble salts, but the types and amounts vary appreciably. The effect of soluble salts on both efflorescence and the more serious problem of disintegration of bricks themselves is largely governed by the strength and pore structure of the bricks. These effects are discussed later in the chapter.

9.1.5 Movement in Bricks

The coefficient of thermal expansion of clay bricks is in the order of 5–6 $\times 10^{-6}$ per °C. This movement is less significant when compared to the irreversible moisture movement which occurs when newly fired bricks absorb moisture. A good deal of potential difficulty can be reduced by not using bricks fresh from the kiln. In addition, it is also recommended that expansion joints be incorporated every 12 m in long runs of unrestrained walls.

9.2 Mortar

9.2.1 Requirements of Mortar

The basic requirements of a good mortar are:

- Workability: A mortar must be sufficiently workable and cohesive to allow it to be easily applied without the constituents segregating.
- Water retentivity: It should be able to retain water for a sufficient length of time for it to be used.
- Strength: It must have a minimum strength to support the loads imposed on it.
- Bond: It must be able to provide a good bond between the units of bricks.
- Durability: It must be durable to weathering and resistant to damage by abrasion.
- Colour and texture: It should possess the colour and/or texture required.

All the requirements can be obtained by using suitable mixes and materials.

Various mortar mixes are available depending on the type of construction; conditions of exposure; risk of frost attack during construction; and risk of sulphate attack. See tables 9.1 and 9.2.

9.2.2 Mortar Strength and Wall Strength

The factors which give rise to variability in mortar strength include mortar composition, water: cement ratio, and batching and mixing methods.

Generally, the strength of brickwork increases as the strength of both brick and mortar increases, but not in direct proportion in both cases (see figure 9.2).

As with concrete, the durability of mortar is enhanced by reducing the water: cement ratio, which can be achieved by adding lime or by using a plasticiser or air-entraining agent. Additives containing calcium chloride should be avoided as they may lead to corrosion of embedded metals and wall ties. Sulphate-resisting Portland cement should be used where attack by sulphates is likely to prevail.

9.2.3 Bonding Strength of Brickwork

The strength ratio for brickwork: brick varies from about 50 per cent to less than 20 per cent.

Table 9.1 Mortar mixes (proportions by volume)
(Source: Seeley, I. H., *Building Maintenance*, 2nd edn, Macmillan, London, 1987)

	Mortar group	Cement : lime : sand	Masonry– cement : sand	Cement : sand with plasticiser
Increasing strength but	i	1 : 0–¼ : 3	—	—
decreasing ability	ii	1 : ½ : 4–4½	1 : 2½–3½	1 : 3–4
to accommodate movements	iii	1 : 1 : 5–6	1 : 4–5	1 : 5–6
caused by settlement,	iv	1 : 2 : 8–9	1 : 5½–6½	1 : 7–8
shrinkage, etc.	v	1 : 3 : 10–12	1 : 6½–7	1 : 8

equivalent strengths
←————————————→
within each group

Direction of changes in properties

increasing frost resistance
————————————→

improving bond and resistance
←————————————
to rain penetration

Where a range of sand contents is given, the larger quantity should be used for sand that is well graded and the smaller for coarse or uniformly fine sand.

Because damp sands bulk, the volume of damp sand used may need to be increased. For cement : lime : sand mixes, the error due to bulking is reduced if the mortar is prepared from lime : sand coarse stuff and cement in appropriate proportions; in these mixes 'lime' refers to non-hydraulic or semi-hydraulic lime and the proportions given are for lime putty. If hydrated lime is batched dry, the volume may be increased by up to 50 per cent to get adequate workability.

Table 9.2 Selection of mortar groups (Source: Seeley, I. H., *Building Maintenance*, 2nd edn, Macmillan, London, 1987)

Type of brick:	Clay		Concrete and calcium silicate	
Early frost hazard[a]	no	yes	no	yes
Internal walls	(v)	(iii) or (iv)[b]	(v)[c]	(iii) or plast (iv)[b]
Inner leaf of cavity walls	(v)	(iii) or (iv)[b]	(v)[c]	(iii) or plast (iv)[b]
Backing to external solid walls	(iv)	(iii) or (iv)[b]	(iv)	(iii) or plast (iv)[b]

continued on p. 190

Table 9.2   continued

Type of brick:	Clay		Concrete and calcium silicate	
Early frost hazard[a]	no	yes	no	yes
External walls; outer leaf of cavity walls:				
—above damp-proof course	(iv)[b]	(iii)[d]	(iv)	(iii)
—below damp-proof course	(iii)[e]	(iii)[b,e]	(iii)[e]	(iii)[e]
Parapet walls; domestic chimneys;				
—rendered	(iii)[f,g]	(iii)[f,g]	(iv)	(iii)
—not rendered	(ii)[h] or (iii)	(i)	(iii)	(iii)
External free-standing walls	(iii)	(iii)[b]	(iii)	(iii)
Sills; copings	(i)	(i)	(ii)	(ii)
Earth-retaining walls (back-filled with free-draining material)	(i)	(i)	(ii)[e]	(ii)[e]

[a] During construction, before mortar has hardened (say 7 days after laying) or before the wall is completed and protected against the entry of rain at the top.

[b] If the bricks are to be laid wet, see text.

[c] If not plastered, use group (iv).

[d] If to be rendered, use group (iii) mortar made with sulphate-resisting cement.

[e] If sulphates are present in the groundwater, use sulphate-resisting cement.

[f] Parapet walls of clay units should not be rendered on both sides; if this is unavoidable, select mortar as though *not* rendered.

[g] Use sulphate-resisting cement.

[h] With 'special' quality bricks, or with bricks that contain appreciable quantities of soluble sulphates.

Generally, the maximum strength of brickwork is obtained with a 1:3 mortar mix of cement:sand by volume.

As its height increases, the strength of a wall constructed in brickwork decreases. The primary cause of this behaviour is elastic instability initiated by stiffness difference from one side of the wall to the other. This stiffness difference, in turn, is caused by such factors as bonding of the bricks; openings within the brickwork; slenderness ratio of the walls; and lateral support. See figures 9.3 and 9.4.

9.2.4 Workmanship Factors in Brickwork Strength

Certain workmanship factors can have appreciable effects on the strength of brickwork. In order of relative importance, these factors are:

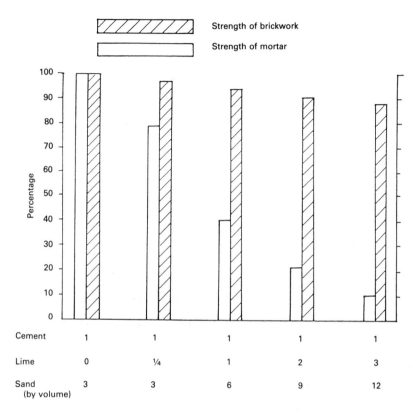

Figure 9.2   Effects of mortar mix proportion on the crushing
strengths of mortar and brickwork built with medium-
strength bricks. Strengths are shown relative to the
strength of a 1:3 cement–sand mortar and the brickwork
built with it (Source: *Strength of Brickwork and
Blockwork Walls: Design for Vertical Load*, BRE Digest
246, Building Research Establishment, UK, 1981)

1 Incorrect Adjustment of Suction Rate in Bricks
To achieve maximum brickwork strength, the suction rate of bricks
should be controlled to prevent excessive removal of water from the
mortar.

It is probable that the water absorbed by the bricks leaves cavities in
the mortar, filling them with air and resulting in a weakened material
on setting.

On the other hand, brickwork built with saturated bricks develops
poor adhesion between bricks and mortar.

Although water extraction reduces the final strength of mortar, it
does not result in serious weakening of the brickwork in compression.

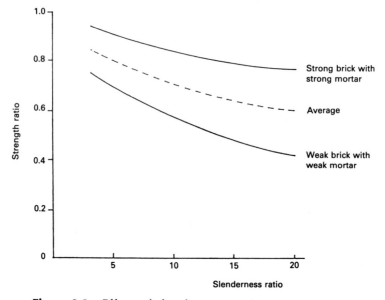

Figure 9.3   Effect of slenderness on brickwork strength

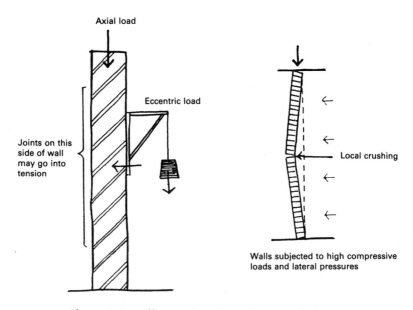

Figure 9.4   Effects of axial and eccentric loads

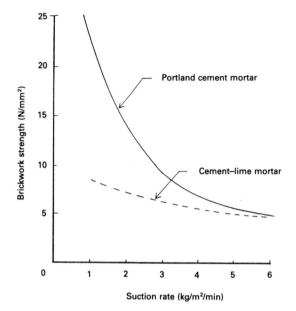

Figure 9.5   Effect of brick suction rate on brickwork strength

However, suction rate has a considerable effect on brickwork strength because dewatered mortar tends to produce a rounded joint during building owing to the loss of elasticity (see figure 9.5).

2 Incorrect Jointing Procedures
Defects can arise from incomplete filling up of joints (see figure 9.6). For example, brickwork with deeply furrowed bed joints would show a reduction of strength of about 33 per cent.

In addition, excessively thick bed joints, say 16 to 20 mm, could reduce the strength of brickwork by about 30 per cent as compared with normal 10 mm thick joints.

In the case of walls with joints filled and unfilled, however, there should not be any significant difference.

3 Deviation from Vertical Plane or Alignment
Any deviation from the vertical plane or alignment can give rise to eccentric loading in a wall under compression and thus reduce its strength.

Comparing the strength of walls with eccentrically applied loads with corresponding axially loaded walls will show a reduction in strength of about 10 per cent. For those off-plumb, the reduction could be about 20 per cent.

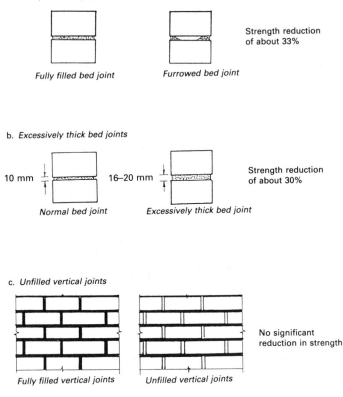

a. *Incomplete filling up of bed joints*

Fully filled bed joint   *Furrowed bed joint*

Strength reduction of about 33%

b. *Excessively thick bed joints*

10 mm   16–20 mm

Normal bed joint   *Excessively thick bed joint*

Strength reduction of about 30%

c. *Unfilled vertical joints*

Fully filled vertical joints   *Unfilled vertical joints*

No significant reduction in strength

Figure 9.6   Effects of incorrect jointing procedures on brickwork strengths

4 Unfavourable Curing Conditions
Newly completed brickwork can be adversely affected by exposure to unfavourable weather conditions, including curing under very hot conditions, frost damage and damage by rain. For example, there would possibly be a 10 per cent reduction in strength of brickwork cured in the sun compared with that cured under cover.

9.3 Brickwork

The diagnosis of brickwork defects is not always easy. Cracking of the brickwork, for example, can be due to one or more of a variety of causes, including foundation movements. Careful study is necessary to identify the real cause.

9.3.1 Ground Movement

If the building settles as a whole unit, it will not suffer much damage. Differential settlements, on the other hand, can give rise to greater problems manifested in the form of cracks developing in the walls.

Differential settlement is brought about by changes in soil strength due to changes in groundwater levels or site drainage, loss of support due to running sand, 'swallow holes', mining subsidence or local vibration effects, and frost heave in chalk.

Settlement cracks are usually diagonal and often appear at door and window openings, these being the weakest parts of the wall (see figure 9.7).

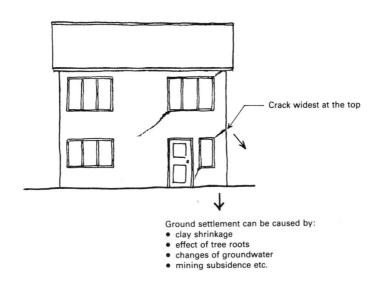

Crack widest at the top

Ground settlement can be caused by:
- clay shrinkage
- effect of tree roots
- changes of groundwater
- mining subsidence etc.

Figure 9.7   Cracking patterns of brickwork caused by ground settlement

9.3.2 Bulging, Buckling and Spreading

Bulging and buckling are caused by the outward spreading of external walls, either vertically between ground level and the roof, or horizontally between the walls (see figure 9.8).

The main causes of this problem are from:

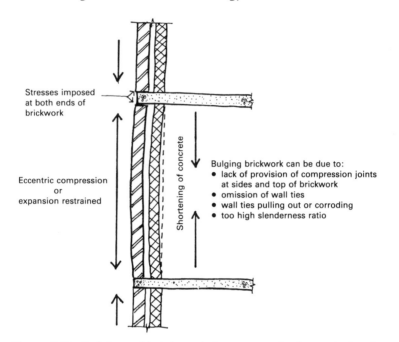

Stresses imposed at both ends of brickwork

Eccentric compression or expansion restrained

Shortening of concrete

Bulging brickwork can be due to:
- lack of provision of compression joints at sides and top of brickwork
- omission of wall ties
- wall ties pulling out or corroding
- too high slenderness ratio

Figure 9.8   Bulging of brickwork in a concrete framed structure

- Vibrations generated by machinery, building plant or traffic.
- Overloading of the structure, for example, by increased loads on floors or by adding more structures.
- The wall having a high slenderness ratio, referring to its inadequate thickness in relation to its height.
- The lack of cross ties between the outer wall structures and the cross walls due to floor joists or beams running parallel to outer walls.

The first signs of this defect take the form of a gap between the wall and the floor at first floor level. The problem must be checked to prevent a collapse of the wall.

Spreading occurs at roof level when the roof sags. This sagging of the roof often produces an outward thrust, thus fracturing the wall (see figure 9.9).

9.3.3 Thermal Movement

Thermal expansion is theoretically reversible, and is so in the case of an individual brick. However, brickwork is not merely a composite material but also laid with varying degrees of skill which undoubtedly will affect its movement characteristics. For example, excessive expan-

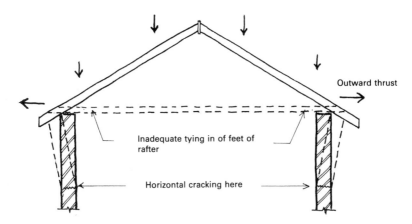

Figure 9.9   Sagging of roof causes outward thrust which can fracture the supporting walls

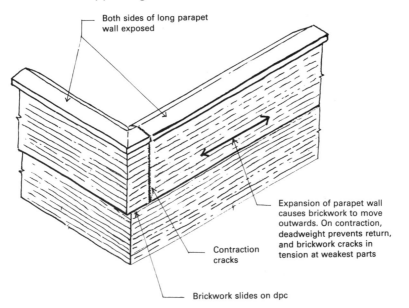

Figure 9.10   Typical crack pattern caused by horizontal movements

sion in long walls of brickwork may cause differential movement fracture on contraction.

Lateral movement may also occur along horizontal damp-proof courses such as parapet walls. In this case, expansion forces the brickwork outwards; but when it contracts upon cooling, it does not return to its original length owing to its own weight, thus resulting in tension cracks (see figure 9.10).

Vertical thermal movements in walls are generally reversible but horizontal movements may only be reversible if the wall does not crack as a result of the expansion or contraction. This depends on the material used for the damp-proof course which appears to be the critical factor.

Temperatures used for calculating expansion should be based on the average wall temperatures. For solid walls, these may be the temperature at the centre of the wall; in cavity wall construction, there may be differential thermal movement between the inner and outer leaves and, in such situations, provision should be made for maximum thermal movement by taking the average temperature of the outer leaf.

9.3.4 Moisture Movement

Fired clay products, like many other building materials, exhibit reversible dimensional changes dependent on their moisture content. In addition, fired clay, while cooling in the kiln, begins to take up a permanent expansion which can proceed, but at a greatly reduced rate, over many years. At least half the total expansion in two years takes place within two days of the commencement of cooling.

If bricks are not built into the work while they are fresh from the kiln, moisture expansion is unlikely to be a major problem.

The moisture content of brickwork depends on whether the walls are external or internal. Bricks themselves vary in their ability to absorb moisture. They may absorb enough moisture to cause expansion, in which case they would probably also dry rapidly and shrink. Excessive expansion and contraction can produce shrinkage cracks which can be very pronounced in some cases.

9.3.5 Efflorescence

Efflorescence on brickwork can be seen as a white or whitish deposit of salts on the exposed surfaces of the bricks.

This phenomenon is caused by the migration of salts from the interior to the surface of the bricks. Any absorbed water drying out in the bricks will leave the salts behind. The process often continues for many years depending on the quantity of salts present and their solubility. The amount seen depends on the quantity and availability of soluble materials and water, and the damage depends on the chemical nature of the salts. Thus magnesium sulphate which crystallises just behind the face of the brickwork causes spalling, while other salts, apart from lifting subsequent decorations, are chiefly unsightly.

The salts may be derived from the walling units themselves, from the mortar and plaster, or from contamination from some other source other than the wall (see figure 9.11). Contamination from outside may occur from groundwater, from substances stacked against the wall, or even from spray borne inland from the sea. Materials may also pick up salts before use if they are stacked on ground contaminated by, say, fertilisers. The presence of nitrates or chlorides in the efflorescence is usually an indication of this type of external efflorescence.

Rainwater may take calcium carbonate or calcium sulphate into solution from limestone or concrete copings, and if this solution does not fall clear of the building, it may be taken up by the brickwork to give rise to efflorescence on subsequent drying out.

The appearance of efflorescence is not a certain indication of the presence of the salts. The solutions may have migrated considerable distances through the brickwork. For example, the use of a very dense, impermeable mortar pointing in conjunction with a more permeable brick wall will allow water to flow into the wall, mainly through the bricks, and dry out the same way; so that efflorescence will appear on the bricks although the salts may have arisen from the bricks or mortar, or both.

External efflorescence, although unsightly, is rarely a serious problem because the salts are washed away by rain. Internal efflorescence or crytoflorescence is usually more troublesome, particularly on plastered and decorated walls. For example, in severe cases, the plaster can be pushed off the walls. Therefore, where efflorescence can be expected, decorative treatments to the walls should not be applied too hastily.

9.3.6 Sulphate Attack

This is a chemical reaction between the sulphate salts in the bricks, the tricalcium aluminate in Portland cement in the mortar and water, which is essential in promoting the reaction. The compound that is formed is called calcium sulphoaluminate, the crystals of which can cause considerable expansion, disintegration of mortar joints and distortion of brickwork.

Sulphate attack is particularly noticeable in brickwork in exposed positions such as gable and parapet walls, free-standing and retaining walls, external walls in more exposed conditions, masonry below the damp-proof course and chimneys.

The first characteristic sign of attack is horizontal cracking of bed joints which will, in severe cases, lead to expansion of the mortar and consequent bowing and disruption of the masonry (see figure 9.12). When attacked, chimneys tend to bow away from the principal source of driving rain. The source of sulphates in the case of unlined chimneys is from the products of combustion. However, some clay bricks con-

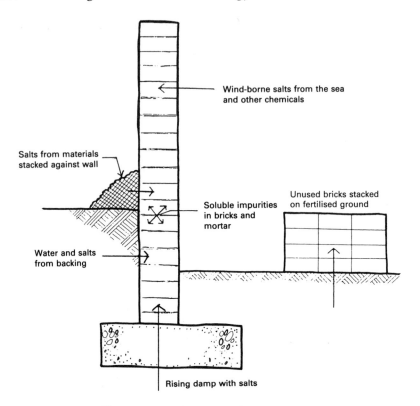

Wind-borne salts from the sea
and other chemicals

Salts from materials
stacked against wall

Unused bricks stacked
on fertilised ground

Soluble impurities
in bricks and
mortar

Water and salts
from backing

Rising damp with salts

Figure 9.11   Sources of soluble salts

tain acid-sulphate and, particularly in foundations, sulphates may be
derived from groundwater, from the soil or from fill. As the damage is
due to the reaction of two chemicals, a possible solution is to remove
one of them. If the sulphates cannot be removed, the risk may be
reduced by using sulphate-resisting cement, as the tricalcium aluminate content of this is limited to a maximum of 3.5 per cent.

9.3.7 Staining

Soluble lime in the form of calcium hydroxide is produced during the
hydration of Portland cement. This substance may be deposited on the
surface of the wall by the movement of rainwater through freshly set
and hardened mortar in a similar manner to that for efflorescence. But,
unlike efflorescence, the calcium hydroxide tends to react with carbon
dioxide in the atmosphere to form calcium carbonate, an insoluble
white crystalline solid. The calcium carbonate forms a disfiguring stain
on the brickwork which will not weather off but will need a dilute acid

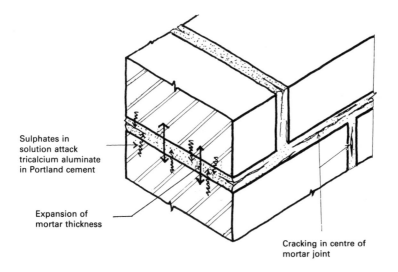

Sulphates in
solution attack
tricalcium aluminate
in Portland cement

Expansion of
mortar thickness

Cracking in centre of
mortar joint

Figure 9.12　Expansion of jointing mortar caused by sulphate attack

for its removal. Protection of partially built or newly completed brick-work with waterproof temporary covers such as polythene sheets is, therefore, necessary if risk of such staining is to be avoided.

Another form of permanent staining is caused by ferrous sulphate (copperas) from the bricks reacting with lime in the mortar to produce brownish hydroxides and carbonates of iron. The decomposition of sodium or potassium vanadates on the surface of bricks will also produce yellow or greenish stains.

9.3.8 Impurities

The presence of lime nodules in clay bricks is frequently due to faulty screening of the materials used in the brick production. These lime nodules usually appear as white particles, averaging about 3 mm in diameter. The nodules are basically composed of quicklime, which, when subjected to air and moisture, hydrate and expand. This can cause spalling in the case of facing bricks and disintegration of plaster in the case of plasterwork.

Bricks can also contain blue or black cores caused by unoxidised carbonaceous materials changing to their ferrous state. Although this condition may not necessarily impair the durability of the bricks, it is often associated with a high salt content.

The presence of vegetable matter will also produce a black colora-tion, sealing carbon in a black core, especially when there is a sudden rise in temperature.

Surface colour may be produced by adding finely ground metallic oxides to sand sprinkled on the bricks before burning, for example, manganese (brown); chromium (pink); cobalt and manganese (black); antimony (yellow); copper (green); and cobalt (blue).

9.3.9 Frost Attack

Failures of brickwork due to frost attack are usually confined to partly built unprotected brickwork or to brickwork subjected to severe exposure conditions such as parapet walls.

Water expands by 9 per cent when it changes to ice, and the damage caused to masonry by the expansion of the freezing water in pores or crevices results in spalling or crumbling of the face of the wall. Generally, the denser the material, the less porous it is, and, therefore, the less liable to frost damage. However, if the pore structure is not interconnected, as in air-entrained concrete and many autoclaved aerated concrete blocks, damage from freezing is unlikely to happen. Although weak mortars are more vulnerable to frost attack generally, the stronger but less flexible mortars containing a high proportion of cement are also susceptible to shrinkage cracking and movement-induced cracking which permits water to penetrate into these cracks more readily. The entrapped water can freeze and cause disruption if it is unable to drain away freely.

Calcium silicate bricks should never be used in situations where they can absorb salts, that is, sea-water, or adjacent to roads which may be treated with de-icing salts, as deterioration can occur when units saturated in such salt solution become frozen.

Precast concrete units in general possess good frost resistance, provided that they are selected according to the recommendations of BS 5628: Part 3.

Some stones are seriously affected by frost action and care should be taken not to use such stones in positions where they may become saturated. With certain stones, including the softer limestones, the use of thin open joint construction is not recommended.

9.3.10 Corrosion of Embedded Ferrous Metals

Iron and steel components which are embedded in brickwork may corrode for various reasons and cause opening of brick joints or cracking of brickwork, and also rust staining. This problem can be alleviated by coating these metallic components with bitumen, anti-corrosion paint or metallic zinc paint.

The corrosion of wall ties in cavity brickwork produces cracking along mortar bed joints where the ties are located (see figure 9.13).

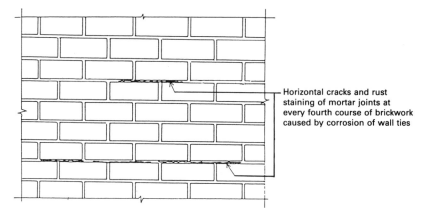

Horizontal cracks and rust staining of mortar joints at every fourth course of brickwork caused by corrosion of wall ties

Figure 9.13   Corrosion of embedded wall ties in brickwork

9.3.11 Atmospheric Impurities

Dust particles coming into contact with bricks and moisture form weak acids. The resulting acids can cause the deterioration of brick surfaces, especially of softer and under-burnt bricks which will allow surface erosion.

The surface dirt can be removed by washing. In addition, all defective bricks should be cut out, the wall rebuilt and then repointed.

9.3.12 Lichens, Moulds and Other Growths

Although these organisms are seldom destructive, nevertheless they tend to disfigure and stain brickwork. In addition, climbing plants and creepers can also cause damage to walls as their roots penetrate into cracks and crevices of mortar joints. Such growths can be prevented or destroyed by applying some toxic washes such as sodium orthopentachlorophenate during a dry spell, after partially removing any thick surface growths. The effectiveness of the treatment depends, however, on the porosity of the surface and the extent to which it is washed by rain.

9.4 Repairing Damage to Brickwork

9.4.1 Strength and Stability of Damaged Walls

It is not always easy to judge from appearance how serious the damage is likely to affect the strength and stability of the damaged structure.

Generally, if the walls are also not too distorted or too much out of plumb, it may be taken that cracking may not be too serious.

A careful check should be made of the walls to assess the condition, and the bearing area of joists, lintels and roof timbers should be inspected to make sure that there is no significant loss of support.

In the case of cavity walls, the effects of bulging or leaning, and of eccentricity of loading, will be more seriously felt than with solid walls. Wall ties must be thoroughly checked for the stability of the wall as a whole, and the external leaf in particular, will depend on them. Rebuilding the whole outer leaf would often be the most suitable measure. Another remedy may be the insertion of new wall ties as detailed later in the chapter.

The additional factors that need to be considered when deciding on the treatment for walls that are apparently sound, except for a slight bulge or tilt, include the following:

- The nature and condition of the wall and of the foundation supporting it.
- The availability of lateral restraints in the form of cross walls, beams, roof trusses and other members.
- Whether upper walls, floors and roofs are liable to exert thrust.
- The probability of vibrations being created by users and traffic.
- The influence on the users or prospective buyers.

9.4.2 Treatment of Structural Damage

To treat brickwork severely damaged by causes such as fires or explosions, the following methods are used:

- Tie rods are fixed at the floor or roof level to anchor the suspect wall to another sound wall or structural member.
- Buttresses are keyed into the suspect wall and carried to a stable base by underpinning to make sure that the buttresses actually thrust against the wall in the correct direction (see figure 9.14).
- Permanent repair involves the rebuilding of the damaged wall either partially or wholly.

Tie rods offer the cheapest and most effective method, but they are very unsightly and may not be acceptable to many owners.

A Portland cement:lime:sand mortar (1:1:6 by volume) is generally suitable for rebuilding work. A stronger mortar is likely to cause cracking between the old and new work, whereas a weaker mix may not be able to withstand initial or long-term movements.

In order to obtain proper structural connection between new and existing brickwork, careful toothing is necessary in addition to dry mortar packing along the full length of horizontal joints.

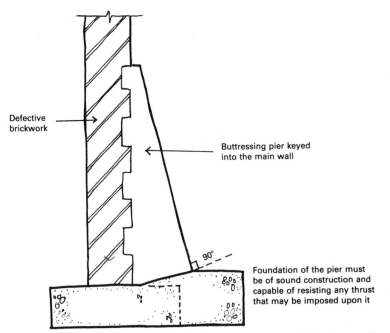

Defective brickwork

Buttressing pier keyed into the main wall

90°

Foundation of the pier must be of sound construction and capable of resisting any thrust that may be imposed upon it

Figure 9.14 Buttressing pier built to support a defective wall

9.5 Other Repairs

When the damage is not sufficient to affect structural stability such as cracks, surface defects and displacements of brickwork, the repairs can be carried out individually.

9.5.1 Cracks

Fine cracks of up to 1.5 mm wide are not very conspicuous. Moreover, if the bricks are absorbent, rain entering the cracks is not likely to pass through the wall. Fine cracks, therefore, are often ignored. However, if repair is necessary, particularly in the case of non-absorbent bricks in a wall exposed to wet winds, the procedure would be to cut out all cracked bricks; rake out the joints along which the cracks appear; rebond with a 1:1:6 cement:lime:sand mortar; fill the cracked joints with the same mix and repoint.

Wider cracks will generally require repair. The procedure will involve raking or cutting out the joints squarely to a depth of about 15 mm; then repoint with a 1:2:9 mortar mix of cement:lime:sand.

With cracks passing through bricks and mortar, cut out and rebond, using a mortar similar to that in the existing wall.

9.5.2 Surface Damage

Frost damage to mortar causes it to crumble and drop out of the joint. In this state it is very water-absorbent and encourages rainwater seepage into the building.

Frost-damaged mortar should be raked out completely to a depth of 15–20 mm to give a square key for new mortar which should be pointed in solidly (see figure 9.15). The raked joints should be brushed and washed to remove dust and to ensure that repointing mortar bonds well with the existing brickwork. They should be moist when the repointing mortar is applied. The appropriate mix and joint profile for the repointing should be selected with regard to the type of brick and exposure conditions. Where the condition of the bricks is good, the profile of the original joint could be used again; otherwise use a weather-struck profile. Care should be taken not to finish the joint proud of the brick arris. It should also not be buttered over as this will encourage rainwater to accumulate in the joint. Strong cement-rich mortars should be avoided as they tend to shrink and crack, leading eventually to poor bonding with the brick and cracking at the brick/mortar interface.

Frost damage of bricks, sometimes called 'spalling', may take the form of a general crumbling of the bricks or a shelling off of their surface. It may be due to the selection of an inappropriate type of brick

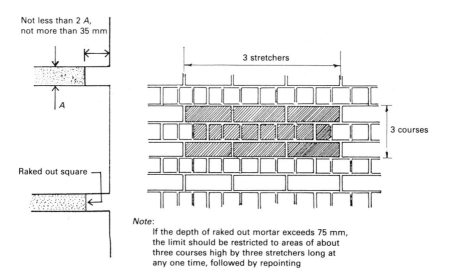

Figure 9.15 Repointing mortar joints

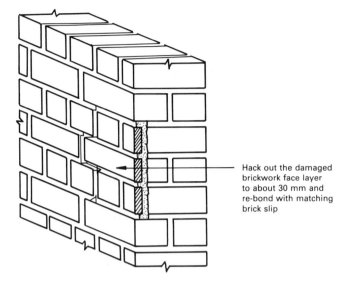

Hack out the damaged brickwork face layer to about 30 mm and re-bond with matching brick slip

Figure 9.16 Replacement of surface-damaged brickwork with matching brick slips

to suit exposure, a fault in the protection against saturation or the accidental inclusion of substandard units in the wall.

Bricks cannot be treated to make them frost-resistant. Replacement of damaged bricks is the best remedy. Sometimes the solution might be simply to turn the other face outwards.

The replacement of single bricks can be more difficult to carry out than replacing small areas of brickwork. A simpler method is to cut back the face of the damaged brick to a depth of about 30 mm and solidly mortar-mix a matching brick slip (see figure 9.16).

Matching, however, may be a problem. If there is any redundant brickwork, slips could be cut from reclaimed bricks.

9.6 Special Treatments

9.6.1 Sulphate Attack

The effects of sulphate attack manifest themselves as expansion of the jointing mortar. On rendered walls the signs are horizontal cracking of the rendering with portions falling off. Advanced stages of attack may make the structure unsafe.

When rebuilding is necessary, the bricks used should be of low sulphate content and the mortar should be of a mix of 1:1:6 sulphate-resisting Portland cement:hydrated lime:sand. In addition, care should be taken to exclude all conditions of dampness.

On rendered walls, the rendering should be removed and the brick-work allowed to dry before reapplying a weaker mix of sulphate-resisting cement, lime and sand.

9.6.2 Insertion of Wall Ties

It is preferable to carry out the work in dry walls. If both walls are wet, assurance should be sought from the resin suppliers that the particular resin grade proposed will set properly in contact with moisture.

Various methods for the replacement of defective wall ties are given in BRE Digest 329. One of the suggested methods involves the following steps:

1 Prepare the ties by cutting to length and slotting one end. The far inner end of the tie should be cut obliquely to improve the mixing action (see figure 9.17). For a 280 mm cavity, the tie should be 215 mm long.
2 Drill through the near leaf using either a tube guide or a bubble level guide to set the 5° fall.

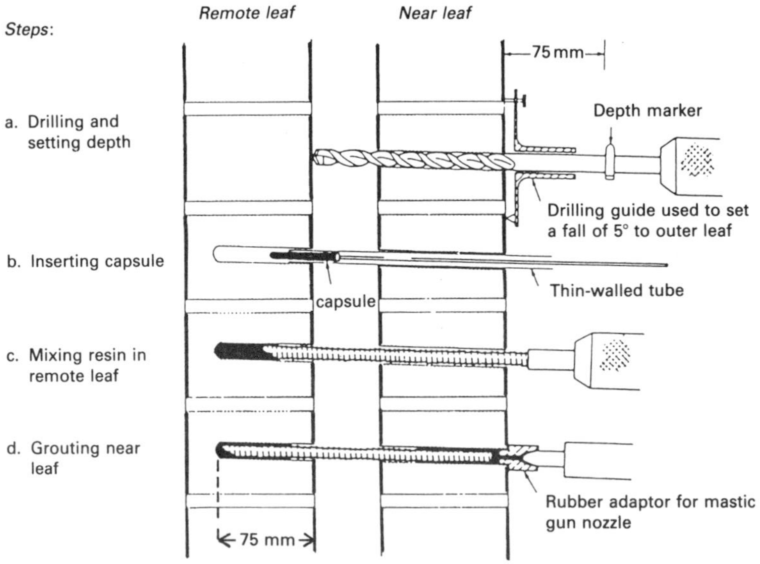

Figure 9.17   Replacement of cavity wall ties using resin-grouted tie rod (Source: *Replacement of Cavity Wall Ties using Resin-grouted Stainless Steel Rods*, Information Paper IP 29/79, Building Research Establishment, UK, 1979)

3 Remove the tube guide, if used, and then push the drill through to bear on the remote leaf and set the depth marker at 75 mm.
4 Drill 75 mm into the remote leaf. Blow the dust and debris out of the hole using the 6 mm tube and air source.
5 Use the thin-walled tube as a guide and the other tube as a push rod to introduce the synthetic resin capsules.
6 Insert the tie, then smash the capsule and drive the tie to the base of the hole using the driving attachment.
7 Allow the resin to set hard. Most resins will give a reasonable strength in one hour and full strength after a day, but the exact time will depend on the ambient temperature.
8 Check that a bond has been made in the remote leaf. If a bond fails to form, check the remote leaf for perforations or excessive dampness.
9 The final step is to grout the near leaf from a gun through a rubber adaptor.

9.6.3 Treatment of Bulges and Fractures

In common with other types of masonry, a careful diagnosis should first be carried out prior to the repair. Fractures are usually caused by local subsidence, failure of lintels, or alterations and additions to the original structure. Bulging may similarly be the result of alterations in loadings and lack of bond between brick skins or straight joints at wall junctions.

From this initial diagnosis a decision is then made to adopt one of the following measures:

1 Leave Alone
This decision is taken only if there is no more danger of fracturing affecting the stability of the wall. Sometimes more damage may be caused by cutting out or attempting to grout than by doing nothing.

2 Cut Out and Point
The decision to cut out and point a fracture would be taken in situations where the cause of fracturing has ceased but the fractures remain a source of water penetration and potential structural weakness.

In this case the fracture should be carefully cut out with hacksaw blades, masonry saws and/or diamond wheels, flushed with water and pointed. If fracturing has extended through some of the bricks, these should be cut out and replaced.

3 Stitch and in situ *Grouting*
The purpose of stitching is to prevent further movement taking place

which would threaten the stability of the structure. The decision to stitch and grout *in situ* would be made where fracturing extends through bricks and joints, and extensive cutting out for the full height of the fracture may be necessary, as for example, in a chimney stack. The fractures could be cut out in lifts of one metre; the fractured bricks replaced with whole ones; and hand grouting and deep tamping of fractured joints or rubble fills carried out.

If the fracturing has resulted in a two-way movement, it may be necessary to introduce concrete stitching at intervals behind the brick facing. This may consist of precast dovetail sections or may be cast *in situ*. In both cases the facing bricks are removed for a depth of, say, three courses, and the opening extended 450 mm either side of the fracture. After the stitch is placed, the bricks are replaced exactly in their former position.

Other forms of stitching include the introduction of brick reinforcement or stainless steel mesh, or wire set into new mortar joints. Special ties may be introduced from an internal face to bond two skins together. Some of these systems rely on an epoxy mortar to anchor the ties and are formed of resin anchors (see figure 9.18). Others lock two elements together such as a patented fixing, consisting of a stainless steel or aluminium bronze tie with an expanding head at each end. These ties are set in an 8 mm drilled hole and the expansion takes place by using a locking key.

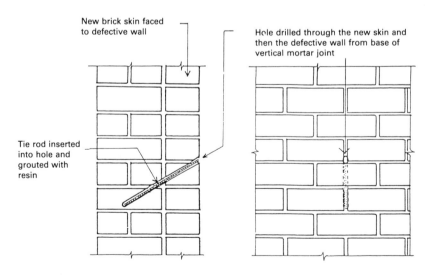

New brick skin faced to defective wall

Hole drilled through the new skin and then the defective wall from base of vertical mortar joint

Tie rod inserted into hole and grouted with resin

Figure 9.18   Attaching a new brick skin to the defective brickwork with resin anchor ties

4 Take Down and Rebuild
In most cases where walls are bulging or leaning and when there is serious displacement around a fracture, the best course of action is carefully to take them down and rebuild, salvaging all possible materials. The rebuilding work should follow the original coursing, bonding and joint profile. It is a painstaking task and is undertaken only when conservation is necessary.

9.6.4 Control of Algae, Lichens and Mosses

Biological growths which should receive attention include unsightly algal slimes on vertical surfaces and pavings, lichens causing deterioration of building materials such as copper, marble or glass, and fouling organisms in drainage systems.

A number of treatments are available which effect an initial kill. But some of the traditional treatments, such as the use of weed killers incorporating calcium chloride, build up residues of damaging soluble salts. In addition, concentrated solutions of zinc or magnesium silicofluoride may produce hard surface skins on limestone which are liable to spall off.

The recommended method for treating masonry covered with algae, lichens, mosses and small plants is as follows:

1 Remove as much of the growths as possible by hand or other aids.
2 Prepare a solution of quaternary ammonium-based biocide according to the manufacturer's specification, and fill a pneumatic garden-type sprayer two-thirds full with the prepared solution.
3 Apply a flood coat, starting from the top of the vertical surface to be treated and moving across horizontally and slowly. The next horizontal pass should be made across the previous run-down.
4 Leave the treated area for at least one week. Brush off as much dead growth as possible, taking care to avoid adjacent gutters and hoppers.
5 Prepare a solution of proprietary biocide based on a quaternary ammonium compound and incorporating tributyl tin oxide or other proven durable biocide according to the manufacturer's specification.
6 Fill a second pneumatic sprayer with the diluted biocide and apply in the same manner as previously described.
7 Allow the surface to absorb and carry out a second application of proprietary biocide as (5) above.

When handling and mixing biocides, take precautions to wear rubber gloves and safety goggles. In addition, take care not to spray in the immediate vicinity of people and animals.

9.6.5 *Control of Ivy and other Creepers*

Decorative climbing plants and creepers may have a beauty and value of their own, but can also become a real problem. Typical problems associated with mature wall creepers or other large plants growing against walls include persistently damp walls; disturbance and blocking of rainwater disposal systems; scouring of soft wall surfaces; difficulties in painting and repairing; and security risks.

In the case of ivy, the much more serious problem is its rapid growth with aerial roots intruding into joints and displacing stones or bricks. Suckers and tendrils also contribute to surface decay, especially of mortar, by the secretion of acid substances. In general, therefore, it is strongly suggested that large plants are kept away from walls unless specifically built into the landscape for the purpose.

To remove ivy growth, a length of the main stem of ivy should be cut out at a convenient height above ground level. The plant may be left in this state to wither of its own accord or sprayed with toxic substances to hasten its destruction.

9.7 Stonework

9.7.1 *Defects in Stonework*

The durability of a stone is affected by its chemical composition and structure. For example, limestones offer the least resistance to weathering; sandstones are harder and more durable than limestones; and granite is extremely durable.

Water is the main vehicle for the attack on stonework, particularly when the water is polluted. In addition, weathering and gradual decay is inevitable in the use of stone.

The main types of defects associated with stonework in buildings are:

1 Attack by Polluted Water
Rainwater, made acidic by dissolved atmospheric gases such as carbon dioxide and sulphur dioxide, can have severe action on stonework, particularly where sandstones and limestones are used. For example, sulphurous and sulphuric acids tend to dissolve limestones to give then a weathered and rough texture.

Where stonework is not frequently washed by rain but merely remains moist, a hard skin of calcium sulphate may be formed which can develop into surface crazing, blistering or exfoliation.

2 Attack by Soluble Salts

All types of soluble salts damage porous building stones in some way. The stone itself may contain excessive amounts of these salts; the salts may be produced on the stonework by chemical reactions between acidic rain and the stone; chlorides may be deposited from sea sprays; and the salts may come from the soils.

The trouble starts with the migration of soluble salts by capillary action in the unprotected porous stone. Crystallisation takes place by evaporation of the water from the surface and this sets up forces that can cause damage to the stonework. The damage is often manifested in the form of efflorescence, exfoliation or spalling.

3 Frost Action

The vulnerability of stonework to frost action in temperate countries is related to the poor structure of the stone. Generally, small-pored stones have a greater capillary effect so that large-pored stones do not hold as much water as their small-pored counterparts.

Most damage is caused to buildings as a result of frost following wet weather. The volume change when water becomes ice is about 2 per cent, but this is sufficient to generate expansive forces which cause damage in stonework.

4 Thermal Stress

During the day, the surface temperature of the stonework is warmer than its inner mass. At night, the condition is reversed. The stonework, therefore, is always subjected to a constant cycle of differential thermal stress between its surface and mass. The main damage to stonework is fatigue which may lead to more serious problems of contour scaling and spalling.

5 Erosion

There is a tendency for softer stones to be eroded by strong winds. For example, in coastal regions, erosion is accelerated by winds carrying sand grains.

6 Lichens, Moulds, Algae and other Growths

These organisms thrive best in damp conditions, particularly outdoors. Stonework which is attacked by these growths contains unsightly stains which are characteristically green, brown or black. Like brickwork, the strength of stonework is not affected, although its appearance may be marred.

The eradication may be more difficult in stonework than in brickwork because the toxic acids normally used in the process may be detrimental to some stones.

9.7.2 Protection of Stonework

Some forms of chemical treatment may be applied to stonework to keep it dry. However, it should be noted that although the treatment may improve the impermeability of the stonework to moisture penetration, it can also drastically affect the appearance of the stone.

Most water repellents are silicone-based products and there are various classes for different types of stone. The repellent acts by lining the pores and inhibiting capillary absorption of moisture. It is dangerous to use silicone-based water repellents on materials containing large quantities of soluble salts.

9.7.3 Repair of Stonework

In much of the repair of any stonework, attention must be paid to cracks, bulges or signs of settlement. Accurate diagnosis is important and may require careful observations and measurements to be taken over a long period of time.

Repair of stonework invariably involves one or more of the following operations:

- Stitching of cracks caused by structural movements to be carried out after underpinning.
- Grouting of cracks not likely to worsen in condition.
- Repointing of mortar joints to improve appearance, reduce water penetration and unify the stones.
- Cutting and removing defective stones and replacing them with compatible ones from similar sources as far as possible.
- All metal anchorages should be examined where they are used and be replaced with bronze or stainless steel ones if they are found to be corroded.
- Re-dressing of the stonework may be possible where the original surface has eroded.
- Creepers and other plants should be removed carefully with a weed-killer which does not have adverse effects on the stonework.

9.8 Cleaning of Brickwork and Stonework

Most buildings constructed of stone are cleaned regularly for aesthetic reasons. The dirt may also retain harmful substances and camouflage decay and structural defects. The choice of cleaning techniques may depend largely on the type and condition of the surface, cost, speed and convenience to the occupants of the building.

The main methods commonly used to clean stonework are as follows:

1 Washing

This simple method of washing away the accumulated dirt from the surface with a water spray and brushes is cheap and the least harmful, but is also the slowest. Moreover, the method is not effective when stubborn dirt has been formed over a long period.

In some limestones, for instance, the dirt adhering to the porous surface of the stone over a long period of time becomes attached to the stone with the development of a binding matrix of calcium sulphate. In such cases, other more aggressive techniques are used.

2 Dry-blasting

In this method, abrasive grit is blown under pressure at the surfaces to scour away the dirt. The size of nozzle is selected according to the demands of the job. Coarser grits are used to remove thick deposits of grime and stubborn dirt, medium grits for general soiling and finer grits for use on delicate surfaces.

Grits of sand and flint are usually used for abrasive cleaning. For best results, the surfaces should be washed rapidly with water after dry-grit blasting to remove traces of dust left behind. A high-pressure water lance is recommended for this operation.

3 Wet-grit Blasting

This technique is very similar to dry-grit blasting, except that water is introduced into the air/grit stream. Although the mixture of wet grit is less harsh on the surfaces, it generates slurry which can be troublesome.

The facade should be well washed after completion of cleaning, preferably with a high-pressure water lance. Drying-out stains are to be expected.

4 Mechanical Cleaning

The abrading media for this type of cleaning include conical carborundum stones, grinding and polishing discs, and rotary brushes attached to power tools.

Hand tools such as chisels, brushes of bristle and stainless steel wire and abrasive blocks, are used to supplement power tools, particularly for ornamental works.

5 Chemical Cleaning

Chemical cleaning methods fall into two major categories: those using acids and those using alkaline chemicals.

Table 9.3 Comparison of cleaning methods (Source: Cleaning External Surfaces of Buildings, BRE Digest 280, HMSO, London, 1983)

Method	Relative speed	Relative cost	Advantages	Disadvantages
Water spray	Slow	Low	No risk of damage to masonry except under frost conditions. No danger to public or operatives. Quiet	Limestone may develop brown, patchy stains. Water penetration may damage interior finishes, hidden timber and ferrous metals. Some risk of drain blockage. Possible nuisance from spray and saturation of surrounding ground. Often requires supplementing with an abrasive method or high-pressure water lance
Dry grit-blasting	Fast	High	No water to cause staining or internal damage. Can be used in any season	Risk of damage to surface being cleaned and to adjacent surfaces, including glass. Cannot be used on soft stone. Possible noise and dust nuisance. Risk of drain blockage. Injurious dust from siliceous materials. For best results, needs to be followed by vigorous water washing
Wet grit-blasting	Fast	High	Less water than with water spray method. Less visible dust than with dry-grit blasting	Similar to dry grit-blasting but greater risk of drain blockage. Some risk of staining limestone. Can result in mottled finish if operatives are unskilled

	Speed	Cost	Advantages	Disadvantages
Mechanical cleaning	Fast	High	No water to cause staining or internal damage. Can be used in any season	Considerable risk of damage to surface, especially mouldings. Injurious dust from siliceous materials. Hand rubbing may be necessary for acceptable finish
Hydrofluoric acid preparations	Medium	Low	Will not damage unglazed masonry or painted surfaces. Quiet	Needs extreme care in handling – can cause serious skin burns, and instant damage to unprotected glazing and polished surfaces. Scaffold pole ends need to be plugged and boards carefully rinsed
Caustic alkalis	Fast	Low	Rapid cleaning of some types of limestone with minimum use of water	Needs extreme care in use; can cause serious skin burns and damage to glazing, aluminium, galvanised surfaces and paint. Only preparations covered by an agrément certificate should be used and only in accordance with the terms of the certificate. Incorrect use can cause serious progressive damage to masonry

Table 9.4   Cleaning of natural stones (Source: Hollis, M. and Gibson, C., *Surveying Buildings*, Surveyors Publications, London, 1983)

Stone	Method	Remarks
Limestone Marble	Clean water spray to soften deposits followed by light brushing. Marbles and hard, polished limestones can be washed with water containing mild detergent, rinsed with clean water, dried with wash-leather and polished with soft cloth	Relatively slow. Not suitable for heavy encrustations, in frosty weather, or where buried ferrous metals or timber might be adversely affected and the method may cause brown stains on limestones. Marble is sometimes difficult to clean. To maintain the colour of dark, particularly green, marbles externally, after cleaning them, beeswax and natural turpentine should be applied and polished several times each year
Granites	Ammonium bifluoride	Acids, particularly hydrofluoric acid, are extremely dangerous in handling.
All stones	Hydrofluoric acid (about 5 per cent concentration)*	Risk of severe damage to surrounding materials, particularly glass
	Grit-blast**: dry	Rapid, even with heavy encrustations. No staining of stones. Requires skill to avoid damage to soft stones. Very dusty process, operatives must have independent breathing supply. Close screening is required but some dust escapes into atmosphere
	wet	Generally as above. Water reduces visible dust, but may give rise to the objections to the water spray process

Table 9.4 continued

Stone	Method	Remarks
	Mechanical: abrasive power and hand tools brushes	Rarely necessary for limestones

* Steam sometimes helps to remove deep seated soiling after acid cleaning.
** Only non-siliceous grit should be used.

Acidic cleaning agents generally consist of an aqueous solution containing organic detergents and acids. For example, a solution of hydrofluoric and orthophosphoric acids is popularly used.

Hydrofluoric acid works by dissolving silica in the material being cleaned; the dirt is released and washed away as the silica that binds it is dissolved. However, its use on limestone is not recommended because it is a hazardous chemical and tends to attack the limestone.

The cleaning process is usually carried out in sections; each section is thoroughly wetted prior to treatment by the chemicals. This practice ensures that the stone does not absorb the acid. Care must be taken to rinse off every trace of the chemical.

Alkaline cleaning agents generally consist of chemicals from the hydroxide group, most notably sodium hydroxide (caustic soda) and potassium hydroxide.

Caustic soda is very effective on limestone, but it must be used with great caution because it tends to leave behind harmful salts.

Table 9.3 compares the various cleaning methods, while table 9.4 summarises the methods used to clean natural stones.

With so many techniques available to clean masonry, it is imperative that selection of the correct method will reduce the possible problems associated with the cleaning process itself. Precautions have to be taken for certain methods. For example, proper protection of windows, including glazed areas, will obviate accidental damage resulting from grit-blasting.

Related and Further Reading

Addleson, L. *Building Failures: A Guide to Diagnosis, Remedy and Prevention*. Butterworth Architecture, London (1989).
Bidwell, T. G. *The Conservation of Brick Buildings: The Repair, Altera-*

tion and Restoration of Old Brickwork. Brick Development Association, UK (1977).

Brick Development Association, UK. *Bricks, their Properties and Use*. Construction Press, London (1974).

Brick Development Association, UK. *Cleaning of Brickwork*. BDA Building Note 2 (1986).

British Standards Institution. *BS 1243: 1978 Metal ties for cavity wall construction*.

British Standards Institution. *BS 6270: Part 1: 1982 Cleaning and surface repair of buildings – natural stone, cast stone and calcium silicate brick masonry*.

British Standards Institution. *BS 6270: Part 2: 1982 Cleaning and surface repair of buildings – concrete and precast concrete masonry*.

British Standards Institution. *BS 6477: 1984 Specification for water repellents for masonry surfaces*.

British Standards Institution. *BS 3921: 1985 Clay bricks and blocks*.

Building Research Establishment, UK. *Clay Brickwork 2*. Digest 165 (1974).

Building Research Establishment, UK. *Replacement of Cavity Wall Ties using Resin-grouted Stainless Steel Rods*. Information Paper IP 29/79 (1979).

Building Research Establishment, UK. *Clay Brickwork 1*. Digest 164 (1980).

Building Research Establishment, UK. *Strength of Brickwork and Blockwork – Design for Vertical Load*. Digest 246 (1981).

Building Research Establishment, UK. *Control of Lichens, Moulds and Similar Growths*. Digest 139 (1982).

Building Research Establishment, UK. *External Masonry Walls: Vertical Joints for Thermal and Moisture Movement*. Defect Action Sheet (Design) DAS 18 (February, 1983).

Building Research Establishment, UK. *Cleaning External Surfaces of Buildings*. Digest 280 (1983).

Building Research Establishment, UK. *Safety of Large Masonry Walls*. Digest 281 (1984).

Building Research Establishment, UK. *Sulphate Attack in External Tiled Brickwork*. Building Technical File No. 11 (October, 1985).

Building Research Establishment, UK. *Brickwork: Prevention of Sulphate Attack*. Defect Action Sheet (Design) DAS 113 (January, 1988).

Building Research Establishment, UK. *Installing Wall Ties in Existing Construction*. Digest 329 (1988).

Building Research Establishment, UK. *Decay and Conservation of Stone Masonry*. Digest 177 (1990).

Building Research Establishment, UK. *Testing Bond Strength of Masonry*. Digest 360 (April, 1990).

Building Research Establishment, UK. *Repairing Brick and Block Masonry*. Digest 359 (March, 1991).

Building Research Establishment, UK. *Building Mortar*. Digest 362 (June, 1991).

Hammett, M. *A Basic Guide to Brickwork Mortar, Part 1: Material Mixes and Selection*. Building Technical File No. 22, Building Research Establishment, UK (July, 1988).

Hammett, M. *A Basic Guide to Brickwork Mortar, Part 2: Working with Mortar on Site*. Building Technical File No. 23, Building Research Establishment, UK (October, 1988).

Hollis, M. and Gibson, C. *Surveying Buildings*. Surveyors Publications, London (1983).

Lees, T. P. and Bowler, G. K. A note on the chemical attack on mortars. *Eighth International Symposium on 'Loadbearing Brickwork'*, London (1983).

Mills, E. D. *Building Maintenance and Preservation*. Butterworths, London (1980).

Ransom, W. H. *Building Failures, Diagnosis and Avoidance*. Spon, London (1987).

Seals, C. L. and Thomasen, S. E. Deterioration mechanisms in sandstone. In Baker, J. M. *et al.* (eds), *Durability of Building Materials and Components*. Spon, London (1991).

Seeley, I. H. *Building Maintenance*, 2nd edn. Macmillan, London (1987).

Thomas, K. Frost attack on masonry. *Building Trades Journal* (March, 1987).

Thomas, K. Repairing brickwork is not always a simple matter. *Building Today* (April, 1989).

Vekey, R. C. de *Corrosion of Steel Wall Ties: Recognition, Assessment and Appropriate Action*. Information Paper IP 28/29, Building Research Establishment, UK (October, 1979).

10 Steel and Other Metals

Metals form a significant group of construction materials because they exhibit high strength in tension. Their high strength is also matched by their high stiffness.

Among the metals, steel is the most popularly used in structural frameworks and reinforcement. Other metals are used as materials for services, weatherproofing, finishes and fixings.

Defects can occur in metals for a number of reasons, particularly corrosion. The source of a defect may be traced back to as early as the design stage. This may be due to the wrong connection techniques employed. Even if the design is sound and the construction satisfactory, environmental factors can affect the performance of the metal during its service life.

10.1 Corrosion

Corrosion may be described as the result of a natural chemical reaction that causes a material to revert back to its natural condition, which, for most metals, is their oxides. All metals will eventually corrode and it is apparent that some metals corrode at a faster rate than others.

An alternative explanation for corrosion in metals is that it is caused by the flow of electricity from one metal to another or from one part of the surface of one metal to another part of the surface of the same metal where conditions permit the flow of electricity. In order for this flow of electricity to take place, an electrolyte must be present.

Corrosion takes one of two forms, depending on the conditions. The metal may react with gases in the atmosphere, resulting in direct chemical attack (oxidation); alternatively, the metal may react with aqueous solutions (electrolytic corrosion).

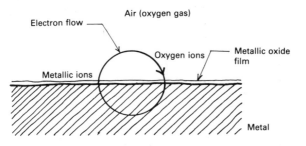

Figure 10.1   Formation of an oxide film (oxidation)

10.1.1 Oxidation

Oxidation implies a reaction between a metal and an atmosphere which may include one or more gases such as oxygen, carbon dioxide and sulphur dioxide. This form of corrosion attacks the surface of the metal and takes place in dry air at ambient or elevated temperatures. The chemical action which takes place tends to produce an oxide film (see figure 10.1).

Oxidation is a special case of corrosion where the electro-chemical processes take place within the corrosion product.

With most metals, the amount of oxidation which takes place at ordinary temperatures is not serious. In fact, in many cases, the oxide layer which rapidly forms on a freshly exposed metal surface tends to protect the metal from further oxidation.

The scale that is formed on iron heated in air acts as the electrolyte and the electron carrier as well as forming a barrier between the metal and atmosphere. In order for oxidation to continue, either oxygen must diffuse through the scale to the metal surface, or metal ions must diffuse through to the surface of the oxide layer. Usually it is diffusion of metallic ions which occurs owing to their relatively smaller size. In this case, the oxidation rate will decrease as the thickness of the oxide layer increases.

In other cases, however, the oxide layer may be porous or it may not adhere to the metal surface. In these circumstances, there will be free access of oxygen to the metal surface. Therefore, the properties of the oxide layer formed determine and control the rate of oxidation in a particular environment.

For example, the oxide layer formed on iron is loose and porous, so that oxidation will continue until the whole metal is oxidised (rusted). In the case of aluminium, however, the oxide layer is adherent and non-porous, so that the thin oxide film formed protects the underlying metal.

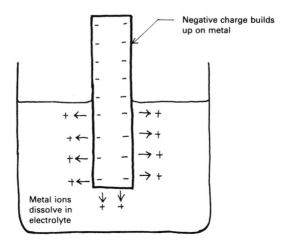

Figure 10.2   Behaviour of a metal in an aqueous solution containing metal ions

It follows that an important method of achieving oxidation resistance is by introducing suitable alloying elements to produce protective films.

10.1.2 Electro-chemical Corrosion

In the presence of water all metals have a tendency to dissolve or corrode, during which the metal discharges positively charged ions into solution (see figure 10.2). This leaves the metal with a negative charge. The greater this negative charge, the greater is the tendency of the metal to dissolve or corrode.

The magnitude of the resulting negative charge on the metal is typical of the particular metal and is called its electrode potential. If a suitable scale is chosen, this characteristic electrode potential can be expressed in volts, with the 'hydrogen electrode' potential taken as zero. In this way, metals can be arranged in order (see table 10.1).

It is clear that the driving force of electro-chemical corrosion is the potential difference between the anode and the cathode, and the current flowing through the circuit determines the corrosion rate. If the circuit resistance is increased, or the potential decreased, the current is reduced and, therefore, the corrosion rate is reduced. The corrosion rate is also affected by the relative areas of anode and cathode. Generally, for a given area of anode, the attack increases as the area of the adjacent cathode is increased (see figure 10.3).

The ability of metals to resist corrosion depends to some extent on their position in the electro-chemical series. The farther the two metals

Table 10.1 Electro-chemical series of pure metals

Metal	Electrode potential (volts)		
		Anodic end	Reactive
Potassium	−2.92	↑	metals
Sodium	−2.71		
Magnesium	−2.40		Increasing
Aluminium	−1.70	↑	reactivity
Zinc	−1.70		
Chromium	−0.56		
Iron	−0.44		
Cadmium	−0.40		
Nickel	−0.25		
Tin	−0.14		
Lead	−0.13		
Hydrogen	0.00	(Reference) ↓	Increasing
Copper	+0.34		nobility
Silver	+0.80		
Platinum	+1.20		
Gold	+1.50	↓	
			Noble
		Cathodic end	metals

Note: The further apart the metals in the series, the greater the accelerated attack on the more reactive (anode) metal.

are separated from one another in this series, the more powerful is the electric current produced by their contact in the presence of an electrolyte and hence, the more severe the corrosion.

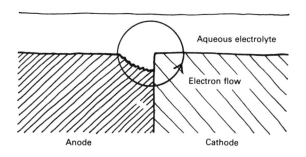

Figure 10.3 Mechanism of galvanic corrosion

10.1.3 Environment of Exposure

It should be noted that the corrosion rate of steel rises sharply when the relative humidity exceeds 60 per cent. More significantly, the rate also increases when atmospheric contaminants such as sulphates and chloride ions are present. For example, in a coastal environment with a high air-borne salt level, the risk of corrosion is high.

In the case of structural steelwork used inside buildings, the effects of the interior environment must be considered. The main factors are relative humidity, temperature, condensation and atmospheric pollutants.

In an environment facilitated by dry-heated and weathertight buildings such as offices and hotels, bare unprotected steel will not corrode seriously. On the other hand, buildings subjected to condensation will face varying degrees of corrosion. For example, occasional condensation in a relatively clean atmosphere poses only a slight corrosion risk; frequent condensation coupled with a polluted atmosphere will constitute a high corrosion risk. See table 10.2.

10.1.4 Other Types of Corrosion Cells

The formation of an anode and cathode need not necessarily be due to contact between dissimilar metals. An electro-chemical cell can be formed between two areas of the same piece of metal if there is some difference between the areas. This difference may be due to one or more reasons, such as:

- In a two-phase alloy, or a metal containing impurities, one phase may be anodic with respect to the other.
- Randomly arranged grain boundary atoms tend to ionise more readily than atoms within a regular crystal lattice, so that a grain boundary tends to be anodic with respect to the grain itself.
- The presence of surface abrasions.
- Differences due to thermal or mechanical effects.
- Differences in composition or concentration of electrolyte.
- The presence of stress areas.
- Differential aeration such as scale adhering to parts of the surface.

Arising from the above situations, corrosion cells other than dissimilar electrode cells may be broadly classified as follows:

1 Stress Cells
The atoms of a highly stressed metal tend to ionise to a greater extent than atoms of the same metal in an unstressed condition. So the stressed metal will be anodic with respect to the unstressed metal.

Table 10.2   Classification of steel corrosion risk level according to types of environment

Environment	Description	Corrosion risk level
Exterior		
Inland: non-polluted	Clean environment: dry atmosphere relatively free from SO_2, chemical and salt pollutions Example: rural and urban areas	Mild
Inland: polluted	Industrial areas: atmosphere of high concentration of SO_2 and other forms of pollution Example: areas in close proximity to chemical plants	Moderate
Coastal: non-polluted	Marine environment: normal inland with high air-borne salt levels Example: areas close to the sea	Severe
Coastal: polluted	Marine and polluted atmosphere: moist, high air-borne salt and highly contaminated industrial air Example: industrial areas located near sea coast	Very severe
Interior		
Normal	Dry, comfortable and weathertight buildings Examples: shops, offices, schools, etc.	Mild
Condensation	Relatively clean atmosphere with occasional condensation problems Examples: unheated buildings, sports halls, laundries, kitchens, etc.	Moderate
Condensation and corrosive	Frequent presence of condensation with a corrosive atmosphere Examples: swimming pools, chemical processing plant, etc.	Severe

Consequently, an electro-chemical cell may be set up in a component in which the stress distribution is uneven. This also applies to an uneven distribution of internal stresses, for example, residual stresses in a cold-worked component.

2 Differential Temperature Cells

This type of cell can occur when pieces of the same metal are at different temperatures in an electrolyte of the same initial composition. Such a situation may occur in heat exchanger units or with immersion heaters.

3 Salt Concentration Cells

When a metal is in contact with a concentrated electrolyte, it will not ionise as much as when it is in contact with a dilute electrolyte. Therefore, if a piece of metal is in contact with an electrolyte of varying concentration, those portions in contact with dilute electrolyte will be anodic relative to portions in contact with more concentrated electrolyte. This type of electro-chemical cell may be set up in situations involving flowing electrolytes in pipes.

4 Differential Aeration Cells

This type of cell is due to differences in oxygen concentration and is more common than salt concentration cells. The differential aeration effect can be used to explain a number of corrosion problems such as the rusting of iron under drops of water (see figure 10.4) and the occurrence of corrosion just below the water-line of steel vessels (see figure 10.5).

10.1.5 Types of Corrosion Attack

The various forms of corrosion attack on metals can be categorised into two main types, namely, uniform and local attack.

1 Uniform Attack

This is the most common type of corrosion. Uniform attack results in the heaviest masses of metal loss, but the rate of attack can usually be reliably determined so that the service life of components can be fairly accurately estimated. However, what is usually far more important than the amount of general surface corrosion is the pattern of the attack.

2 Local Attack

If the attack is localised, the corrosion rate is accelerated, being almost directly proportional to the ratio of the areas of cathode to anode. This

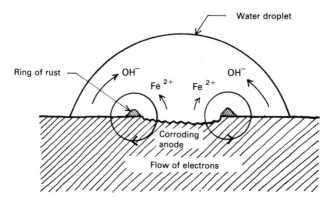

Figure 10.4 Corrosion of steel under a drop of water

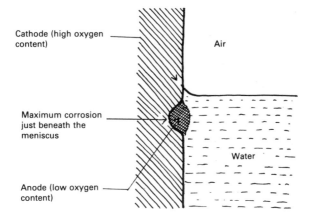

Figure 10.5 Effect of differential aeration

type of attack may cause premature failure, such as leaking of tanks. Local attack may take the following forms:

- Pitting is caused mainly by differential aeration or by the presence of stress. The initial depression in the surface may be due to a break in a protective film or the presence of scale. Once a pit is formed, the corrosion proceeds rapidly because the surface of the metal (cathode) has greater access to oxygen than the bottom of the pit (anode). Corrosion is accelerated because the surface area of the cathode is much greater than that of the anode. The corrosion product accumulates at the mouth of the pit and aggravates the corrosion by making access to oxygen more difficult (see figure 10.6).
- Intergranular corrosion occurs by localised attack at grain bound-

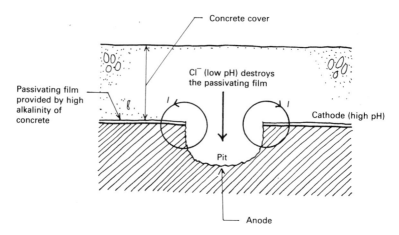

Figure 10.6   Pitting corrosion in steel embedded in concrete

aries which behave as anodes to the larger surrounding cathodic areas. Incorrectly heat-treated austenitic stainless steels and duralumin-type alloys are prone to this type of attack, as are plain carbon steels in the presence of nitrite solutions.

- Stress corrosion cracking may be defined as the premature failure of a material due to the combined action of a static tensile stress and a corrosive environment. In stress corrosion cracking there is usually very little overall corrosion, but the metal breaks by the passage of a microscopically sharp narrow crack across the axis of tensile stress. Stress corrosion cracking may be intergranular or transgranular, and the appearance of the fractured surface is similar to that after brittle fracture.

10.2 Prevention of Aqueous Corrosion

10.2.1 Good Design

In combating corrosion, the importance of good design cannot be over-emphasised because this helps to reduce contact with the corrosive medium.

Deterioration can be avoided by attention to such design details (see figure 10.7) as:

- Both parts of the structure should be accessible for maintenance or, if this is not possible, the members should be provided with some form of permanent protection.
- Select structural shapes which have a minimum of exposed surface;

for example, from the standpoint of minimising corrosion, a T-section is better than double angles.

- Avoid shapes or details which will catch dirt or debris.
- Eliminate pockets, low spots and crevices which will trap water; for example, channel sections should be provided with drain holes.
- Column bases should be protected with concrete encasement projecting above ground line or floor level.
- Avoid details which include narrow crevices that cannot be sealed or painted.
- For riveted or bolted joints, or for sections placed back-to-back, inhibit water penetration between the plates or shapes by ensuring that all adjacent metal surfaces are drawn tight.
- Pipes or tubular columns should be concrete filled or sealed airtight.
- Isolate dissimilar metals to avoid galvanic corrosion.

10.2.2 Keeping the Structure Clean

Corrosion will be much accelerated if dirt or debris is allowed to accumulate in contact with the member. The reason is that the dirt retains rain or wash water, or may even soak up moisture from the atmosphere and maintain this moisture in contact with the steel surface. Furthermore, in industrial areas the accumulated dirt often consists of soot containing a heavy concentration of corrosive sulphur compounds. Also, the accumulation of dirt tends to hide underlying defects and make proper inspection difficult.

No matter how well the steel may be painted or otherwise protected, it is essential to sweep, blow or hose off the dirt, frequently from accessible parts and periodically from parts which are less accessible. The importance of regular inspection and cleaning in preventing corrosion is well established. In fact, regular cleaning and inspection are more important than painting.

10.2.3 Modification of the Environment

An aqueous environment may be modified by the removal of its oxygen or by the addition of inhibitors. Examples of the above include deaeration of boiler water.

Dissolved gases may be removed by increasing the temperature or by holding at low pressure and flushing with an inert gas such as nitrogen. Chemical deaeration may be achieved by adding sodium sulphite to alkaline solutions, or hydrazine to neutral or acidic solutions.

Inhibitors are substances which, when added to a corrosive aqueous environment, stifle the corrosion reaction.

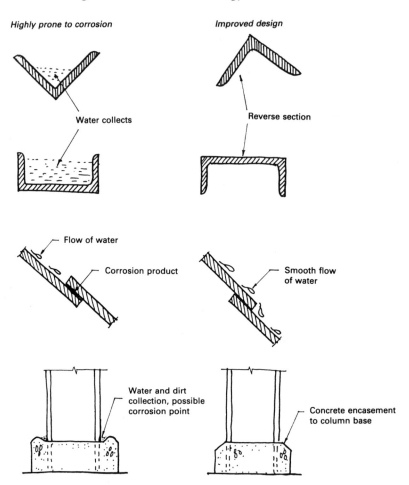

Figure 10.7   Good design practice to minimise corrosion

10.2.4 Modification of the Material

The corrosion resistance of many materials may be improved by alloying. Alloys are used which simulate noble metal behaviour by passive oxide film formation. Therefore, aluminium, chromium, titanium, nickel–chromium alloys and stainless steels are used for specific environments.

The resistance of mild steel to atmospheric attack may be increased by small additions of copper or chromium which render the oxide film more protective.

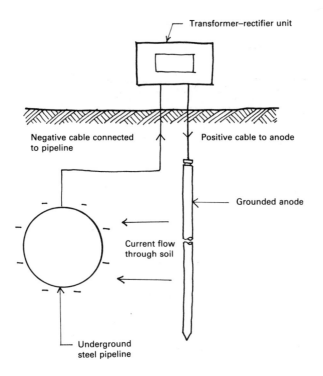

Transformer–rectifier unit

Negative cable connected
to pipeline

Positive cable to anode

Grounded anode

Current flow
through soil

Underground
steel pipeline

Figure 10.8   Typical cathodic protection of underground steel
pipeline by impressed current

10.2.5 Cathodic Protection

In this method of protection, galvanic cells are deliberately formed and
the metal to be protected is made the cathode. Metals which are
strongly anodic with respect to steel, such as zinc, magnesium and
aluminium, may be used as sacrificial anodes to prevent the corrosion
of buried steel pipes (see figure 10.8).

The sacrificial anode maintains a supply of excess electrons to the
material which is to be protected, thus ensuring that the latter is the
cathode. The replacement of consumed anodes is usually an easy and
relatively inexpensive operation.

10.2.6 Protective Coatings

One of the commonest methods of minimising corrosion is to isolate
the material from its environment by using a protective coating. Coatings may be metallic or non-metallic, and afford protection either by

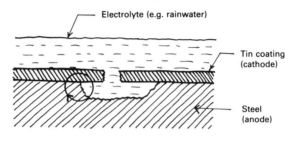

a. *Cathodic metallic coating*

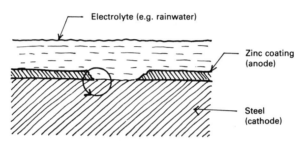

b. *Anodic metallic coating (sacrificial protection)*

Figure 10.9   Cathodic and anodic metallic coatings

excluding direct contact with the environment or by sacrificial cathodic protection. With all coatings, proper surface preparation is vital, which means that scale and rust must be removed by acid pickling or abrasive cleaning, while grease and oil can be eliminated by solvents.

1 Metallic Coatings

The coating metal may be either anodic or cathodic with respect to the base metal (see figure 10.9). With a cathodic coating, such as tin on steel, any flaw in the coating will accelerate the corrosion of the steel by galvanic action. But in the case of an anodic coating, such as zinc on steel, any break in the coating will cause the zinc to corrode sacrificially and the steel will be protected so long as the zinc is present.

Metallic coatings can be applied by various methods such as:

- Hot-dipping in which the material to be protected is immersed in a molten bath of the coating metal, usually of low melting points, such as zinc, tin, lead or aluminium. However, good adhesion and coating thickness are difficult to control.

- Electroplating is used to deposit a metal on to both metallic and non-metallic surfaces. The surface to be plated is made the cathode in an electrolytic cell. The electrolyte is usually the solution of a salt of the metal to be deposited. The anode is made of the coating metal which dissolves into the electrolyte and is then deposited on the cathodic metal. Gold, silver, chromium, nickel, copper, cadmium, tin and some alloys can be deposited in this way.
- Cladding is applicable mainly to the production of cladding panels in which the metal to be protected is sandwiched between two pieces of the coating metal and then hot or cold rolled to the required thickness. It is essential that the coating metal and base metal must have similar deformation characteristics. Alclad, which is duralumin coated with pure aluminium, and Niclad, which is nickel-clad mild steel, are the most popular of these products.
- Spraying can be employed to coat surfaces with a wide range of molten metals, though zinc is most often used. No alloying occurs, however, and the base metal must be roughened to receive the coating. This method is useful for applying an *in situ* coating to existing structures.
- Cementation enables the protective metal to diffuse into the surface of the component to be protected at a sufficiently high temperature. Sheradising, for example, allows a thin uniform coating of zinc to be formed by heating the mild steel and zinc powder together at about 370°C.

2 Inorganic Coatings

Besides metallic coatings, protection can also be afforded by applying inorganic coatings to the base metal on the same principle of forming a barrier against corrosive agents.

The various types of inorganic coatings are:

- Vitreous enamels or porcelain enamels which are essentially glass coatings fused on to the metal, usually steel. Glass formulations with very high silica, aluminosilicate and borosilicate compositions have the highest corrosion resistance to a wide range of environments. The greatest disadvantage comes from mechanical damage to the coating which can result in localised corrosion of the base metal.
- Phosphate coatings, though not used to provide corrosion protection, give a good base for the retention of paints, by ensuring good adherence of the paint to steel and decreasing the tendency for corrosion to undercut the paint film at points of defect.
- Oxide coatings are also not used to protect against corrosion but are used to provide an improved base for paints. Anodised aluminium can be obtained in different colours for aesthetic purposes.

- Chromate coatings are produced on zinc, imparting a yellowish colour and protecting the metal against spotting or staining by condensed moisture. The life of zinc will be extended to some extent when exposed to the atmosphere.

3 Organic Coatings
The most commonly used organic coating is paint. The corrosion resistance of the paint is dependent on the specific properties of these resins which can be thermoplastic or thermosetting. Thermosetting resins differ in that a chemical change takes place after application and solvent evaporation. This curing can take place at room temperature or at elevated temperatures. High temperatures or exposure to solvents do not cause the coating to soften.

Table 10.3 summarises the optimal coatings for steel according to the environment in which it is to be located.

10.3 Atmospheric Corrosion

Most metallic materials are liable to attack by pollutants present in the atmosphere. Such pollutants include both solid and gaseous substances such as carbon (soot), water vapour, sulphur dioxide, hydrogen sulphide, ammonia and chlorides. The type of pollutants present depends very much on the geographical location. In marine areas, for example, the air contains significant amounts of chlorides and ozone, while in industrial districts the atmosphere has a higher concentration of sulphur dioxide and carbon and its compounds.

The rate of corrosion is influenced by climatic variables such as temperature, rainfall, relative humidity and wind. The amount of moisture present is particularly important and corrosion is more severe where relative humidity is higher, as in tropical countries. However, rainfall may wash away corrosive substances and hence may be beneficial. Solid, air-borne impurities are very important because they may absorb reactive gases to form an electrolyte with condensed water vapour. Of all the gaseous contaminants in the atmosphere, sulphur dioxide is the most injurious because of its easy tendency to form acids.

10.4 Corrosion in the Soil

The basic electrochemical process of corrosion is the same in soils and depends on moisture content, oxygen content, pH value, electrical conductivity and bacterial content. These factors are in turn largely

Table 10.3 Coating treatment for steel according to corrosivity of environment

Steel surface	Corrosion risk level		
	Mild	Moderate	Severe
Main structural members (e.g. stanchions, beams, girders, etc.)	Metallic coating. Red lead, metallic lead primer plus micaceous iron oxide paint (painting only for appearance)	Metallic coating and painted. Aluminium sprayed with or without painting. 2 coats of zinc-rich paint. Heavy-duty bitumen, coal-tar or coal-tar/epoxy paints	Metallic coatings with micaceous iron oxide paint. 3 coats of heavy-duty bitumen or coal-tar or coal-tar/epoxy paints. Anti-corrosive wrappings
Other structural members (e.g. trusses, purlins, braces, etc.)	As above. Metallic coating with or without painting	As above. Wrapped with anti-corrosive paste and tape	As above
Non-structural members (e.g. railings, chain link fencing, etc.)	Metallic coating with or without painting. Red lead or metallic lead primers. 2 coats of aluminium or gloss paint	Metallic coating and painted. PVC coatings. 2 coats of red lead, metallic primers plus 2 coats of aluminium or gloss paint	Replace by aluminium metallic coating. PVC coatings

continued on p. 238

Table 10.3   continued

Steel surface	Corrosion risk level		
	Mild	*Moderate*	*Severe*
Cover sheetings (e.g. roofing, cladding, etc.)	As above. PVC coatings. 2 coats of zinc chromate primers	PVC coatings. Metallic coating and painted. Bitumen coated	Vitreous enamel or PVC coatings. Replace by plastic or aluminium sheet. Bitumen coating (factory applied)
Door and window frames	Metallic coating with painting. Stoved zinc chromate factory primer with gloss paint	Replace by PVC, aluminium, or timber. Metallic coating with painting. Zinc-rich paint for re-painting (if corroded)	Avoid using steel. Replace by PVC, aluminium or timber

Exposed pipework	Thin bitumen coatings and wrappings. 2 coats of zinc-rich paint. Bituminuous or coal-tar paint	Anti-corrosive wrapping. Bitumen coating. 2 coats of red lead, metal lead plus gloss paint	Thick bitumen coating and wrapping. Anti-corrosive paste and tapes
Rainwater goods (gutters, downpipes and brackets)	Metallic coating. 2 coats of red lead, metal lead plus gloss paint externally. Coal tar paint internally	Metallic coating and painted. 2 coats of red lead, metal lead plus gloss paint externally. Bitumen or tar coating internally	Avoid using steel. Replace by PVC or aluminium. Heavy-duty bitumen, coal-tar or coal-tar/epoxy paints

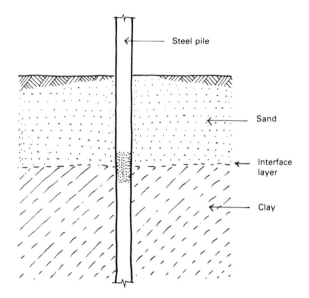

Figure 10.10   Corrosion attack on a steel pile at the interface
between different types of soil

governed by the chemical composition of the soil and its particle size.

The moisture content of soils can vary from a dry sandy type to waterlogged conditions. Wet soils are more corrosive than dry ones. The ability of a soil to retain water and oxygen is controlled by particle size; a coarse gravel usually retains more oxygen than clay. Clays, alluvial soils and all saline soils are therefore more corrosive because atmospheric oxygen may be unable to come into contact with the metal surface to form a protective film which can reduce the subsequent rate of corrosion (see figure 10.10).

The depth of the water table also has an important influence on corrosion, and the rate depends on whether the metal is permanently below or above it. Soils which permit alternate cycles of wet and dry conditions are particularly vulnerable to serious corrosion.

The conductivity and pH value of a soil will be determined by the chemical composition of the soil. In general, the higher the conductivity, the more corrosive the soil. The pH value of soils is usually between 5 and 8, but dissolved carbon dioxide may make it more acidic.

Bacterial content in the soil can also cause chemical changes that can result in corrosion. For instance, sulphuric acid may be formed by the oxidation of sulphur-containing compounds.

Differences in soil resistivity, water content and oxygen concentration can all lead to the creation of potential differences over pipelines embedded in soils and the formation of electrolytic cells. Generally, sound protective coatings on the principle of cathodic protection can alleviate this problem. In the case of piles, however, the problem is more acute because the protective coatings are often damaged during the process of driving.

10.5 Abrasion

Deterioration of steel members caused by abrasion is easily identified by the worn, smooth appearance of the abraded surface. Abrasion is associated with the working of moving parts in contact; for example, with portions of members immersed in a moving fluid. The general solution to the problem of abrasion is armouring.

10.6 Fatigue

Fatigue is the fracture of a structural member due to repetitive fluctuating loads occurring at stresses below the usual allowable design values. The symptoms are small fractures perpendicular to the line of stress. If not detected, these cracks may result in collapse without warning. Repair of members showing signs of fatigue cracks requires restoration of lost strength by plating.

10.7 Loosening of Connections

Rivets and bolts in connections tend to work loose with time. Loosening of the connections induces slip in joints, causes distortion of the structure, creates areas of extreme stress concentration and increases the vulnerability of the structure to fatigue failure (see figure 10.11).

Accordingly, the connections of steel structures which are subject to impact loading should be checked periodically. Loose rivets should be cut out and replaced, either with new rivets or with high-strength bolts, and loose bolts should be retorqued or replaced.

10.8 Weld Defects

Cracking is often caused by large depth: width ratio of weld bead, high arc energy or the pick-up of sulphur or phosphorus from the parent metal. Surface cracks are detected by visual examination, magnetic particle or penetrant inspection, whereas the detection of internal cracks requires the use of ultrasonic or radiographic techniques.

Porosity resulting from entrapment of gas may give rise to cavities in the solidified weld metal.

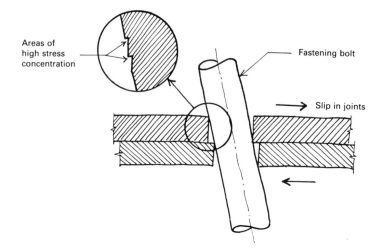

Figure 10.11   Stress corrosion from misaligned bolt

Poor welding techniques will cause imperfect shapes of the welded metal. Typical examples include linear misalignment, excessive reinforcement, overlap, undercut and excessive penetration.

Figure 10.12 summarises some common defects in welds.

10.9 Impact Failure

Exposed steel sections are sensitive to damage from the impact of moving objects. This sensitivity is due to the use in steel design of sections having relatively thin flanges and other projecting parts.

Impact damage is characterised by local distortion of the affected members, usually in the form of a bow or crimp. Defective members may be repaired by either plating or encasing.

10.10 Repair Procedures

Assuming that significant deterioration has occurred and that a decision has been taken to repair the affected members, the following methods are suitable:

10.10.1 Plating

Plating can be done by taking plates or rolled sections, running them alongside and past the deteriorated member or portion, and splicing them into the structure in areas where the structure is still sound. The

a. *Solidification cracking*

b. *Lack of fusion*

c. *Excessive reinforcement*

Figure 10.12 Some common welding defects

method is also used to repair members which have cracked, buckled or suffered from local crushing. However, it is not recommended if appearance is of prime importance.

Fabrication and installation of plating should follow the standard procedures for new construction. Care should be taken to provide a close fit between the new and existing members. New sections should be ground and fitted to the fillets of the existing sections.

Before installation of the plates, the contact surfaces between the new and existing members should be cleaned and the whole assembly cleaned and painted after plating. Dust, scale or dirt should be removed from the existing surfaces. The contact surfaces should be primed and painted before plating is done.

Figures 10.13 and 10.14 show details of some typical strengthening operations.

10.10.2 Replacement

Where the entire member is severely corroded, if there is no room to add new plates or if appearance is a consideration, replacement offers the solution.

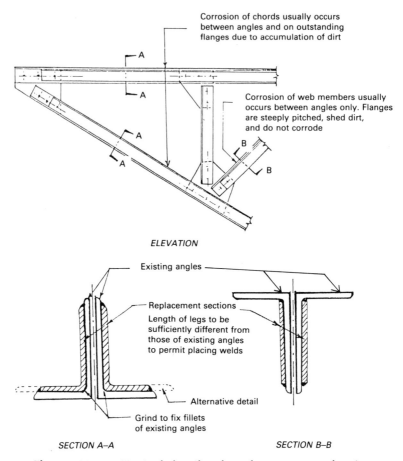

Corrosion of chords usually occurs between angles and on outstanding flanges due to accumulation of dirt

Corrosion of web members usually occurs between angles only. Flanges are steeply pitched, shed dirt, and do not corrode

ELEVATION

Existing angles

Replacement sections

Length of legs to be sufficiently different from those of existing angles to permit placing welds

Alternative detail

Grind to fix fillets of existing angles

SECTION A–A   SECTION B–B

Figures 10.13 Typical details of roof truss strengthening

If this is to be done, care should be taken to ensure that temporary propping be carried out, if necessary prior to the dismantling of any structural member.

10.10.3 Encasement with Concrete

This method is a means of preventing deterioration due to corrosion and abrasion. It is also a good and effective way to reinforce a deteriorated section, provided that there is room for the enlargement of the section, the section is strong enough to carry the added weight and the encasement is not unsightly.

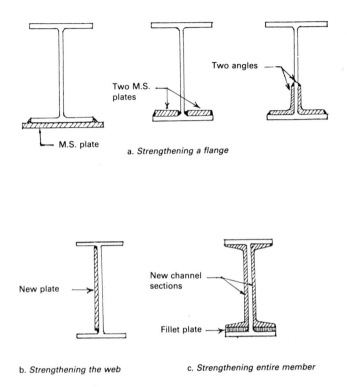

a. *Strengthening a flange*

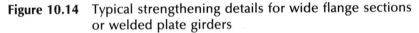

b. *Strengthening the web*   c. *Strengthening entire member*

Figure 10.14 Typical strengthening details for wide flange sections or welded plate girders

10.11 Planned Maintenance

The protective treatment of steelwork usually implies planned maintenance at regular intervals. Regular inspection of structural steelwork, carried out in a careful and systematic manner, is necessary to keep an acceptable standard of appearance for a minimum cost. Unless repainting is carried out before the protective paint film begins to break down to a marked degree, the cost of preparation will greatly increase. Breakdown of the paint in the early stages is indicated by rust stains, chalking, cracking and blistering of the surface, followed by the breakthrough of rust and the flaking of paint in the advanced stages.

10.12 Non-ferrous Metals

10.12.1 Copper

Copper is extensively used where good resistance to atmospheric conditions is required. Its resistance is due mainly to the ability to develop adherent protective layers of corrosion products. Initially the protective patina may be brown, but it gradually changes to a typical green and is basically copper sulphate. Exposure to a marine atmosphere will hasten the formation of the green patina.

Seawater, despite its high salinity, causes only negligible corrosion of copper, provided that the protective patina adheres to the parent metal.

Generally, when copper fails to meet satisfactory performance standards, it is the result of design or operational features rather than the properties of the metal.

10.12.2 Zinc

The behaviour of zinc in conditions of moderate pH is such that passivity is attained in a wide variety of practical applications. Passivity is attained by the initial formation of zinc oxide but, after prolonged exposure, additional zinc salts such as carbonate and sulphate develop. Zinc is also capable of giving sacrificial protection to exposed and connected surfaces of most metals except aluminium or magnesium, and is thereby itself preferentially corroded.

In dry air, zinc is very resistant and, once a surface layer of oxide has formed, it is not susceptible to atmospheric corrosion even on prolonged exposure. For this reason, zinc is used extensively for coating and galvanising ferrous metals.

Zinc resists most natural waters satisfactorily unless the water is acidic or deaerated, or solid deposits form differential aeration cells wherein the protective oxide layer cannot form. Pitting of the surface may occur under any of these conditions.

10.12.3 Aluminium

Aluminium is characterised by its low density, good thermal conductivity, ductility and low mechanical strength. The alloys of aluminium are generally slightly less corrosion-resistant than aluminium itself.

At pH values between 4.0 and 8.5 at room temperatures, aluminium is tolerant to changes in conditions, passing readily from the immune to the passive state after only a very limited phase of reactivity. The rapid formation and self-healing properties of an invisible film of aluminium oxide lead to satisfactory performance in most natural environments. However, low or high pH values, the absence of oxygen, or the presence of film destructive ions such as chloride occurring locally, may all cause the breakdown of this oxide film with resultant pitting attack.

Atmospheric exposure weathers aluminium to a dull grey colour upon which carbon deposits may cause black stains after some time. This is not known to initiate corrosion, however, and once the surface film is well developed, neither hydrogen sulphide nor carbon dioxide has adverse effects.

Contact with marine environments invariably promotes initial pitting. Under immersed conditions, the pits are fewer but are large and shallow. In fast-moving seawater, however, the pitting may well be continuous.

Related and Further Reading

Allen, M. D. and Lewis, D. A. Cathodic protection in civil engineering. *Corrosion in Civil Engineering*. Institution of Civil Engineers, London (1978).

Avoiding trouble by regular painting. *Building Maintenance and Services Journal* (July/August, 1977).

Building Research Establishment, UK. *Corrosion of Metals by Wood*. Digest 301 (1985).

Building Research Establishment, UK. *Zinc-coated Steel*. Digest 305 (1986).

Butler, G. and Ison, H. C. K. *Corrosion and its Prevention in Waters*. Leonard Hill, London (1966).

Harrison, H. W. *Inspecting Steel Houses*. Information Paper IP 14/87, Building Research Establishment, UK (August, 1987).

Higgins, R. A. *Materials for the Engineering Technician*. English Universities Press, London (1972).

Johnson, S. M. *Deterioration, Maintenance and Repair of Structures*. McGraw-Hill, New York (1965).

Matteson, E. *Basic Corrosion Technology for Scientists and Engineers*. Ellis Horwood, Chichester, UK (1989).

Narayanan, R. Protection of steel buildings from atmospheric corrosion. *Proceedings of 4th Conference on 'Durability of Building Materials and Components'*, Singapore (1987).

Ross, T. K. *Metal Corrosion*. Oxford University Press (1977).

Taylor, G. D. *Construction Materials*, Longman, London (1991).

11 Roofs and Roof Drainage

The roof is the most vulnerable part of a building and hence its performance requirements have to be stringent. Although most roofs are structurally stable, problems do occur because of poor design and construction. All roof coverings are expected to be durable under a wide range of conditions. But this durability is often short-lived because the roof is invariably exposed to the extremes of temperature, solar radiation, snow loadings and wind action as well as to chemical, biological and mechanical agents.

11.1 Flat Roofs

The reputation of flat roofs for poor performance is partly the result of inadequate on-site workmanship and detailing, and partly poor design. However, by paying careful attention to the design and by cautious selection of materials for the service conditions, it is still possible to reduce significantly potential problems associated with flat roofs (see figure 11.1).

11.1.1 Primary Structure

The primary structure is the load-bearing element which transmits the dead and superimposed loads of the roof to the walls or columns of the building. The choice between a deck of reinforced concrete slabs or cast concrete *in situ*, and lightweight materials of troughed metal or timber, will be dictated mainly by the overall design concept for the building.

The weight and high thermal capacity of concrete give it satisfactory thermal performance generally. Metal decks have high resistance to the passage of vapour from within the building. But timber and other board materials show considerable movements under changing moisture content, thereby inducing high stresses in insulants and coverings that overlie them.

One of the major causes of ponding is insufficient slope provided to the roof. Although a designed fall of 1 in 80 is normally considered as adequate, variations in construction accuracy, sagging and thermal and moisture movements demand a bigger gradient of 1 in 40, according to BS 6229.

Local areas of the roof, too, can deviate markedly from the overall falls. Ponding, rather than shedding of rainwater, can occur, leading to serious seepage of water into the roof structure. Other sources of water leakage include the entrapment of water during construction, interstitial condensation and rainwater penetration through defective roofing membranes.

11.1.2 Insulation

A large variety of materials is available commercially for use as insulation. But the choice of insulating material must be exercised with care for the particular roof design and conditions of service.

There has been an increasing tendency to use warm deck designs with the insulation put on the roof deck to meet the enhanced standards of thermal insulation. This method has the added advantage of minimising thermal movement of the roof structure due to solar radiation.

However, the placing of some insulation below the roof structure ensures a warmer ceiling and reduces the risk of condensation, especially in instances where the rooms beneath the roof are prone to high humidities, such as kitchens and bathrooms. Excessive moisture in the fibrous insulation can cause rotting of the material and serious ponding problems.

In the inverted roof design, the insulation layer is placed above the waterproof membrane to act as a temperature buffer. The weathering surface placed above the insulation protects the covering from temperature fluctuations and solar heat.

The movement characteristics of insulating materials vary considerably. This behaviour of the insulating material determines whether the waterproofing membrane is to be fully bonded, partially bonded or protected from movement by using a more stable insulation as an overlay to the main insulation board before applying the membrane.

Fibrous materials, such as wood fibreboards, glass fibre and mineral wool, suffer little movement from temperature effects and it is usual to bond the membrane fully to these insulants since fatigue failure is unlikely to occur.

Foam insulants, such as foamed polyurethane and phenolic foam, however, have high coefficients of expansion and a rapid response to

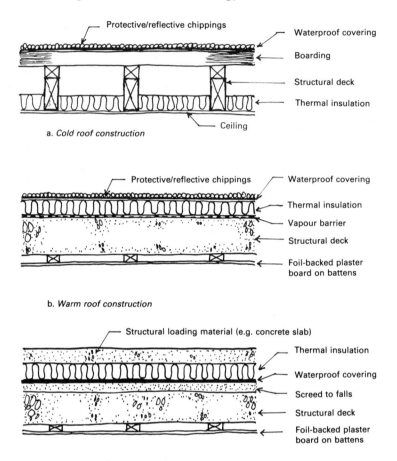

a. *Cold roof construction*

b. *Warm roof construction*

c. *Inverted roof construction (protected membrane roof)*

Figure 11.1   Types of flat roof construction

temperature changes. Although they tend to absorb deck movements, they also impose their own type of movements, which should be considered when specifying their use.

Expanded polystyrene, on the other hand, moves substantially as temperature changes. Therefore, it is necessary to use an overlay of a more stable insulating material to reduce movement of the expanded polystyrene being transmitted to the waterproofing membrane.

11.1.3 Parapets

Water penetration due to defects in parapet detailing and construction is a common problem in flat roofs. It is often difficult to suggest a single cause for this failure.

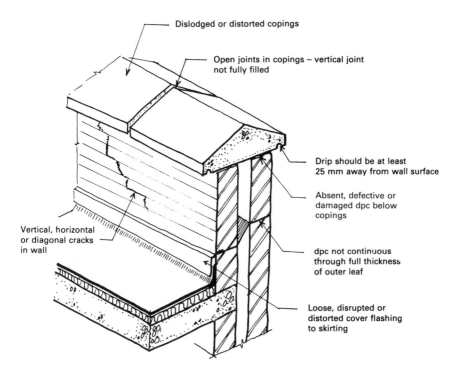

Dislodged or distorted copings

Open joints in copings – vertical joint
not fully filled

Drip should be at least
25 mm away from wall surface

Absent, defective or
damaged dpc below
copings

dpc not continuous
through full thickness
of outer leaf

Loose, disrupted or
distorted cover flashing
to skirting

Vertical, horizontal
or diagonal cracks
in wall

Figure 11.2   Faulty construction of parapet walls

The presence of a damp-proof course in the parapet will reduce water penetration. But this is often not found in very old construction.

On any occasion where the interior of the building has shown indications of water penetration or condensation, a careful investigation of the construction should be carried out. Common symptoms of failure include defective installation and location of damp-proof courses, failure to install damp-proof courses beneath the coping and the closing of the cavity by the construction of a floor slab to the back of the outer leaf of cavity brickwork (see figure 11.2).

If there are signs of leaking at the roof perimeter, it will be necessary to examine the coping details, particularly its size, how it has been bedded and throat details. Frequently, this failure is due to an under-sized coping being constructed with insufficient overhang for the drip channel to be effective. The problem will be compounded if the up-stand between the roof finish and the coping is too small, making it easier for water to splash up the joint.

The best method of repair is to remove the existing coping and replace it with a new one of sufficient size to permit adequate over-hang with adequate throatings. Where the upstand is small, a sealant should be incorporated at the edge of the upstand in addition to the normal bedding of the coping. If it is necessary to retain the existing coping for whatever reasons, it should be carefully removed and cleaned. The existing bedding should be cleared away and the coping replaced on a layer of roofing sheet bonded to the existing roofing and carried over the parapet. The mortar bed should be protected by using a sealant on both sides.

11.2 Flat Roof Coverings

For the majority of applications, the performance of waterproof membranes for flat roofs must satisfy three important parameters, namely tensile strength, elongation to failure and fatigue resistance. While it is not necessary to specify very high standards of performance in terms of tensile strength and degree of elongation, there must nevertheless be a minimum value in order to guarantee the integrity of the membrane. The dominant parameter in the assessment of the performance of a waterproofing membrane lies in its resistance to fatigue in combating the effects of thermal and moisture movements.

11.2.1 Mastic Asphalt

Asphalt is an inherently durable material and is highly impermeable. The material is laid in two layers on isolating felt to allow movement, and is held in place by its own weight. The substrate should preferably be rigid, like concrete, rather than lightweight materials, since asphalts tend to crack under excessive flexing.

The common types of defects found in asphalt roofing include the following:

1 Surface Crazing
When asphalt is exposed to sunlight for some time, it tends to harden. The hardening at the surface induces stresses within the material, resulting in a pattern of random cracks on the surface. As the asphalt continues to harden with prolonged exposure, the cracks become progressively deeper and the surface gives the appearance of alligator hide.

If alligatoring is allowed to proceed, the cracks may enlarge and deepen, and pieces of asphalt may break away to expose the underlying felt. As soon as the felt becomes exposed to the weather, it may subsequently permit penetration of water and then deteriorate.

Application of additional coatings of asphalt over the crazed surfaces is unlikely to be useful since shrinkage will continue and rapidly crack up the new asphalt too. Repair work, therefore, requires the use of reinforcing materials such as felts or fabrics to resist the stresses that caused the crazing and prevent them from rapidly breaking the new surface.

2 Ponding

The common symptom of ponding is manifested in the form of small puddles of water remaining on the asphalt roofing during rain. Ponding frequently occurs as a result of faulty construction or a subsequent failure in the roof which has allowed a settlement in the finish.

The possible causes of ponding are:

- Inadequate fall of the roof towards drainage points arising from poor design or construction.
- Flexing of the lightweight substrate owing to the self-weight of the decking and asphalt roofing, leading to 'dishing' and subsequent ponding at the centre of the roof.

If the ponding occurs around drainage outlets, there is a need to inspect the drainage system because of possible blockage by fallen debris or poor installation of an outlet pipe, which can result in it standing proud above the general roof level.

Persistent ponding on the roof at the same location is undesirable because it can lead eventually to deterioration of the membrane as well as serious water penetration.

3 Fractures

Fractures refer to deep cracks which cut through the thickness of the asphalt layers and permit water penetration. The most common causes of this problem (see figure 11.3) are the result of:

- The high coefficient of thermal expansion of asphalt which leads to its continuous expansion and contraction induced by solar gain.
- The roof deck bending excessively under load, particularly for lightweight construction. This tends to cause overstressing of the asphalt.
- Differential movements between the membrane and the underlying structural deck which are evidence of cracks being coincident with joints provided in the structure.

If the cracking is due to differential movement between the membrane and its substrate, a movement joint should be provided. This is effected by making a chase in the substrate that is filled with a backing strip and sealant, and then covered with a synthetic rubber strip bonded to the waterproofing membrane.

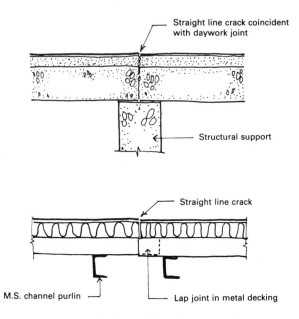

Figure 11.3   Movement failure of mastic asphalt roofing in high
stress regions

4 Blistering

Blistering of asphalt is most common in hot weather. It can happen
during, or soon after, the laying of the roof, and is particularly likely to
occur if no solar protection is provided.

The blisters are caused by entrapped water being expanded by solar
radiation that has also softened the asphalt. Where the blisters are cut
out and repaired, those caused by construction water in the concrete
slab are not likely to recur.

However, if the blisters are caused by leaks or interstitial condensation, their formation is likely to continue. The underlying problems
should be dealt with first before resorting to repair of the asphalt.

5 Blowing

Asphalt is relatively hard, stiff and heavy, and is less prone to blistering, but it does pose special problems from trapped moisture and air.

The hot asphalt expands the entrapped air rapidly and raises the
temperature of moisture droplets above the boiling point to cause
steam pressure. The result is the formation of blows or bubbles on the
surface.

Blowing occurring during the application of the first coat may increase the difficulty of achieving a satisfactory adhesion of the second
coat because of the dampness caused by the defect.

It is important that the second coat is applied as soon as possible after the first coat in order to minimise deposits of dirt and dust which could prevent the formation of a full adhesion between the coats. These deposits could also cause the entrapment of sufficient air and moisture to give rise to blowing.

6 Defects at Parapets and Junctions
Poor detailing at junctions of walls, parapets and verges has often been a source of failures in asphalt roofing. The failures include:

- Extensive cracking in or around the asphalt fillet due to differential movement between the deck and the parapet (see figure 11.4).

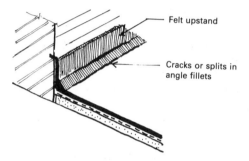

Felt upstand

Cracks or splits in angle fillets

Figure 11.4 Cracking in fillets between upstands and roof covering

- Slumping of the asphalt both at upstands and within the roof area can lead to leaks (see figure 11.5). This is caused by unrestrained asphalt applied on vertical surfaces moving under the force of gravity if sufficiently softened by heat.
- Deflection of the roof deck can also cause the asphalt to pull away from the upstand. Provided that the structure has completely

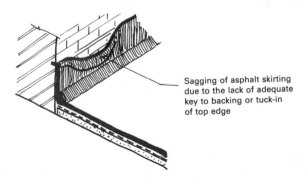

Sagging of asphalt skirting due to the lack of adequate key to backing or tuck-in of top edge

Figure 11.5 Slumping of asphalt skirting

settled, the asphalt work should be repaired and strap reinforcement applied to all the fillets.

Repairs to defective asphalt layers can be carried out quite easily. Asphalt melts when heated and small areas can be softened for removal in this way. The area is then cleaned out, prepared and the new asphalt laid. It is important to pay careful attention to the joint with the old surface so that both the old and the new surfaces will anneal satisfactorily together.

For example, in the repair of blistered asphalt, carefully remove strips of asphalt where the blisters occur after softening the material. The edges of asphalt remaining should then be softened to allow the removal of material to a depth of half its thickness.

Having removed the asphalt, the bottom half of the asphalt layer and the felt should be eased free of the base by warming. A new strip of sheathing felt is inserted to form 50 mm laps with the existing. The asphalt should then be eased back into position after warming and new asphalt applied to complete the repair. Finally, apply two coats of solar reflective paint (see figure 11.6).

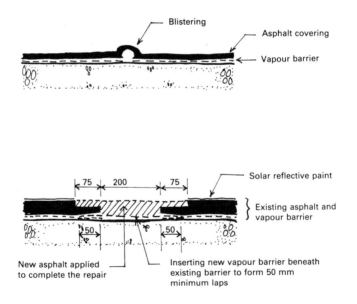

Figure 11.6 Repairing blistered asphalt roof covering

If the total area of asphalt is to be relaid, then precautions must be taken to keep the insulation dry by incorporating a vapour barrier beneath the insulation. Skirtings can also be easily relaid by applying asphalt over a layer of expanded metal lathing.

11.2.2 Bituminous Felt

Roofing felts constitute a group of organic or inorganic fibres which are impregnated or coated with bitumen. Their greatest weakness is their inability to accommodate movements without splitting. It is because of this property that the lowest layer of the usual 3-ply felt system is recommended to be only partially bonded to the substrate.

The principal defects associated with bituminous felt roofing include the following:

1 Splitting

Splitting has many causes, acting singly or in combination. Among these causes are movement of the substrate accompanying thermal contraction, deck deflection and insufficient allowance having been made for movement of the membrane.

The symptoms are narrow ridges in the felt covering, extending the whole length of the roof at regular intervals, and splitting in the felt which coincides with joints in the deck or structure.

The most likely reason for this defect is water that has been trapped in either woodwool or chipboard decking during its construction, which caused the material to swell (see figure 11.7). When this moisture dried out, the decking sheets shrank at the end joints. The felt over these joints has stretched to accommodate this movement, so that when the subsequent inevitable thermal expansion happened, it caused the already stretched felt to buckle upwards to absorb the movement. Over time, this cyclical thermal expansion and contraction will cause fatigue and splits in the felt.

One method used to repair split felt is to strip back the covering along the line of the joint for a width of at least 250 mm. A new piece of felt is then inserted into this gap, followed by another two or three layers of new felt bonded down over the first loose layer to form a slip plane (see figure 11.8). This will allow free movement of the substrate without harming the felt. An alternative method is to introduce a rubber or plastic pipe over the joint, and then lay new felt layers over it.

2 Blistering

Blistering is frequently caused by vapour pressure building up in localised areas beneath the felt or between layers of felt. The pressure can develop as a result of solar heat vaporising moisture that is trapped within the felt layers, insulation or roof structure.

If the waterproofing membrane has suffered an irreversible stretch, subsequent cooling will not cause the air pocket to return to the original size and a partial vacuum occurs in the now partly developed blister. Air and water vapour may be drawn slowly through the sub-

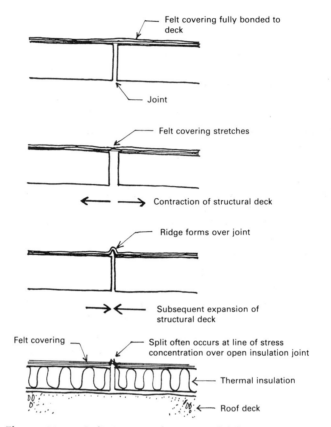

Felt covering fully bonded to deck

Joint

Felt covering stretches

Contraction of structural deck

Ridge forms over joint

Subsequent expansion of structural deck

Felt covering

Split often occurs at line of stress concentration over open insulation joint

Thermal insulation

Roof deck

Figure 11.7　Splitting mechanism of felt covering

strate to refill the original pocket of air, now slightly increased in size and ready to start another cycle of development of the blister when the temperature rises.

Disruption of the waterproof covering by vapour pressures takes many forms.

Full membrane blistering refers to the blistering of the whole waterproof membrane from the substrate without any separation between the individual layers of felt. To prevent full membrane blistering, part bonding of the felt is often specified.

Inter-layer blistering, on the other hand, usually takes the form of a blister formed under the cap sheet of the membrane (see figure 11.9).

Blisters which are not punctured should be left undisturbed. Repair is necessary only if there is water seepage, in which case it is necessary to star-cut the blister, rebond to the underlying layer and patch with high performance material. Reinstatement of the solar reflective chip-

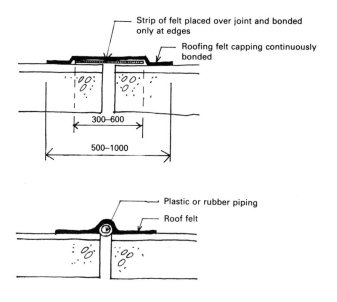

Figure 11.8 Repair methods to incorporate narrow expansion joint

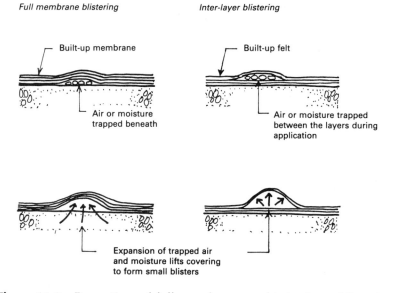

Figure 11.9 Formation of full membrane and inter-layer blistering

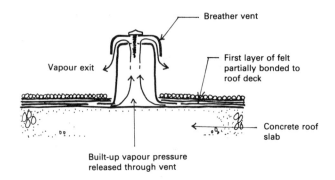

Breather vent

Vapour exit

First layer of felt
partially bonded to
roof deck

Concrete roof
slab

Built-up vapour pressure
released through vent

Figure 11.10   Use of breather vent to release vapour pressure

pings is also vital. Alternatively, mineral surfaced roofing or liquid surface coatings can also be used.

In some cases, provision of vapour vents may be necessary (see figure 11.10).

3 Ridging

Long undulations or ridges may form in felt to give a rippled appearance (see figure 11.11). The causes vary according to the condition of the defect when pressure is applied. For example, if the ridges are firm when pressed, the possible causes are due to:

- The substrate, particularly lightweight woodwool slabs, chipboards and insulation boards, was uneven before the felt was installed or has distorted because of moisture movement during service.
- Thermal and/or moisture movements of the substrate with or without vaporisation of moisture entrapped below the waterproofing membrane. This defect occurs invariably over joints between the decking material.

If there are leaks and the defect seriously interferes with roof drainage, it is necessary to remove the felt, rectify the defective material and then relay entirely. If the distortion is caused by thermal movements, replace existing felt with new felt on fibre boards bonded with hot bitumen to the substrate.

Undulations in roofing felt which yield to pressure, on the other hand, are caused by:

- Felt being distorted at the time of laying because the rolls were stored flat, instead of upright on their ends.
- Inadequate pressure applied during laying.
- Insufficient or unevenly distributed bitumen compound.
- Vaporisation of entrapped moisture in the roof deck.

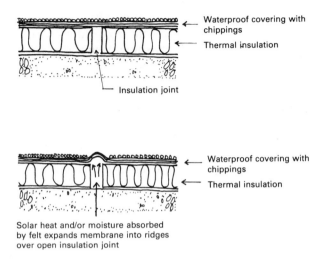

Waterproof covering with chippings

Thermal insulation

Insulation joint

Waterproof covering with chippings

Thermal insulation

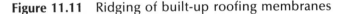

Solar heat and/or moisture absorbed by felt expands membrane into ridges over open insulation joint

Figure 11.11 Ridging of built-up roofing membranes

For these defects, generally no remedy is necessary unless entrapped moisture is the principal cause of the problem. In this case, it may be necessary to repair the defective felt, using the same procedure as for blistering.

4 Crazing and Pitting
Built-up bituminous felt is further subjected to the combined effects of solar radiation and atmospheric oxidation of the bitumen compound, a process commonly referred to as 'heat ageing'. Where there are chippings, the bitumen used to bond them to the surface of the felt cracks first, followed by the top layer of felt. Where there are no chippings, the ageing process is accelerated.

Generally, no remedial work is necessary, except for a solar reflective treatment, if the cracking is superficial and shallow. If the cracks have penetrated the membrane but are localised, partial reinstatement is required; if cracking is widespread on the roof, then complete replacement is needed.

5 Ponding
Bituminous felt suffers from similar problem of ponding as asphalt membrane, primarily from insufficient fall. Likewise, if ponding occurs around rainwater outlets, there is a high possibility that the outlets may be choked, in which case they will require rodding and clearing; or that the outlets have been fixed proud of the covering so that rainwater could not be drained off effectively. In the latter case, there is no other

choice but to refix the outlet and covering after correcting the faults.

Ponding on flat roofs is an indication of differential settlement, structural shrinkage, poor workmanship, design defects and lack of maintenance.

6 Defects at Upstands

Upstands at parapets, balconies, around pipes, flues, rooflights and plant rooms, and at raised expansion joints and drainage gutters, pose problems of membrane failure owing to the following causes:

- Inability to accommodate the movement imposed upon it at that point.
- Lack of support.
- Turning through too tight an angle.

Any change in direction from the horizontal to the vertical must be gradual so that the felt is not stressed. This can be achieved by using fillets.

Sometimes differential movement between the vertical and horizontal structures may cause cracking of the felt around the fillet. An expansion joint must then be incorporated in this case, possibly with a loose flashing over the felt.

7 Other Minor Defects

Minor defects commonly found in bituminous felt roofing include the following:

- Lifted lap joints of felt caused principally by poor bonding. The remedial measure involves rebonding of the lifted membrane.
- 'Pimpling' and 'crocodiling', caused by solar radiation attack on the bitumen. The defect is not as serious as pitting and is often rectified by applying protective reflective treatment where this is absent.
- Mechanical damage by movement of heavy objects over the surface and by placing or dropping heavy loads on to the surface. This problem is particularly prone to occur around blistered and ridged felt. Patch repair is often necessary if the felt has been punctured.

11.2.3 Metal Roofing

The common metals used for roofing are lead, copper and zinc. Generally, well-laid metal roofs can last for many years but they can also suffer from design and construction faults.

A major factor determining the durability of metal roof coverings is the behaviour of the metal oxide on the surface when exposed to the atmosphere. For example, the metal oxides formed from certain metal ions tend to be porous, thus allowing oxidation to proceed into the mass metal. Where the oxide is of similar size or larger than the parent metal ions, then virtually impervious layers are formed.

It is essential that the design and construction of the roof takes into account the particular properties of the various metals for roofing purposes so that their inherent advantages are exploited.

The more common defects associated with metals in roof construction include the following:

1 Creep

This phenomenon occurs over long periods of time and tends to pull the sheets apart, opening up joints and causing stress concentrations at junctions and any changes of direction.

The problems associated with creep in copper and zinc are fewer than those in lead. For this reason, the zinc/copper/titanium alloy gives a generally improved resistance to creep over the zinc/lead type, enabling it to cover areas up to 6 m² without the need for expansion joints.

Where creep is minor, extra nailing and adding clips at overlaps and abutments would be sufficient. If it is more marked, a new covering is needed; new lead will not be cost-effective and zinc should be substituted.

2 Water Ingress

The coverings are designed to be impervious to moisture. Joints are often sealed by lapping, so moisture penetration by capillary action leading to timber decay should always be checked. Care is needed not to split coverings, especially where they become more brittle with age.

The possible sources of water ingress are:

- Lap failure due to creep, thus allowing water to penetrate and cause decay of timber members.
- Leaking rolls occur when the waterproof clenching is ineffective. Where the roll has sharp arrises and irregular surfaces, cracks may develop in the lead or zinc sheets. Such cracking indicates poor workmanship and the likelihood of other defects. The repair of minor perforations by soldering may be satisfactory; otherwise it is necessary to replace the damaged sheets.
- Abutment failure can occur from thermal movement of the upstand brought about by severe exposure to a range of temperatures. There may be cracking where the metal has been bent too sharply into the junction between wall and roof. If damage is localised, it can be patched.
- Leaking drips can occur when the weathertightness of the beaded or

welted joints at the top of the drips has failed. Where drips are provided with insufficient height, capillary action can cause leakage.
- Gutters and cesspools require careful detailing and construction. Debris can accumulate and produce acidic concentrations that attack the metal.

3 Corrosion

All metals are liable to corrode electro-chemically. The position of zinc in the electro-chemical table means that for many practical situations zinc will become the anode in any electrolytic corrosion cell.

Very occasionally, there is reaction between the lead and copper nails at rolls and drips, but by then the lead is usually damaged too so that both metals become brittle.

In the case of copper, for example, corrosion will normally be associated with anodic metals in contact with the copper. Damage will not take place on the copper sheets.

11.2.4 Single-layer Membranes

Single-layer membranes are increasingly being used for flat roof covering. Most of these membrane materials are based on compositions of polyvinyl chloride, chlorinated polyethylene, chlorosulphonated polyethylene, ethylene, propylene diene-terpolymer or polyisobutylene.

Some of these membranes are laid loose on the substrate; some are bonded and/or mechanically fastened to the substrate; and all have bonded laps or beams.

The type of defects in these membranes are very similar to those found in bituminous felt, but because they are laid in single layers, good workmanship in their installation is very essential. The causes of defects are due to:

- Laying the membrane on sharp objects such as pieces of grit, stones or debris, and then subjecting the membrane to foot traffic during laying or subsequently.
- Absence of a separating layer between the membrane and the underlying substrate which is of a chemically incompatible material.
- Lack of exceptionally good workmanship, especially at laps, corners and fixings.
- Puncturing of membrane.

If the defective area is not very large, local repair of the membrane is sufficient to rectify the problem. But for extensively damaged areas, it becomes necessary to strip membranes completely and then reinstate, care being taken not to repeat the same mistakes as in the original installation.

11.2.5 Replacement of Weatherproofing Membrane

Replacement should be considered if the membrane is failing because of ageing, if the materials underneath have deteriorated over a substantial part of the roof, or if the defects are widespread. The following points should be noted:

- The fabric of the original membrane must be made good. For example, blisters and splits should be patched.
- All loose materials must be removed.
- This is an ideal time to improve the thermal insulation economically rather than doing it later.
- Any other maintenance that is required should be carried out while the scaffolding is in place.
- Make sure the repair work is done by experienced contractors.

There are usually three options available for replacement: installing an additional membrane only, thermal upgrading and additional membrane and complete re-roofing when the materials underneath the membrane are also unsound.

11.3 Pitched Roofs

Pitched roofs are usually of framed construction, with timber mainly used as the structural material. They are usually covered with small impervious units such as tiles and slates, although larger-sized coverings such as asbestos cement and metal are also available.

Generally, pitched roofs perform better and give fewer problems than flat roofs because of their design and construction. But inspecting a pitched roof externally for defects is more difficult.

11.3.1 Roof Structure

The timber used for the construction of pitched roofs is mainly light and medium hardwoods which are liable to be attacked by fungi and insects.

Fungal attack can either be wet rot or dry rot. The former attack is caused by continuous exposure of the timber to persistently damp conditions such as those found where roof coverings leak. Dry rot, on the other hand, thrives on more confined conditions such as unventilated roof spaces.

Insect attack can be caused by the powder-post beetle which can inflict considerable damage to the framing members. To control or reduce both forms of attack, all timbers for roof construction, particularly those to be used in damp conditions, should be properly and adequately treated with preservatives.

In addition to fungal and insect attacks, roof members such as rafters, braces, purlins and ties are also subjected to other forms of defects which may affect their strength and stability.

These defects (see figure 11.12) include the following:

- Spreading of pitched roof at the eaves in older buildings, resulting in horizontal cracks in the external walls near eaves level. Remedial work will depend on the findings of the inspection. Structural members with timber decay should be removed and renewed with fresh preservative-treated timber; the rest of the roof timbers should also be treated.
- Sagging of roof, resulting in a dished appearance in the tiling or slating, including the ridge area. Several causes acting independently or together may be attributed to this problem: roof timbers become bowed from long-term loading and dimensional changes; corroded nails and fixings holding the structural members; weakening of members attacked by fungal decay or insect; movements induced by general deterioration of members; and under-sizing of supporting members.
- Distorted trusses, for example, incorrectly sized or positioned tank bearers, can cause deflection that can result in leaking plumbing installations.

Remedial work depends on the extent of the defect according to the inspection. Unless the roof leaks, there is no urgent need for remedial work until the roof is approaching an unacceptable state of structural instability.

If structural fixings have perished, they should be replaced. If fungal decay or insect attack are evident, they should be treated without further delay.

Once bowed, timber gradually takes on a permanent set. But it is possible to fix additional struts at suitable positions to support the roof and prevent further sagging, though they are unlikely to be useful in restoring the roof to its original condition.

11.3.2 Underlays

Sometimes the sarking felt is not supported at the eaves to enable water to drain over the fascia into the gutter, so water ponds on the dip in the surface of the sarking felt behind the eaves fascia board. This water may penetrate at unsealed laps and usually down the inner face of the inner leaf of the external cavity wall either directly or through the cavity. Alternatively, the sarking felt is not carried over barge-

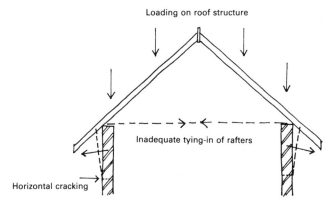

Loading on roof structure

Inadequate tying-in of rafters

Horizontal cracking

a. *Spreading of roof members at the eaves*

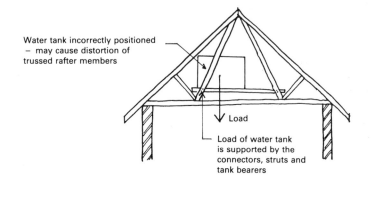

Water tank incorrectly positioned — may cause distortion of trussed rafter members

Load

Load of water tank is supported by the connectors, struts and tank bearers

b. *Sagging of roof members*

Figure 11.12   Common causes of spreading and deflection of roof members

boards, so water can penetrate between the bargeboard and the wall (see figure 11.13).

If ponding is present, the roofing should be removed and sprockets or fillets should be installed at the eaves under the sarking felt to support it, ensuring that it is carried over the bargeboard. Severely degraded felt should be replaced.

The same problem can also be associated with perforations such as pipes or chimney stacks through the roof. In this case, the tiles or slates should be removed to expose the pipe (or chimney stack) and the sarking felt. The old felt should be repaired by patching and bonding properly with the new felt. A cross-cut should then be made in the centre to accommodate the pipe with the cuts pointing upwards.

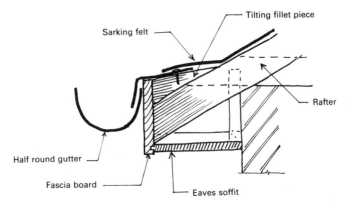

Tilting fillet piece

Sarking felt

Rafter

Half round gutter

Fascia board

Eaves soffit

a. *At projecting eaves*

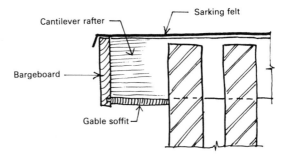

Cantilever rafter

Sarking felt

Bargeboard

Gable soffit

b. *At projecting verge*

Figure 11.13   Detailing of sarking felt in pitched roof

Careful attention should be paid to the seal around the pipe. Finally, reinstate the tiles or slates, including the flashing.

Around chimney stacks, the sarking felt should be carried up the wall of the stack and sealed to it, ensuring that water from the back of the stack can drain down the sides of the stack.

11.4 Pitched Roof Coverings

The first sign that something is wrong with the roof is usually a damp patch on the ceiling below. It would be wrong to assume immediately that the defect is directly above the dampness, for water may have travelled along other parts of the roof before surfacing as the visible damp patch. For a proper diagnosis, the whole roof, including the coverings, must be inspected thoroughly and systematically.

11.4.1 Roofing Tiles and Slates

Tiles and slates are fixed to horizontal battens which are laid across the supporting framework of the roof. These small units can either be nailed on to the battens or hooked over with nibs cast on the underside of the tiles. Deterioration of roofing tiles or slates takes the following forms:

- Slipping and displacement of the tiles or slates from their original positions (see figure 11.14). This defect can be caused by the secondary effect of a structural roof failure or by the failure of the fixing. If the nibs of the tiles are found to have disintegrated, it is usually due to crystallisation of salts that have been transferred by water from the lower exposed part of the tile to the upper part which is protected by the overlying tiles. This problem can further be caused by decaying battens which support the units and deterioration of nails.

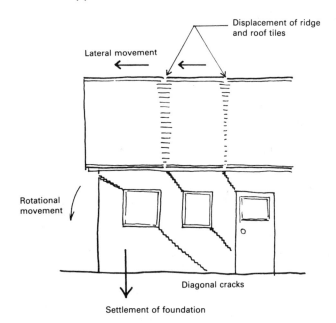

Figure 11.14   Displacement of roofing tiles caused by foundation settlement

- Tiles or slates breaking across their width and falling away owing to excessive pressure on their surface. The pressure could come from snow loads or human beings walking on the roof during regular maintenance.
- General softening of the tile structure which results in surface

deterioration. This is mainly caused by the action of atmospheric impurities and weathering effects.

- Spalling of some clay tiles may be evident if inadequate screening of the aggregate during their manufacture produces inferior tiles containing limestone or silica.
- Tiles may have a laminated structure because of the method of production. Deterioration results when the surface laminations break away with the assistance of atmospheric moisture and frost. Slates can also delaminate because of acid rain attacking the calcium carbonate.
- Corrosion of fixing nails will loosen the tiles or slates. During strong winds, the tiles or slates around hips, ridges and gables are most liable to be dislodged.
- Leakage is liable to occur at single-lap joints at the head and side of the tile, particularly if they are not properly fixed. Tiles may also be slightly lifted, causing a gap through which leakage conditions are made worse by the suction action of the wind.

Generally, it is quite simple to repair a tiled or slated roof. If the units are simply dislodged without signs of leakage, they can be easily but carefully pushed back into position. If the nibs of the tiles are missing, the tiles have to be replaced with new ones.

Where timbers have decayed, these members must be renewed, together with the underlay.

11.4.2 Asbestos Cement Sheets

This form of covering is extensively used in industrial buildings such as factories. Corrugated asbestos cement sheets are generally satisfactory in performance, unless they become brittle with age. Nevertheless they are liable to deteriorate in the following ways:

- Cracking of asbestos cement sheets, usually either along the crown having the fasteners or along the crown at mid-sheet width, may be caused by shrinkage cracks, overtightening of the fasteners, excessive imposed loadings or restraint from movements (see figure 11.15).
- Moss and lichen growths may cause surface deterioration and continuous contact with their acidic waste products, and cement content of the sheets may result in softening of the material.
- Gradual erosion of the surface, which tends to expose the strands of asbestos fibres.
- The fixings may corrode and cause loosening and dislodgement of the sheets. Eventually the problems may include staining and water penetration.

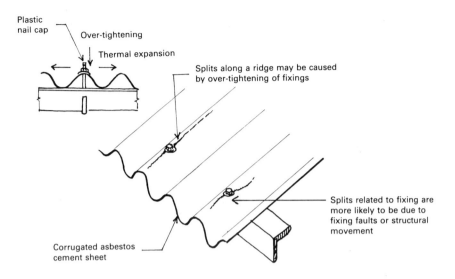

Plastic nail cap

Over-tightening

Thermal expansion

Splits along a ridge may be caused by over-tightening of fixings

Splits related to fixing are more likely to be due to fixing faults or structural movement

Corrugated asbestos cement sheet

Figure 11.15   Splitting of corrugated asbestos cement roofing sheet

Asbestos poses serious hazards to health and the Advisory Committee on Asbestos, HMSO (1979), recommended that the use of asbestos should be phased out.

Cleaning of biological growths on asbestos cement sheets can be done with a high-pressure water lance but some skill and caution is required in the process of cleaning. Frequently, the life of such roofs can be extended after cleaning by some surface sealing treatment, for example, using a good-quality exterior emulsion paint.

Damaged corrugated asbestos sheets should be renewed rather than repaired, making sure that non-corrodible fixings be used. A better policy would probably be to replace with aluminium alloy sheets.

11.4.3 Profiled Metal Roofing Sheets

All metal roofs have to take into account the high coefficient of linear expansion of the metal. The metal used in the construction of the roof is inclined to move a substantial amount because of the temperature variations that occur daily. This makes it necessary to lay the metal in small panels.

The vulnerability of metal roofs is at the fixing points and lap joints. Failure at both areas will allow rainwater to penetrate into the ceiling below. Leakage through fixings usually occurs because the fixing has loosened owing to:

- Corrosion of the fixing or the metal sheet at the location of the fixings.
- The use of inappropriate fixings or inadequate spacers.

A careful examination of the roof and fixings should determine the most likely cause. Even if only one sheet appears to have loosened, all the fixings should be checked, particularly for signs of bimetallic corrosion.

If the roof covering has become corroded to the extent that the fixing holes are enlarged, a new roof covering will be required.

Failure at lap joints is commonly caused by inadequate overlaps or sealing of overlaps, particularly when the pitch is low and the roof exposed to severe weather conditions. In addition, excessive loading on the roof can cause the laps to gape. Whenever leakage occurs through the laps, it becomes necessary to lift the upper sheet and re-apply sealant between the sheets as a temporary measure.

Corrosion is primarily a problem that can occur with steel sheet roofs when the protective coating breaks down. Sometimes the damage is often not apparent until the corrosion has caused pitting. The remedial work depends on the extent of the corrosion. Where rusting is not serious, the rust can be removed completely prior to application of a proprietary protective coating. If corrosion is very extensive, the sheets will need to be replaced.

11.5 Rainwater Discharge Systems

Generally, all good roof design should include the provision of adequate discharge systems to carry all rainwater from the roof away to a storm drainage system. It is important that the stormwater be taken away from the perimeter of the building to prevent damp penetration through walls and to avoid subsoil erosion. All gutters require regular maintenance to avoid deterioration and overflowing.

11.5.1 Eaves Gutters

Gutters made in cast iron may corrode, become perforated or crack as a result of normal deterioration. Jointing materials often fail and require rejointing; fixing brackets may deteriorate by corrosion and will need to be replaced. Poorly designed discharge systems may result in the installation of undersized gutters which are not large enough to carry the rainwater to the downpipes quickly and lead to overflows. In addition, gutters may have been laid to insufficient falls because of bad workmanship. Both faults can lead to unsightly damp patches, usually accompanied by staining of the walls around them.

Gutters made from plastics are now frequently specified. These gutters are non-corrodible but cannot withstand heavy snow loads and significant expansion and contraction with changes of temperature. They usually need little maintenance other than being kept clear of silt deposits, fallen leaves and other debris. Metal gutters, on the other hand, require additional regular maintenance such as repainting in order to keep them in good condition.

11.5.2 Downpipes

Rainwater downpipes are positioned to convey the large volumes of roof water to storm drains located at ground level. They must be constructed of sound materials and must also be well maintained in a watertight condition. Regular maintenance is essential as small defects may develop and cause other defects in adjacent structures and materials.

Deterioration and failure may be caused by:

- Fracture of the rainwater pipes, particularly those fabricated from plastics, arising from impact. This results in damage and distortion of the pipes.
- Corrosion of metal pipes as a result of peeling paintwork and a lack of preventive maintenance.
- Pipes becoming filled and blocked with silt and leaves at the base, bends and rainwater heads and outlets. This causes water to over-flow or leak from defective joints.

Regular maintenance in the form of painting, rejointing and clearing of silt and other blockages is essential. In addition, it is necessary to maintain free and adequate outlets from gutters and uninterrupted discharge to drainage systems at ground level.

Badly damaged downpipes can be removed easily and replaced as required. Repairs are normally effected by replacing damaged pipes with new ones. When fitting pipes, it is best to keep them clear of the wall for subsequent maintenance purposes.

Small pitting can be repaired by filling with a glass fibre mat; clean the corroded area with a wire brush; then burnish with wire wool. The glass fibre mat has to be bonded to the pipe, using a mixture of resin paste and a catalyst; then with a putty knife, apply glass fibre in layers after each layer has hardened.

11.5.3 Prevention of Roof Drainage Defects

The following are some recommendations to reduce defects occurring in rainwater discharge systems installed at the roof:

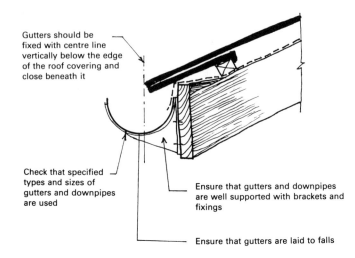

Gutters should be fixed with centre line vertically below the edge of the roof covering and close beneath it

Check that specified types and sizes of gutters and downpipes are used

Ensure that gutters and downpipes are well supported with brackets and fixings

Ensure that gutters are laid to falls

Figure 11.16   Correct detailing of gutter in pitched roof

- Check that specified types and sizes of gutters and downpipes are used.
- Ensure that gutters are correctly positioned and aligned (see figure 11.16). For example, gutters should be fixed with the centre line vertically below the edge of the roof covering and close beneath it.
- Check that gutters are not twisted or tilted sideways.
- Ensure that gutters and downpipes are well supported with the specified type of fixings. For example, fascia or rafter brackets should be no more than 1 m apart. Additional support for gutters will be needed at angles and outlets, and intermediate supports for downpipes over 2 m long.
- Ensure that gaps for thermal movement are left when jointing plastic gutters and downpipes.

Related and Further Reading

Addleson, L. *Building Failures: A Guide to Diagnosis, Remedy and Prevention*. Architectural Press, London (1982).

Bisset, A. H. How a flat roof failure occurs. *Buildings, Maintenance and Services* (November, 1978).

British Standards Institution. *CP 143: Parts 1–16 (1958–74) Code of Practice for sheet roof and wall coverings*.

British Standards Institution. *BS 5247: Part 14: 1975 Code of Practice for sheet roof and wall coverings, corrugated asbestos cement*.

British Standards Institution. *BS 6229: 1982 Code of Practice for flat roofs with continuously supported coverings.*

British Standards Institution. *BS 6577: 1985 Specification for mastic asphalt for building (natural rock asphalt aggregate).*

British Standards Institution. *BS 747: 1977 (1986) Specification for roofing felts.*

British Standards Institution. *BS 6925: 1988 Specification for mastic asphalt for building and engineering (limestone aggregate).*

British Standards Institution. *BS 5534: Part 1: 1990 Code of Practice for slating and tiling Part 1, Design.*

Building Research Establishment, UK. *Asphalt and Built-up Felt Roofing: Durability.* Digest 144 (1972).

Building Research Establishment, UK. *Slated or Tiled Pitched Roofs: Ventilation to Outside Air.* Defect Action Sheet 1 (1982).

Building Research Establishment, UK. *Slated or Tiled Pitched Roofs: Restricting the Entry of Water Vapour from the House.* Defect Action Sheet 3 (1982).

Building Research Establishment, UK. *Pitched Roofs: Thermal Insulation Near the Eaves.* Defect Action Sheet 4 (1982).

Building Research Establishment, UK. *Pitched Roofs: Sarking Felt Underlay – Drainage from Roof.* Defect Action Sheet 9 (1982).

Building Research Establishment, UK. *Condensation in Insulated Domestic Roofs.* Digest 270 (1983).

Building Research Establishment, UK. *Felted Cold Deck Flat Roofs Remedying Condensation by Converting to Warm Deck.* Defect Action Sheet 59 (1984).

Building Research Establishment, UK. *Flat Roof Design: The Technical Options.* Digest 312 (1986).

Building Research Establishment, UK. *Cavity Parapets – Avoiding Rain Penetration.* Defect Action Sheet 106 (1987).

Building Research Establishment, UK. *Flat Roof Design: Thermal Insulation.* Digest 324 (December, 1987).

Building Research Establishment, UK. *Mastic Asphalt for Flat Roofs: Testing for Quality Assurance.* Information Paper 8/91 (May, 1991).

Ellis, N., Hutchinson, B. D. and Barton, J. *Maintenance and Repair of Buildings.* Butterworth, London (1975).

Hinks, J. and Cook, G. Metal roofs need regular inspection for damage. *Building Today* (18 May 1989).

Holden, C. Roofs, renew or patch: Which is the best policy? *Buildings, Maintenance and Services* (July/August, 1976).

March, F. *Flat Roofing: A Guide to Good Practice.* Tarmac Building Products Ltd, UK (1982).

Property Services Agency. *Technical Guide to Flat Roofing.* Department of the Environment, UK (March, 1987).

Property Services Agency. *Parapet Gutters – Rain Penetration*. Feedback Digest, Technical File No. 1 (April, 1988).

Ransom, W. H. *Building Failures: Diagnosis and Avoidance*. Spon, London (1987).

Royal Institution of Chartered Surveyors. *A Practical Approach to Flat Roof Covering Problems – Guidance Note*. Surveyors Publications, London (1985).

Seeley, I. H. *Building Maintenance*, 2nd edn. Macmillan, London (1987).

Thornton, M. Lead for roofing. *Traditional Homes* (October, 1988).

12 Wall Claddings

The term 'cladding' is taken to mean a method of enclosing a building structure by the attachment of elements capable of spanning between given points of support on the face of the building or as infill panels between members of a structural frame.

Claddings have been popularly used in high-rise buildings because they are lighter and save space and construction time. Another advantage of their use is that claddings permit greater architectural expression by allowing the designer more freedom in exploiting the utilisation of new materials. However, one great danger in the use of new materials in buildings is that such materials have not been sufficiently tested under serviceability and their performance may not be totally satisfactory. Furthermore, with the introduction of larger storey-height panels, accessibility to carry out maintenance of these claddings may present problems which can be very difficult and costly to resolve.

12.1 Failure of Structural Members

12.1.1 Deflection and Deformation

Total structural failures of buildings are rare unless their design is faulty and inadequate. Isolated member failures, however, are not uncommon. The most readily identifiable problem with individual structural members is deflection or deformation caused by movements acting on columns, beams and floors.

For example, elastic deformation under service loads can cause deflection of horizontal members such as suspended floor and roof slabs, beams or spandrels. The deflection may be continuous or intermittent under live loads and long-term under dead loads.

Other causes of deflection or deformation of structural members include:

- Elastic shortening of columns under load.
- Deformation initiated by wind and earthquakes.
- Differential foundation settlement.
- Vibrations generated by heavy vehicles, machinery or underground railways.

Forces such as these must be taken into account in the design of both the structural frame and the cladding (see figure 12.1). If not, they can produce glass breakage, panel failures and failure of attachments between the panels and the frame (see table 12.1).

12.1.2 Differential Movements

Differential movements between cladding and the structure can always be expected to take place. It is critical, therefore, to consider those dimensional changes in service which will produce relative movements between cladding and structure or background.

Relative movements may be reversible (for example, seasonal or diurnal), or irreversible (for example, shrinkage of concrete or creep under sustained load). In addition, movements with different causes (both reversible or irreversible) may operate at the same time and may be characteristic of either cladding or structure or both.

The main causes of relative movements between cladding and structure are:

1 Thermal Movement
It is likely in practice that the cladding will be subjected to greater movement, either of expansion or contraction, than the structural backing because the cladding is more exposed to the weather. The relative movement is greater when the cladding is thin and the structure is massive.

The movement is intermittent, characterised by alternating cycles of expansion and contraction with diurnal or seasonal frequency. All materials and components are affected by thermal movement. The nature and extent of damage is governed by:

- The thermal coefficient of the material.
- Exposure condition of the component.
- Colour of the material.
- Insulation provided by the backing material.
- Time over which the temperature change occurs and the frequency.

If movement is restrained, the damage inflicted by temperature changes is likely to be greater.

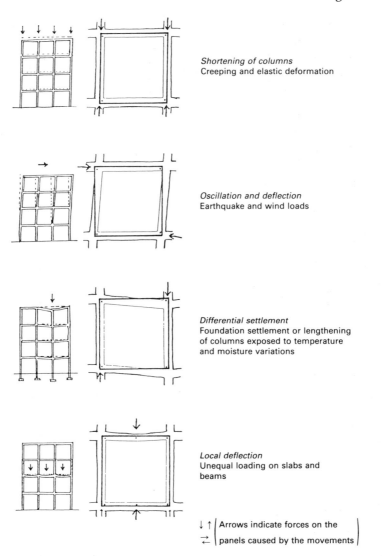

Shortening of columns
Creeping and elastic deformation

Oscillation and deflection
Earthquake and wind loads

Differential settlement
Foundation settlement or lengthening
of columns exposed to temperature
and moisture variations

Local deflection
Unequal loading on slabs and
beams

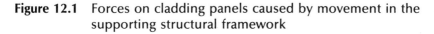

↓ ↑ | Arrows indicate forces on the
⇄ | panels caused by the movements

Figure 12.1   Forces on cladding panels caused by movement in the
supporting structural framework

2 Moisture Movement
Cladding is usually fixed to steel or concrete structures. Moisture
movement does not occur in steel, but in the case of concrete, shrinkage takes place after erection as its moisture content slowly reaches
equilibrium with the surrounding atmosphere. An irreversible shrinkage between 0.03 and 0.04 per cent can be expected for normal gravel
aggregate concrete. The rate of loss of water depends on the moisture

Table 12.1 Movement affecting performance of wall claddings (Source: *Wall Cladding: Designing to Minimise Defects due to Inaccuracies and Movement*, BRE Digest 223, HMSO, London, 1979)

	Cause	Effect	Duration, frequency	Examples of materials or components affected	Significance for design
1	Temperature changes	Expansion and contraction	Intermittent, diurnal, seasonal	All. Where restrained, distortion or damage may occur. Distortion may also result from temperature gradients or from non-homogeneity	Extent of movement is influenced by thermal coefficient, exposure, colour, thermal capacity, insulation provided by backing
2	Moisture content changes:				
(a)	Initial moisture absorption	Irreversible expansion	Relatively short term owing to absorption of moisture after manufacture	Brick and other ceramic products	Depends on age of product; most movement occurs within first 3 months of product's life
(b)	Initial moisture release	Irreversible contraction	Relatively short term	Mortar, concrete, sand-lime bricks	May require measures to control or distribute cracking
(c)	Alternate absorption and release of moisture in service	Expansion and contraction	Periodic, e.g. seasonal	Most porous building materials, including cement based and wood or wood-based products. Restraints,	Generally less significant for cladding than are thermal movements but wood experiences large moisture-induced

				movements across the grain
		humidity gradients or non-homogeneity may produce distortion. Laminates of dissimilar materials may bow, particularly if their construction is asymmetrical		
3 Loading on structure:				
(a) Elastic deformation under service loads	Normally insignificant in vertical members but horizontal members may deflect	Continuous or intermittent under live loads; long term under dead loads	Suspended floor and roof slabs, beams, edge beams or spandrels, of all materials (whether they support or 'contain' the cladding)	Needs consideration in relation to fixings and bearings for cladding and to possible compression of 'contained' cladding: deflections in prestressed concrete members may be relatively large
Creep	Contraction of vertical and deflection of horizontal members	Long term	Reinforced and prestressed concrete components as above	Needs consideration as above. May also be significant where load-bearing concrete walls or columns have cladding such as mosaic or other tiling directly bonded

continued on p. 282

282

Table 12.1 continued

Cause	Effect	Duration, frequency	Examples of materials or components affected	Significance for design
4 Wind loading on cladding	Deflection	Intermittent	Lightweight cladding, including fixed and opening glazing; sheet siding	Extent of deflection depends on exposure for a given stiffness. Deflection is commonly designed not to exceed 1/240 of the span in order to avoid damage to sealants or glazing
5 Chemical changes: (a) Corrosion	Expansion	Continuous	Iron and other ferrous metals	Depends on protection or on corrosion resistance of material; electrolytic corrosion may require consideration. Corroding fixings can seriously disrupt cladding

(b) Sulphate attack	Expansion	Continuous	Portland cement based products in construction where soluble sulphate salts (e.g. from high-sulphate bricks) and persistent dampness present	Significant for cladding where the construction affected has cladding such as mosaic or other tiling or rendering, bonded directly to it
(c) Carbonation	Contraction	Continuous	Porous Portland cement products, such as concrete, lightweight concrete, asbestos-cement	Not very significant unless distortion might result – for example, asbestos cement sheets painted on one face only
6 Vibration (from traffic, machinery, wind forces)	Generation of noise, possible loosening of fixings, disturbance of glazing seals	—	Lightweight cladding, sheet siding	Noise discomfort to occupants; possible rain penetration past seals by 'pumping' action of glazing or spandrel panels. Natural frequency of cladding or panels may influence response

continued on p. 284

Table 12.1 continued

Cause	Effect	Duration, frequency	Examples of materials or components affected	Significance for design
7 Physical changes:				
(a) Loss of volatiles	Contraction, loss of plasticity	Short or long term depending on materials, exposure	Some sealants, some plastics	Contributes to age-hardening of some sealants. May lead to embrittlement and distortion of some plastics
(b) Ice or crystalline salt formation	Expansion and possibly disruption in some building materials	Dependent on weather conditions	Porous natural stones, very exposed brickwork	Damage usually confined to spalling and erosion of surfaces

content of the mix, the size of concrete members and atmospheric conditions. Drying shrinkage is restrained by the bond between concrete and reinforcement to the extent that concrete in heavily reinforced members shrinks less than in lightly reinforced sections.

Although it is true that concrete also undergoes a reversible moisture movement between 0.02 and 0.06 per cent, it is unlikely that the concrete structure will become sufficiently wet in use for it is protected by the cladding or building. It is, therefore, the irreversible drying shrinkage of the structure that is of primary importance.

3 Creep

Creep takes place in structural concrete because of the dead and imposed loads acting on it to produce permanent deformation. It is a long-term phenomenon, the extent of which is related not only to the applied stress in the concrete, but also the nature of the concrete mix and type, and placing of the reinforcement.

The gradual creep of concrete may continue for many months and result in shortening of columns. Like drying shrinkage, creep is restrained by reinforcement. It is important to consider this problem at the design stage in relation to fixings and bearings for the cladding, as well as to the possibility of compression of infill panels caused by deflection of beams.

12.2 Fixing Failures

Fixings between cladding and structure are of two main types, namely, supporting and restraining. The former type is designed to support the dead weight of the cladding and to transfer this load to the structure. Restraining fixings are designed to tie cladding units to their structural frame. Both types are also designed to position the cladding units in relation to each other and to the structure.

12.2.1 Dimensional Changes of Cladding and Structure

The design of fixings has to take into account the overall relative movements between the panels and the structure without sacrificing mechanical soundness and rigidity. Alternatively, the forces resulting from any restraint of movement should be allowed for in the design.

Allowances must be made for dimensional changes in buildings arising from the following causes:

• Drying shrinkage and moisture movement associated with precast concrete panels diminish with time, but provision is still necessary unless sufficient time is allowed to elapse from the time of casting of the components and the structure before the panels are used, in order to minimise the effects.

- Elastic deformation under load takes place from the dead loads of the structure and cladding. Fixings should accommodate the dimensional changes resulting from these deformations.
- Creep of concrete under sustained load may be long-term and will be greater in the vertical than the horizontal direction owing to gravity.
- Thermal movements (see figure 12.2) occur in both the structure and the cladding, although cladding panels are not directly affected. Panels with dark-coloured surfaces exposed to the sun will tend to reach higher temperatures and expand proportionately more than light-coloured panels. For example, glass used as lightweight cladding curtain walling can suffer from thermal fracture through differences in the rate of response to changes in temperature between it and the framework of metal into which it fits.
- Foundation settlement can also induce movements in the elements of the structure which will have to be allowed for at the fixing points.

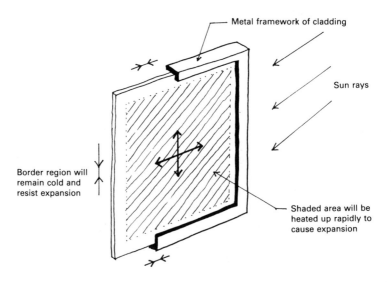

Figure 12.2   The generation of thermal stress in a glazing panel

There is, therefore, a need to provide for movements, where necessary, following careful consideration of amounts and directions of movements.

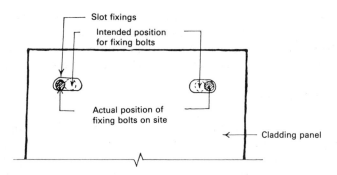

a. *Inaccuracies in setting-out*

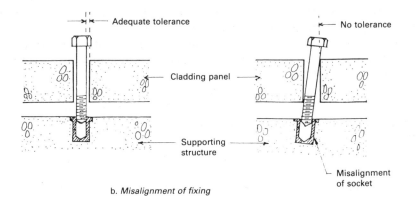

b. *Misalignment of fixing*

Figure 12.3   Typical examples of improperly installed fixing in cladding system

12.2.2 Inaccuracies in the Building

A fixing must be designed to provide adjustability necessitated by inaccuracies arising from the building and manufacturing processes (see figure 12.3). Provision for adjustability should be treated separately from provision for movement. Although some fixings may be primarily intended to give adjustability, they also permit some movement; others may be provided to take account of relative movement but place greater demands on accuracy.

The consequences of providing fixings which are not designed for adjustability may include an improperly installed fixing, haphazard cutting of cladding panels or the structure, or other unproductive work in an attempt to make adjustments on the site.

Generally, it is advisable to provide a few strong fixings rather than to rely on the correct relative positioning of many small ones.

12.2.3 Corrosion

It is of paramount importance that no part of a fixing assembly is subjected to conditions that promote corrosion so that its performance in service can be maintained without any impediment.

In practice, fixings will usually be protected from the direct effects of wet weathering. But there may be situations where the fixings may be exposed to condensation and humidities above the critical level for steel corrosion. The hydrated oxide formed may set up damaging expansive forces that can cause the failure.

To avoid bimetallic electro-chemical corrosion, care must be exercised to make sure that dissimilar metals within the fixing assembly or near to other metallic parts in the framing members do not come into direct contact in potentially damp conditions. Mild steel, in particular, is most vulnerable to this type of corrosion.

Exposure in marine or industrial environments may be relatively severe and warrants special attention. In this context, fixings should ideally be accessible for regular inspection. This can be facilitated with the use of a fibre optic probe.

12.3 Failure of Joints

Joints fall into two main categories: rigid joints that permit no movements such as welded or bolted joints and flexible joints which allow for both expansion and contraction such as open joints and sealant filled joints.

Inaccuracies and movements influence both the performance of joints and the durability of jointing materials. The larger the components, the more difficult it is to produce them accurately, to place them properly and to provide for the larger movements associated with them. Their impermeability also means that the rainwater striking the surfaces of the components may be discharged readily over the joints.

12.3.1 Open-drained Joints

The most common fault of open-drained joints used in conjunction with large concrete panels is the deterioration of the baffles (see figure 12.4). Metal and non-metal faced baffles tend to deteriorate at their

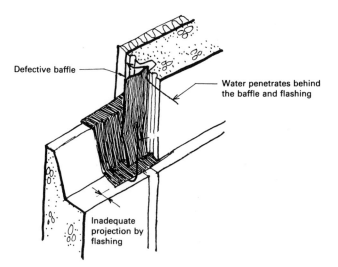

Defective baffle

Water penetrates behind the baffle and flashing

Inadequate projection by flashing

Figure 12.4   Defective baffle and flashing used in conjunction with large concrete panels

ends and laps. Problems also occur at the intersection of vertical and horizontal joints.

If the flashing edge is recessed behind the outer face of the concrete panel, rainwater may penetrate underneath the flashing and there is no protection from further water penetration. If there is no flashing, protection behind the baffle is greatly reduced.

12.3.2 Sealant-filled Joints

Ageing is the most common fault with this type of joint, particularly where the seal is exposed to the elements. Under such conditions, seals tend to fail through a loss of adherence or elasticity.

Different types of sealant can accommodate different amounts of movement; and wide joints can accommodate greater movements than narrow ones (see figure 12.5). A likely cause of failure is the inability of the sealant used to accommodate the movement that is taking place. This can result in splitting, folding or excessive extrusion.

Extrusion of the sealant from the horizontal joints is another problem. It is a symptom that there is insufficient allowance being provided for movement, particularly when all the sealant is extruded so that the edges of the cladding panels come into contact (see figure 12.6). If this problem is left unattended, there will be further risk of cracking, spalling or displacement of the panels.

Sometimes the sealant can be wrinkled at an angle to the line of the

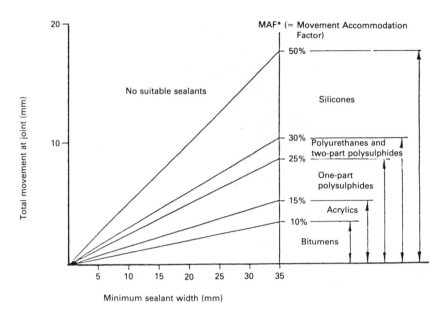

*Where given in product literature as, for example, ±15% use MAF = 30%

Figure 12.5   Minimum joint width related to allowable movement and suitable type of sealant (Source: *Large Concrete Panel External Walls: Re-sealing Butt Joints*, Defect Action Sheet DAS 97, Building Research Establishment, UK, March 1987)

joint. This is a sign of differential movement between cladding units in the direction of the line of the joint.

To reduce the danger of serious defects, all joints should be inspected externally as well as internally. Any defective joint must be checked to deduce the cause of the defect.

During the inspection, it is important to look out for signs that are common to both vertical and horizontal joints. For example, hardening and splitting of the sealant indicate ageing of the material rather than faults in the joints. On the other hand, symptoms that are different in both vertical and horizontal joints indicate possible relative movements.

12.4 Sealant Failures

The types of sealants which are in common use to fill joints are butyl, acrylic, polyurethane, polysulphide, silicone and bitumen. Those which are also resinous in composition are seldom used.

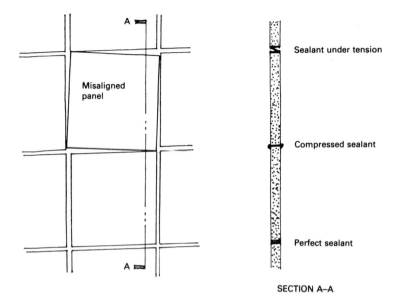

Figure 12.6 Symptoms of sealant-filled joint failures

With the exception of oil-based types, most sealant materials are slow-curing and durable. Polysulphide, for example, has a life expectancy of at least 20 years under normal use.

Failures arising from degradation of jointing materials cannot be totally avoided because they are less durable than the cladding itself. Most sealant failures occur because of the following reasons:

- The application of the sealant has been too thin.
- The sealant has not been applied on a properly primed surface.
- The sealant has been wrongly selected for the joint.
- Poor workmanship on the site in the actual application of the sealant.

12.4.1 Adhesive Failure

This type of failure (see figure 12.7) may be recognised by the pulling away of the curved sealant bead from the joint interface, and results from loss of adhesion of the sealant.

Adhesive failure may be caused by any one of the following reasons:

- Poor preparation of the joint interfaces prior to the application of the sealant material. For example, some sealants require priming, especially to porous surfaces.

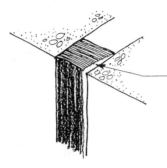

Adhesion failure indicated
by the pulling away of
the sealant bead from
the joint interfaces

Figure 12.7   Adhesive failure of sealant

- Failure to clean joint interfaces, thus preventing a good bond.
- Some sealants cure upon contact with atmospheric moisture. However, adhesion may be affected if the surface is damp at the time of application.
- The sealant in the joint is expected to perform within known tolerances caused by expansion and contraction. If joint movement is obstructed in any way, the sealant material can be affected.
- Some sealants take a considerable period of time to reach their full flexibility. For example, polysulphides can take up to four days to cure completely throughout the joint. Therefore, any movement that takes place during that time may cause rupturing of the sealant.
- Insufficient depth of sealant being provided which can result in straining of the sealant. This problem could arise even when the design depth was adequate if the workmanship was faulty.
- Incompatibility of subsequent surface coating being applied over the sealant and resulting in breakdown of the sealant material.

12.4.2 Cohesive Failure

Cohesive failure (see figure 12.8) occurs when the sealant material itself shows signs of splitting as opposed to adhesive failure which is seen as the sealant breaking away from the interface of the joint.

This kind of failure may be caused by any one of the following reasons:

- When thermal movement is too great, the joint may widen beyond the capacity of the sealant to accommodate the movement and failure occurs.
- High thermal movement occurring prior to complete curing of the sealant. For example, the vulnerability of polysulphide and silicone sealants to early movements can result in cohesive failure.

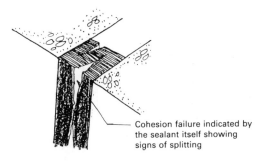

Cohesion failure indicated by
the sealant itself showing
signs of splitting

Figure 12.8   Cohesive failure of sealant

- Inadequate depth at the centre of the material arising from poor application.
- Poor-quality sealants being used at the expense of strength and durability. For instance, butyl and bitumen sealants have limited tolerances for movement.
- Incorrect use of bond breakers at the rear of the joint due to poor design or defective installation.
- Entrapment of air behind the sealant can lead to subsequent expansion of the air which may fracture the material.
- Poor mixing of the sealant components.

12.5 Workmanship Problems

Poor workmanship is the most contentious area. In most cases of failure, workmanship has been blamed. However, apart from the obvious causes arising from quality of work and disregard for instructions issued, the reasons for failures under this category often involve deeper study.

The common causes usually include the following:

- Faulty installation because of unskilled and incompetent workers who lack an appreciation of the importance of accuracy and good workmanship.
- Omission of essential fixings, especially at critical locations, which can be caused by inadequate design provision or accidentally.
- Misuse of fixings which include such acts as overtightening, hammering into undersized holes and forcibly bending the fixings in an attempt to overcome dimensional discrepancies on the site.
- Site alteration without due consideration for consequences. For example, making changes to mortices in stone cladding panels which may cause direct damage to the cladding.

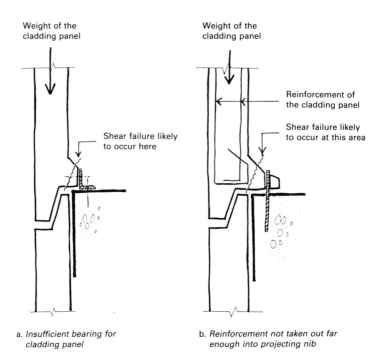

a. *Insufficient bearing for cladding panel*

b. *Reinforcement not taken out far enough into projecting nib*

Figure 12.9   Shear failures of supporting nib of large concrete panels

- Excessive stress can be caused to supporting nibs when the heavier cladding units of stone and precast concrete have inadequate bearing on them.
- Supporting features, compression joints and fixings have often not been designed or placed to allow for the likely inaccuracies over the whole building. This problem occurs in addition to differential movement.
- Reinforcement is often not taken out far enough into the projecting nibs, which may lead to shear failures (see figure 12.9).

Frequently, the need to speed up the construction process may lead to irresponsible acts by site operatives to meet target completion. For example, when a fixing cannot be installed because of some misalignment or inaccuracy, an alteration is made on site to accommodate the fixing. This invariably leads to more adjustments to be made to the cladding or subsequent fixings so much so that it becomes impossible to position the last fixing in a run and the obvious solution is to omit it. Such acts of irresponsibility are very difficult to overcome. In the final analysis, good site supervision is essential in order to reduce many of the problems associated with shoddy and careless workmanship.

12.6 Remedial Work

12.6.1 Infill Brickwork

Large panels of infill brickwork often fail because compression joints are not provided at interfaces with columns and beams. The resultant damage is manifested in crushing and cracking as well as serious misalignment.

Generally, the solution is to cut out damaged brickwork and provide a sliding dowel or similar fixing into the structure to form a flexible compression joint against the structural members (see figure 12.10).

Alternatively, if the panels are very long, a joint can be sawcut at intervals along the brickwork. This method will only be satisfactory if

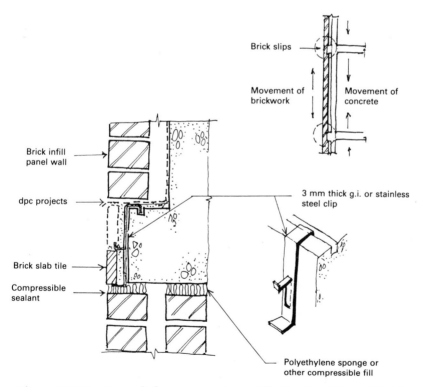

Figure 12.10   Remedial measures to rectify the buckling of brick slips used to cover the edge of a floor slab

the wall has the correct number of ties. However, if this is not the case, then some form of slot has to be attached to the backing structure and more ties provided.

12.6.2 Concrete Panels

Precast concrete panels are very heavy and movement forces tend to damage the fixings. The most common form of failure is due to movement and lack of sufficient expansion joints. Often it is found that units have been bolted together with little allowance for compression and contraction in the connection. Flexible joint separators should generally be employed.

Many precast unit failures occur through corrosion of the reinforcement, resulting in spalling of the concrete. This form of damage is not primarily a fixing problem, and often calls for concrete or epoxy mortar repair.

Precast panels generally require individual attention. For example, repair to open-drained joints of precast concrete cladding panels can be effectively carried out without much difficulty.

12.6.3 Stone Cladding

Failure of stone cladding can usually be attributed to the omission of fixing cramps or misaligned dowels. Sometimes it could also be due to inadequate provision of joints.

It is not a simple matter to repair stones *in situ* because of the difficulty in ascertaining what is behind the cladding and in actually drilling through the stone while it is still in place. It is unlikely that a suitable drill and bit could be used without shattering it.

Generally, if only a few stones are damaged, it may be acceptable to face-fix and plug. On the other hand, if the damage is extensive, it would be more economical to remove the stones completely and then refix them.

Related and Further Reading

Addleson, L. *Building Failures: A Guide to Diagnosis, Remedy and Prevention*. Butterworth Architecture, London (1989).

Anderson, J. M. and Gill, J. R. *Rainscreen Cladding: A Guide to Design Principles and Practice*. Butterworths, London (1988).

Barry, R. *The Construction of Buildings*, Volume IV, 3rd edn. Collins, London (1986).

Beech, J. C. Selection, performance and replacement of building joint sealant. *Building Technology and Management* (September, 1983).

Beech, J. C. and Aubrey, D. W. *Joint Primers and Sealants: Performance between Porous Claddings*. Information Paper IP 9/87, Building Research Establishment, UK (1987).

Bonshor, R. B. *Jointing Specification and Achievement: A BRE Survey.* Current Paper CP 28/77, Building Research Establishment, UK (1977).

British Standards Institution. *BS 5606: 1978 Code of Practice for accuracy in building.*

British Standards Institution. *BS 8200: 1985 Code of Practice for design of non-loadbearing external vertical enclosures of buildings.*

Brookes, A. J. *Cladding of Buildings*. Construction Press, London (1983).

Brookes, A. J. *Concepts in Cladding: Case Studies on Jointing for Architects and Engineers*. Construction Press, London (1983).

Building Research Establishment, UK. *Reinforced Plastics Cladding Panels*. Digest 161 (1974).

Building Research Establishment, UK. *Wall Cladding Defects and their Diagnosis*. Digest 217 (1978).

Building Research Establishment, UK. *Wall Cladding: Designing to Minimise Defects due to Inaccuracies and Movement*. Digest 223 (1979).

Building Research Establishment, UK. *Fixings for Non-loadbearing Precast Concrete Cladding Panels*. Digest 235 (1980).

Building Research Establishment, UK. *Large Concrete Panel External Walls: Resealing Butt Joints*. Defect Action Sheet (Design) DAS 97 (March, 1987).

Coad, J. R. and Rosaman, D. *Site-applied Adhesives – Failures and How to Avoid them*. Information Paper IP 12/86, Building Research Establishment, UK (1986).

Eaton, K. J. *Cladding and the Wind*. Current Paper CP 47/75, Building Research Establishment, UK (1975).

Edwards, M. J. *Weatherproof Joints in Large Panel Systems 1: Identification and Typical Defects*. Information Paper IP 8/86, Building Research Establishment, UK (1986).

Edwards, M. J. *Weatherproof Joints in Large Panel Systems 2: Remedial Measures*. Information Paper IP 9/86, Building Research Establishment, UK (1986).

Edwards, M. J. *Weatherproof Joints in Large Panel Systems 3: Investigation and Diagnosis of Failures*. Information Paper IP 10/86, Building Research Establishment, UK (1986).

Hollis, M. and Gibson, C. *Surveying Buildings*. Surveyors Publications, London (1990).

Josey, B. Light cladding systems. *The Architect* (September, 1987).

Marsh, P. *Fixings, Fasteners and Adhesives*. Construction Press, London (1984).

Parkes, L. Sheet cladding: review of performance and effectiveness. *Buildings Maintenance and Services*, UK (July/August, 1976).

Ransom, W. H. *Building Failures: Diagnosis and Avoidance*. Spon, London (1987).

Rostron, R. M. *Light Cladding of Buildings*. Architectural Press, London (1964).

Thornton, C. H. Avoiding wall problems by understanding structural movement. *Architectural Record* (December, 1981).

13 Finishes and Decorations

Despite developments in building technology, building defects of the non-structural type are still common. Each year, a large amount of money is spent on rectifying defects in finishes. These defects arise from errors in design or construction, many of which could have been avoided if proper and closer supervision had been enforced during the design and construction stages. Other causes include the varying site conditions, occupational use of buildings, lack of maintenance, and climatic effects on the finishes and decorations.

13.1 Floor Finishes

13.1.1 Cement and Sand Paving

This form of floor finish is made with ordinary Portland cement and concreting sand, with water added as required. A rubber latex such as polyvinyl acetate or styrene butadiene may also be added to the mix as a bonding agent to increase adhesion to the base concrete, reduce drying shrinkage and improve surface abrasion.

The main problems associated with cement and sand paving are:

1 Cracking from Consolidation of Hardcore

Hardcore can consolidate after the building is completed because of inadequate compaction or degradation of materials. When consolidation takes place, the ground floor slab loses its support and cracking will appear on the concrete slab as well as the paving, particularly towards the edges under which the depth of hardcore is greatest (see figure 13.1). The first sign is usually the appearance of gaps between the floor and skirting boards, followed by cracks in partitions.

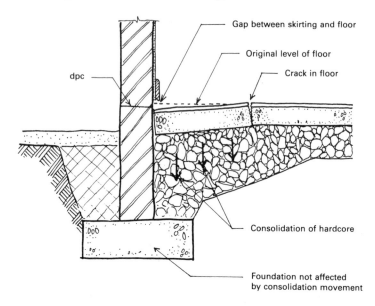

Figure 13.1 Cracking of floor slab caused by consolidation of excessively thick hardcore

2 Drying Shrinkage Cracking

If the paving is allowed to dry rapidly, the risk and extent of cracking is increased because it is unlikely to withstand the shrinkage forces generated. A simple protection by covering with a polythene sheeting for at least seven days can control this problem. If repair to hairline cracks is needed, it is necessary to hack grooves along the line of the crack and then patch it up with cement and sand grout or epoxy. For large areas of damage, it is preferable to hack away all defective areas and then relay the paving.

3 Bond Failure

Bond failure occurs if the base concrete is not properly prepared to receive the paving. This problem is less likely to happen with monolithic construction. However, if monolithic construction is not possible, the concrete base must be hacked to roughen the surface and cleaned before the paving is laid.

Bond failure is usually detected by the hollow sound obtained when the surface is tapped with a hammer. If hollowness is fairly local, repair may not be necessary. But if bond failure results in lifting of the paving such that it is likely to break under superimposed loads, extensive repair is required by cutting out and relaying the defective areas.

4 Curling
If large areas of paving are placed in one operation, there is a tendency for random cracking to occur. This can be reduced by laying the paving in alternate bays. However, this practice often leads to curling and unevenness at the junctions of bays. The remedial work involves grinding down of the edges and making good with a levelling compound.

5 Sulphate Attack
Groundwater or hardcore materials containing soluble sulphate salts can be responsible for chemical attack. The combination of sulphates with tricalcium aluminate present in Portland cement forms calcium sulphoaluminate which can result in disintegration and expansion of concrete slab and paving.

The remedial measures necessary where defects of this type have occurred are expensive. The repair work involves removing the paving, concrete slab and fill, and then replacing with an inert hardcore and a new floor. The proper incorporation of the damp-proof membrane will further assist in controlling the problem of sulphate attack.

6 Dusting of Surface
Dusting is often caused by excessive water in the mix which leads to the formation of laitance and a relatively weak surface. Laitance is a thin layer composed of water, cement and fine particles of aggregate that may form on the surface of concrete. Excessive trowelling may bring cement to the surface where it may craze and dust.

Slight dusting may be ignored. But if the surface is weak and friable, it may be necessary to hack out the paving and relay a new one, paying special attention to avoid the same problem.

7 Wear
Wear resistance of a floor finish is reduced by excessive water in the mix which results in capillary action bringing the fine cement particles to the surface. It can also be due to the loss of chemical adhesion from the use of very old cement which has deteriorated.

The best remedy is to hack off existing paving and then relay the whole area.

8 Potholes
Potholes are caused by the presence of foreign materials or excessive water in the cement mix which may create air bubbles below the surface. These bubbles may become deflated by wear.

For small localised areas, it may be necessary to hack out, clean and then apply one coat of bonding agent before relaying the paving. For larger areas, complete replacement of the paving is preferable.

13.1.2 Granolithic Flooring

Granolithic concrete is a good, wear-resistant flooring material. It is hard and durable, provided that selected aggregates and suitable mixes are used. The common problems with granolithic concrete include cracking, poor bonding to the base concrete and surface crazing.

1 Shrinkage Cracking

It is important that the aggregates should be clean and should not contain any deleterious substances. Too much water in the mix will result in excessive shrinkage which can lead to cracking of the finish. Care should be taken, therefore, to control rapid evaporation of water by covering the newly laid flooring with a polythene sheeting.

2 Loss of Adhesion

Like the cement and sand paving, it is preferable that the granolithic flooring be laid monolithically with the base concrete to ensure a good bond between the two layers. When a granolithic flooring has to be laid separately on a hardened concrete base, it is important to make sure that the surface of the latter is thoroughly hacked and cleansed of all dirt, dust, oils and the like. Just before laying the granolithic material, the whole of the prepared concrete base is wetted with clean water and any surplus water removed.

A two-course operation is often adopted with the bottom layer made drier than the top layer to allow some absorption of water from the top course. But the bottom course should not be too dry, otherwise a bonding problem with the base concrete will occur.

3 Surface Dusting

Final trowelling of the finish should be done when the surface has a moist but not watery appearance in order to avoid dusting of the surface. An incorrect practice is to sprinkle cement on to the surface in an attempt to accelerate its drying; this produces a weak cement skin on the surface of the finish which flakes off easily.

Patching of defective areas of granolithic flooring is seldom satisfactory. If this is absolutely necessary, it is advisable that either a resin emulsion is used in the mix or the area is replaced with an epoxy resin composition.

13.1.3 Terrazzo

Terrazzo is a popular floor finish consisting of a mix of cement and a decorative aggregate, such as marble chippings, laid on a screed. Most of the problems associated with *in situ* terrazzo are similar to those found in granolithic flooring because the method used in their installation is essentially the same. For example, the risk of surface crazing is high when the newly laid terrazzo is allowed to dry too rapidly. There is, therefore, a need to cover the terrazzo with a sheeting initially.

Crazing and cracking may mar the appearance of the flooring but these defects are usually not serious. One way to control crazing and cracking is to lay the *in situ* terrazzo in smaller bays, each separated by brass or PVC strips. Alternatively, the use of terrazzo tiles may overcome the problem of crazing and cracking.

13.1.4 Clay Floor Tiles

Clay tile floorings such as ceramic tiles are also popular because they provide a very durable surface which is relatively cheap to maintain. The main problems with clay floor tiles are:

1 Arching and Lifting

The main failure is caused by differential movement between the base concrete or screed and the clay tiles because they have different coefficients of thermal expansion (see figure 13.2). When clay tiles are laid on a new screed, the drying shrinkage of the screed may be opposed by the irreversible expansion of the tiles derived by absorption of moisture from the ground or atmosphere. The stresses built up by the contraction of the screed and the expansion of the tiles are manifested in arching of tiles over a large area or ridging over one or two rows. Eventually, these tiles will separate from the bedding and lift off.

Another possible cause arises from poor preparation and contamination of the concrete base which can lead to loss of adhesion.

The best way to avoid failure is to control the movements which cause the problem. For example, new tiles should not be used fresh from the kiln. In addition, the tiles should be bedded in mortar on to a separating layer of building paper or polythene sheet. Movement joints are also required around the perimeter of the floor (see figure 13.3).

2 Tile Edge Failure

This problem is manifested by cracking from top face to the edges of the tiles. The main cause is often due to compression of tile edges resulting from inadequate allowances provided for expansion, arching, curling, shrinkage of bed or flexing of the substrate.

The remedy is to remove and replace the defective tiles after correcting any faults in the joints and screed.

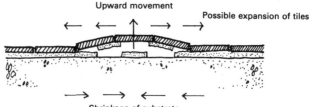

a. *Movement between tiles and substrate*

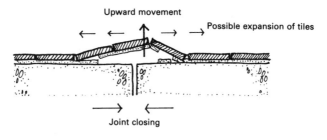

b. *Movement at joint in substrate*

Figure 13.2   Arching and lifting of clay tiles

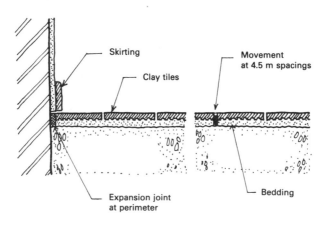

Figure 13.3   Provision of expansion joints in clay tile flooring

3 Broken Tiles
Mechanical damage or extensive movement on the tiles will result in areas of broken tiling. The risk of damage is greater when the tiles are

not properly laid on the bed. The only remedy in this case is to remove the broken tiles completely and replace them.

4 Staining
In the case of new tiles, stains are frequently caused by the bedding cement or jointing cement deposits. If the stains are found on older tiles, the fault may arise from rust deposits from corroded services pipes and connections embedded in the floor. Permanent stains may be due to spillage of chemicals. Most of these stains can be removed by suitable acidic solutions or detergents.

5 Failure of Joints
Failure of joints may come from the wrong choice of jointing material which can result in loss of support for tile edges and complete failure of the tiling. For example, a common occurrence in jointing systems with cementitious beds is the failure to rake out properly the bedding to a sufficient depth. This can lead to a loss of jointing material in isolated areas with bedding exposed or with hollow areas beneath the jointing, where chemical attack has taken place. Consequently, the jointing material may collapse into the void created by the fault.

The remedy involves raking out and repointing.

13.1.5 Thermoplastic Sheets and Tiles

Sheet and tile flooring made from thermoplastic binders such as polyvinyl acetate are usually laid on a screed. They are resistant to oils and grease. The common problems, however, are:

1 Lifting of Tiles
Thermoplastic sheets and tiles can be affected by moisture from the screed which attacks the adhesives used to fix the flooring. The sheet or tile then becomes loosened, the edges lift, and damage may be caused by traffic movement on the floor.

Other possible causes of this problem include excessive water used in cleaning of the floor; poor workmanship in their fixing; the use of inferior or unsuitable adhesives; too long a delay between spreading of the adhesive and laying of the tiles; or thermal expansion of the tiles.

Before any repair is started, it is essential that the source of water penetration should be eliminated. For example, a defective damp-proof membrane in the floor can cause rising dampness from the ground to attack the material. In this case, it becomes necessary to apply a layer of two-ply bituminous felt over the concrete base before the tiles or sheets are relaid. If the defect is due to construction water, it is necessary to remove all the tiles, to allow the concrete base to dry out, and then relay the tiles.

2 Surface Irregularities

Thermoplastic tiles and sheets need a very smooth and level base concrete or screed, otherwise surface irregularities will show prominently through the relatively thin floor finishes. The preparation of the screed is, therefore, of significance.

3 Rippling

This defect usually occurs with thin flooring materials and is caused by moisture movement of the screed as a result of shrinkage and expansion (see figure 13.4). The edges of the screed at construction joints or cracks curl on drying and, in the process, lift the tile or sheet. Subsequently, the screed expands on absorbing moisture and flattens. However, the previously expanded thermoplastic flooring does not flatten, but instead it ripples.

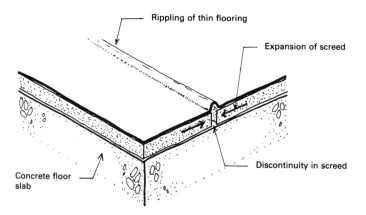

Figure 13.4   Rippling of sheet flooring

Rippling may also be caused by storing the rolls of material flat on the ground rather than on their ends vertically.

The remedial work consists of cutting out the rippled flooring and filling the gap in the screed to its full depth with a material capable of resisting movements. Finally, reinstate the flooring. Suitable filling materials include a 3:1 sand:cement mix or a 6:1 thermosetting resin:sand mix.

4 Indentations

Indentations are caused by concentrated loadings greater than those with which the floor finish can sustain without serious defects. Such

concentrated loadings come from machinery and furniture placed on
the floor. If the marred appearance is objectionable, it may be necessary to replace the affected tiles.

5 Disfiguring Marks
These marks come from rubber footwear and protective studs of furniture owing to anti-oxidant staining. Dragging of heavy cabinets, furniture and equipment can also scratch and damage the surface of the
flooring. Unsightly markings can be removed by gently rubbing them
with scouring powder, using a fine steel wool or by using suitable
detergents.

13.1.6 Timber Flooring

Timber finishes, whether of board, strip, block or parquet, need to be
protected against dampness and outbreaks of dry rot. These finishes
are usually nailed to timber fillets which are embedded in the screed.
The main problems are:

1 Loss of Adhesion
A common defect associated with wood blocks or parquet is expansion
of the timber due to uptake of moisture. When the expansive forces
can no longer be accommodated by compression of the blocks, the
latter will usually lift and arch, and then separate from the adhesive
which fixed them to the base (see figure 13.5).

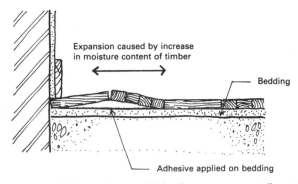

Figure 13.5   Lifting of wood blocks or parquet flooring

Moisture penetration arises from failure to provide an adequate
damp-proofing membrane under the blocks. It is essential that wood
flooring be laid at a moisture content close to that of the environment.
It is also necessary to provide a compression joint, for example, of cork

strip, around the perimeter of the floor where the full impact of the expansion will be felt.

If the source of dampness is of a temporary nature, it will usually suffice to relay the flooring after drying out the moisture. However, care must be taken to make sure that the timber is free from fungal attack.

2 Wear
Another common defect of timber flooring is unevenness resulting from unequal wear, particularly at locations vulnerable to heavy traffic movements.

This problem can be remedied by planing and sanding down, or replacing badly worn timber flooring.

13.2 Repair of Concrete Floors

13.2.1 General Patching and Repairs

If there are existing plans to reconstruct the building in the near future, a temporary method of repair may be used for joints and cracks. However, the following points should be noted:

1 Preparation
The areas to be repaired must be cleaned and all contamination by oils or grease must be removed. All areas of weak and defective concrete should be cut out and loose particles or dust removed (see figure 13.6).

The prepared and cleaned surfaces of concrete should be well wetted overnight before new concrete or mortar is placed, but any standing water should be removed.

2 Choice of Repair Material
Generally, a mortar is used for the repair. Either ordinary Portland cement or rapid-hardening cement can be used as the case may demand. A rubber latex can also be added to the mortar to improve its durability.

3 Repair to Joints
The actual method of repair for defective joints should only be carried out after careful investigation of the causes of the problem. The following steps are recommended:

- Cut away all defective concrete along the line of joint.
- Clean thoroughly the enlarged joint.

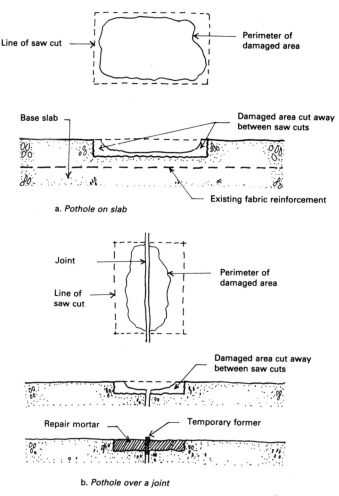

Line of saw cut

Perimeter of
damaged area

Base slab

Damaged area cut away
between saw cuts

Existing fabric reinforcement

a. *Pothole on slab*

Joint

Perimeter of
damaged area

Line of
saw cut

Damaged area cut away
between saw cuts

Repair mortar

Temporary former

b. *Pothole over a joint*

Figure 13.6 Repairs to pothole in concrete floor

- Repair sides of joint with epoxy resin mortar.
- When mortar has set, seal the joint with a preformed sealant or neoprene.

4 Repair to Cracks

The main reasons for repairing cracks are to prevent spalling of the edges and liquid penetration. Cracks can be repaired in several ways as follows:

- Chisel out loose cement, remove dust and debris and then brush a thick grout or epoxy resin well into the cracks; allow to set.

- Prepare as described and use a rigid mortar such as cement and sand, cement and sand and latex, or epoxy resin and sand.
- Use flexible materials such as rubber bitumen, polysulphides, polyurethane, epoxy resins or neoprene.

13.2.2 Resurfacing Concrete Floors

The method chosen for resurfacing a floor depends on the general condition of the floor, the use of the floor after repair and any restrictions on raising of the finished floor level.

The following are some of the recommended methods:

1 Resurfacing with in situ *Concrete and Bonded Topping*
Bonded toppings can only be successfully used when the base concrete is sound and of reasonably good quality, is free from cracks, is at least 100 mm thick and is free from oil and grease contamination.

The best preparation requires thorough scrabbling by some mechanical means, followed by vacuum cleaning to remove all traces of dust. Oil and grease must also be removed because they can affect the bonding.

The day before the topping is laid, the prepared surface of the base concrete should be wetted. The topping should be laid in bays of not more than 15 m² and be well compacted and cured.

All joints in the base concrete should be carried through the new topping.

2 Resurfacing with in situ *Concrete and Unbonded Topping*
The amount of preparation required is usually minimal and consists of simple sweeping and filling-in of badly worn areas and potholes with cement/sand mortar or fine concrete.

It is important to incorporate a layer of polythene as a separating membrane to prevent cracks in the old concrete slab being reflected through in the new topping. The membrane can also provide a slip layer so that the new topping can move independently of the old concrete below. Full movement joints in the old slab should, however, be carried through the new topping.

The usual practice of laying the concrete in small bays should be observed.

3 Resurfacing with Precast Slabs
This particular method is only suitable for a floor which will not be covered with any other surfacing material.

Some preparation needs to be given to the existing floor, such as cleaning, repairing potholes and levelling up.

The slabs should be fully bedded on a layer of mortar 25–40 mm thick. Joints should be narrow and can either be filled with mortar as the slabs are laid or slurried in later with a thin mortar or thick grout. All surplus mortar or grout should be wiped off before it hardens.

All movement joints in the base must be carried through the slabbing and, in addition, a movement joint should be incorporated around the perimeter of the floor and around all columns or other structural members which pierce the floor.

4 Resurfacing with Tiles
A deteriorated concrete floor can be resurfaced successfully with tiles to give an impervious, easily maintained and attractive floor.

The same preparation of the base concrete is required as described before. But the tiles should be laid with a separating layer of polythene sheet on top of the prepared concrete base slab.

13.3 Wall Finishes

13.3.1 Plastering

Internal plastering serves two main functions: it provides a continuous smooth and level surface to walls and ceilings, and a background suitable for receiving a decorative finish.

Porosity or suction, roughness and shrinkage of the background are the main factors that can influence the performance of cement, lime and gypsum plaster finishes. Some examples of defects which arise from these factors are as follows:

1 Crazing and Cracking
Crazing and cracking of finishing coats are frequently caused by shrinkage of the background or shrinkage of the undercoat. The former can occur in the case of immature blocks while the latter often occurs after the application of the finish coat. In both instances, however, the cracking is invariably reproduced in the finish coat. The use of good-quality sands, suitable mix proportions and adequate time set aside for shrinkage to take place between coats can reduce the risks of this defect.

Very fine crazing on neat gypsum finish coats can arise from application faults. High suction of the background, too rapid drying or too late final trowelling can be responsible for this defect. Usually a thin wash of plaster is sufficient to fill up the fine crazing. The crazing can also be camouflaged by decorative treatment such as painting.

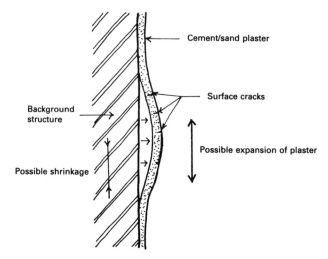

Figure 13.7   Shelling of cement/sand plaster

2 Shelling
Another common problem with plaster finishes is shelling because of
the loss of adhesion (see figure 13.7). Plasters rely for their adhesion
largely on mechanical means. For this reason, their backgrounds must
be adequately prepared to provide a good key, either naturally by
using porous and specially keyed materials or mechanically with raked
joints, roughened surfaces, keyed materials like expanded metal lathing or specially formulated bonding agents.

The set plaster can easily be removed from its background by movement of the background or even the plaster itself. The various forces
that generate these movements include adhesive forces, forces due to
the weight of the material and the effects of shrinkage.

The usual remedial work involves applying a polyvinyl acetate type of
bonding agent to the backing coat before re-skimming. The bonding
agent provides a good bond for the new plaster and should reduce the
risk of shelling.

3 Blowing
Blowing starts as a bulge on the plaster. The bulge then develops into a
fine crack which tends to be circular in form. In the advanced stage of
attack, the circular patch of plaster lifts and falls away, leaving a small
conical hole.

The cause is generally due to the presence of lime nodules in the
plaster materials. These nodules can hydrate and expand after the
plaster has set. Sometimes the blows are the result of particles of chalk
in the materials which can be converted to quicklime by the burning

process used in the production of bricks or blocks. The expansion of the quicklime on slaking produces a 'blow' on the plaster surface.

4 Efflorescence

Small quantities of soluble salts such as the sulphates and carbonates of calcium can cause efflorescence under conducive conditions. These soluble salts are then carried to the surface of the plaster by the water in the background or plaster, and effloresce out as the water evaporates.

In order to prevent damage to decoration as a result of efflorescence, an oil-based or varnish-type sealing coat can be applied over a plaster surface before the decorative coat. But the best preventive measure is still to delay decorating newly constructed walls until they are dry.

5 Rust Staining

The corrosion of electric conduits, switch boxes, nails and other metallic components which are fixed behind the plaster can cause stains to appear on the plaster.

The best prevention against corrosion is to use galvanised components. But in the course of handling and fixing, the galvanised coating can be damaged. In order to reduce the risk of staining from corrosion, all ungalvanised metallic parts should be given a generous coat of aluminium paint before plastering.

Where staining has taken place, the affected plaster should be removed to expose the metal, and the latter should then be treated with aluminium paint. The plaster for making good is ordinary Class B retarded hemi-hydrate gypsum plaster gauged with a small amount of lime.

13.3.2 Rendering

A render serves two main functions: it performs as a cladding to improve the weather resistance of the building to which it is applied, and also serves as a decorative finish. Because a render is used externally, it is subjected to very severe changes of conditions, such as frequent cycles of wetting and drying, and background movements. These factors contribute to the deterioration of a render.

In view of the vast similarities between plastering and rendering, including the materials used in the mix, many of their problems are identical, including the following:

1 Crazing and Cracking

Renders may crack, craze and become detached from their substrate through differential movements between the background and the render. As renders are mostly cement-based materials, there is bound to be shrinkage which tends to transfer tensile stresses to the material and cause cracking. The cracks may then allow rainwater to pass through and loosen the bond between the render and the substrate. Differences in drying shrinkage characteristics between the top coat and the undercoat of the render can also lead to similar defects.

To avoid cracking, it is essential that the background or substrate should be firm and not liable to move. If this is not possible, it is important that the work is divided into smaller panels with separating movement joints.

Any remedial work, when cracking occurs and extends into the background, necessitates the complete removal of the weak rendering coats, particularly the hollow areas. Patching should be carried out with a suitable rendering mix over a well-prepared substrate or metal lathing.

2 Sulphate Attack

Moisture trapped behind a render can result in sulphate attack. The reaction between the tricalcium aluminate in cement and lime with soluble sulphates is accompanied by expansion. This expansion can force the rendering coat from the background. Parapet walls and other free-standing brick walls are most susceptible to sulphate attack.

Where the presence of sulphates is suspected, it is advisable to use sulphate-resisting cement for the rendering mix. Another way is to avoid direct contact between the render and the background by using bituminised expanded metal.

3 Shelling

The adhesion of the render to the background may be reduced by the penetration of water, inadequate bond or key, too strong a render for the background or preceding coats, and other movements in the background. Additional problems arise with defective rainwater gutters and downpipes which tend to keep a render saturated for prolonged periods of time.

Loose renders should be cut away to a firm edge before washing and filling up with a new material. If structural movement is present, it is preferable to fix expanded metal lathing before application of the repair material.

13.3.3 External Wall Tiling

The use of tiles and mosaic on external walls of buildings has the advantage that the surface is virtually self-cleansing and often requires very little maintenance. The usual practice is to 'dub-out', apply one or two coats of rendering, and then bed the tiles in either a cement/sand mortar or a proprietary adhesive.

The failure of external wall tiling is invariably due to loss of bond. In very serious cases, loss of bond can result in dislodgement of the tiles from the wall. With high-rise buildings, falling tiles are extremely dangerous.

The main causes of bond failure may be categorised as follows:

1 Interface Between Concrete and Rendering
The reasons for failure under this category include:

- Poor preparation of the concrete background, for example, lack of mechanical key and contaminated concrete surface.
- Weak concrete background without sufficient strength to hold the combined weight of the rendering and tiles.
- Presence of impurities such as clay, silt and organic substances in the rendering.
- Inadequate protection and curing of the rendering.
- Corrosion of reinforcing steel in the concrete that can cause cracking and spalling after completion of tiling.

2 Interface Between First and Second Coat of Rendering or Between Rendering and Bedding Material
The reasons include:

- Lack of key due to failure to 'comb' surface of rendering.
- Use of very rich mix over a leaner mix.
- Presence of impurities, inadequate protection and curing of rendering and corrosion of reinforcement as described.

3 Interface Between Bedding and Tiles
The reasons include:

- Failure to make sure that tiles are solidly bedded.
- Over application, resulting in too thick bedding material used.
- Too rich a mix for the bedding mortar.

4 Movements
Tiles and supporting layers are subjected to considerable thermal movement. The stresses which are built up in the various layers due to the thermal gradient from outside to inside can have serious disruptive effects on the tiling.

Careful site investigation of the tiling is necessary before any remedial work begins. The procedure includes tapping to detect 'hollow' debonded areas, visual inspection, and removal of defective tiling and rendering to facilitate closer scrutiny of the defect. The process can be expensive, particularly for high-rise buildings where cradles and scaffolding will be required.

In executing the repair work, all tiles and rendering which show signs of loss of bond should be removed back to a sound substrate. The tiles can be refixed with an approved proprietary bedding mortar as soon as possible to prevent water getting down behind the existing tiles. Vertical and horizontal movement joints should be provided wherever it is practical to do so. It is also prudent to use reinforcement in the rendering to prevent dislodged rendering and tiling from falling dangerously off the building.

Some methods of repair include the injection of a polymer resin at the interface between the tiles and the substrate to improve the bond.

13.4 Paintwork

Paints are widely used today as a surface coating to protect, preserve and decorate many materials such as timber, steel and plaster. They often display faults despite extensive research and scientific control exercised by the manufacturers.

The common defects associated with painting and paintwork can be categorised as follows.

13.4.1 Defects Due to Poor Workmanship

The maximum durability of a paint film is only achieved when the surface has been carefully prepared. The manner and circumstances by which the paint is applied will also influence the performance of the paint system. Such factors as weather conditions at the time of painting, the standard of care taken during painting applications and the actual method of applying the paint are also very important.

1 Crazing and Cracking
The elasticity of oil-based films diminishes as oxidation proceeds with ageing. The loss of elasticity is also caused by application of hard drying paint over a soft undercoat, application before previous coat has dried sufficiently or application over contaminated surfaces.

The effects of crazing and cracking of paintwork are:

- Cracking of film extending through the entire paint system to the substrate.

- Crazing which describes shallow breaks in the paint system not reaching the substrate.
- Alligatoring, a term used for pronounced wide cracks over the entire surface but not reaching the substrate.

Prevention includes using compatible paint systems and allowing the primer or undercoat to dry properly. Rubbing down and redecorating will remove slight crazing. In more serious cases, the existing paint must be stripped and the full paint system properly applied.

2 Curtaining
The defect occurs when very thick coatings fail to dry flat. The causes are uneven application or heavy application over the wet edge.

The prevention of the problem lies in the use of good painting techniques and practice. Remedial measures include sanding down the dry film and recoating.

3 Grinning
The opacity or ability of a paint to hide the surface depends on the thickness of the film, the type of pigment used, its absorption and reflectance characteristics.

Poor opacity can be due to one or more of the following reasons:

- Overthinning of the paint.
- Applying paint too thinly or unevenly and covering too wide an area.
- Pigment content of the paint is too low.
- Drastic colour change with too few coats.
- Knots in timber not properly treated.

Most of the preventive measures involve use of reliable materials and good workmanship in the application. The remedy is to apply more coats of paint over the entire surface evenly to obtain a satisfactory coating.

4 Drying Problems
Sometimes the paint remains soft for a long time after application. The possible causes of this problem are:

- Too thick a coat being applied.
- Use of unsuitable thinners.
- Applying under wrong climatic conditions.
- Presence of oil, grease or wax on the surface.

The remedy is to scrape off existing film, clean the surface thoroughly and then re-apply a new coat of paint evenly. Care should be taken to ventilate the painted work.

5 Sinkage
This term refers to the wet paint being absorbed into the surface. The obvious cause of sinkage is surface porosity. For example, this problem is common in hollow concrete blocks.

To obviate the problem, it may be necessary to apply more coats of sealer or undercoats to the surface before the finishing coats.

6 Faults in Painting
Poor painting techniques or the failure to take care during the painting process can result in other faults which can become visible shortly after painting. These faults include the following:

- 'Holidays' or misses in the coating resulting from working under poor lighting conditions; undercoat of similar colour to the top coat; or careless application.
- Lifting, which is some disturbance of the previous coat on application of a new coat resulting from the use of too strong solvents for the new coat; or previous coat not dry when the new coat is applied.
- 'Pimpling', usually on a sprayed paint film, due to wrong air pressure used; paint not properly mixed; wrong thinner used; or spraying too close to or too far away from the surface.

The rectification process ranges from simply applying another coat to the surface to a complete rubbing down or removal of paint film and then repainting.

13.4.2 Discoloration of Paints

Discoloration of a paint film can occur gradually over several months or even years. The most common causes encountered are poor light-fastness of certain coloured pigments, excessive chalking, bleeding, and mould or algae growth.

1 Chalking
Chalking is the condition of a paint surface which, having lost most of its gloss, is coated with a white powder. Generally, chalking appears on whites or light tints and is the result of photochemical breakdown of the surface layer of its binder with consequent release of pigment.

The main causes of chalking are:

- The use of unsuitable pigments.
- Ageing of paint film.
- Repeated condensation on the film followed by drying out.

A good washing will remove the deposits and restore the gloss or colour. In more serious cases, when the paint film has perished, it is necary to remove and reapply the full paint system.

2 Bleeding

Bleeding is a discoloration of the paint film by some ingredient of the coating or surface below. In the case of woodwork, the defect is caused by painting on creosote or bitumen without sealing; knots not properly treated; unclean surface; or red pigments in the previous coatings.

The remedy is to use a specially formulated sealer or an aluminium paint.

3 Loss of Gloss

Gloss is the degree to which a painted surface reflects light. There is a gradual decrease from high gloss to matt finish.

The following are the common causes of loss of gloss:

- The materials to be painted are highly absorbent, for example, new plaster and new wood, and so sealing is essential to prevent sinkage.
- Poor application of paint which gives rise to uneven surface and poor gloss in the finish.
- An excessively rough surface.
- Painting in damp or foggy conditions.

4 Mould or Algae Growths

Paintwork affected by these organisms develops various coloured spots, patches or stains in black, red, green or brown.

Moulds are encouraged by damp conditions and feed on the decorations indoors or outside. Algae also need damp conditions, usually on the external side, but do not feed on the paint.

To obtain the best paint performance it is very important that the surface is clean and not infested with growth prior to painting, because the fungicide and algicide in a paint are chosen to resist surface growth occurring after painting only.

In mild attacks the organisms can be scrubbed off, otherwise it may be necessary to strip off the old paintwork. The wall is then treated with a fungicidal wash, allowed to dry and redecorated with a special fungicidal paint.

13.4.3 Chemical Attack

Paintwork is also susceptible to chemical attack by various substances in the substrate on which the paint is applied. The principal forms of attack are efflorescence and saponification.

1 Efflorescence

Efflorescence is caused by salts from the structure being carried to the surface by water and deposited on drying. The salts may push off the paint film or appear over it.

To control the problem of efflorescence it is necessary to remove all the salts by brushing and washing. Avoid water-thinned paints if possible or use them over an alkali-resistant primer if the surface is heavily contaminated with salts.

2 Saponification
The alkalinity of lime plasters, cement-rendered surfaces and concrete results in the breakdown of oil-based paints by saponification.

The degree of breakdown depends on the strength of alkali present, the sensitivity of the paint film in contact, and the duration of wet conditions to maintain the activity of the alkali.

Paint films attacked by alkalis first become soft and sticky and partially water soluble. Under severe attack and where moist conditions prevail, sticky runs may develop a yellow or brownish liquid, or watery sticky blisters may be present. Upon drying out, the stickiness may disappear, but peeling, cracking and flaking may then occur, as the film will have lost its binder and become brittle.

Where the attack is severe, the film should be removed preferably by scraping and, only if necessary, washing down with water, as the use of water may result in further reactivation of alkali in adjacent areas. Allow to dry out thoroughly and then seal the surface by application of an alkali-resisting plaster or cement primer. Standard types of finishes may then be applied.

13.4.4 Loss of Adhesion

Many problems in paintwork are caused by loss of adhesion brought about by movements in the background or by moisture trapped behind the paint film. This category of defects include blistering and flaking.

1 Blistering
In most cases, blistering is due to the liquids or gases trapped in or underneath the film. While water is the most common cause of blistering and associated failures such as cracking and peeling, even very small quantities are often sufficient to cause blistering, particularly on timber substrates.

Dampness promotes rapid hydrolysis of linseed oil in primers and can give rise to breakdown products which become liquid in warm weather and destroy the adhesion of the paint film; then the expanding air blows up as blisters.

Blistering on metallic substrates is often due to the presence of residual corrosion products. On galvanised metal, the zinc coating may be porous, particularly after weathering, and the pores are liable to retain soluble zinc salts. Water, which permeates through the super-imposed paint film, is absorbed by the zinc salt, thus initiating the blistering process.

2 Brittleness and Flaking

Flaking of a film is usually preceded by cracking; both faults resulting from internal stresses set up in the film during the initial contraction when drying. Films remain intact on a rigid substrate while movement of the substrate, such as dimensional changes in wood due to moist-ure, can result in cracking and adhesion failures giving rise to flaking.

The main causes of brittleness and consequent flaking are:

- The use of an excessively short-drying oil medium will result in a brittle film. When this is applied over a longer drying oil undercoat, cracking or crazing will probably take place.
- Absorption of moisture, resulting in swelling and loss of adhesion.
- Painting over a loose and friable surface.
- Presence of moisture on the surface will impair adhesion of paint film.

The only appropriate and satisfactory remedy is complete removal of all defective paintwork and then repainting.

13.5 Repainting Existing Surfaces

Repainting usually arises from a planned maintenance programme or because the protective coating has deteriorated. The procedure for repainting depends very much on the type and condition of the exist-ing surfaces.

13.5.1 Repainting Woodwork

Paintwork which is chalked or dirty, but otherwise sound, needs thorough washing before repainting, preferably with a mild soap solu-tion. Once the dirt is removed, the surface should be washed with clean water, the surfaces rubbed down with abrasive paper and allowed to dry. Cracks should be stopped; knots should be sealed over; bare timber primed with aluminium primer; undercoats applied; and finally followed by finishing coats.

If the existing paintwork is soft, very chalky or eroded, cracked and peeled, it should be completely removed. Decayed timber should be cut out and replaced; both old and new timber should then be brushed over with a coat of preservative, including the end grains. The bare wood should be rubbed down with abrasive paper and the painting process continued as for new work: knotting, priming, stopping, undercoats and finishing coats.

13.5.2 Repainting Steelwork

Repainting steelwork should not be delayed beyond the appearance of the first traces of rust. This avoids more costly work later. The old painted surfaces can be rubbed down and finished with one or two suitable coats. Any small patches of rust can be removed and treated with a rust-inhibiting primer.

If rusting is serious, complete removal of the paint, followed by proper surface preparation, are necessary. Paint removal can be done with scrapers, solvent removers or flame burning, depending on the circumstances.

For example, severely rusted window frames must have all putty and glazing removed to allow thorough cleaning by brushing and scraping. Two coats of red lead or zinc-rich primer should be applied before reglazing.

13.5.3 Repainting Plastered Surfaces

All loose materials must be removed by washing and brushing off. Dirty surfaces must be thoroughly cleaned. If necessary, touch up existing surfaces to cover all irregularities.

Surface defects most likely to affect painting will be those caused by dampness from direct rain penetration, rising damp or condensation and the only really effective remedy is to stop the damp penetration. A compromise solution is to use a permeable paint that will allow salts and moisture to escape. Persistently damp conditions encourage mould growth and improved ventilation is often a better remedy than using fungicidal paints.

Existing surfaces that have previously been painted with emulsion paints may be redecorated with other materials provided that the emulsion paint is sound and adhering well. It should be rubbed down wet before redecorating and then allowed to dry.

Related and Further Reading

Addleson, L. *Building Failures*, Architectural Press, London (1989).
Allen, R. T. L. and Edwards, S. C. *Repair of Concrete Structures*. Blackie, London (1987).
British Standards Institution. *BS 3260: 1969 Semi-flexible PVC floor tiles*.

British Standards Institution. *CP 204: 1970 In situ concrete floor finishes.*

British Standards Institution. *BS 2592: 1973 Thermoplastic flooring tiles.*

British Standards Institution. *BS 3261: Part 1: 1973 Homogeneous flooring. Unbacked flexible PVC flooring.*

British Standards Institution. *BS 5262: 1976 Code of Practice for external rendered finishes.*

British Standards Institution. *BS 5385: Part 2: 1978 Code of Practice for external ceramic wall tiling and mosaics.*

British Standards Institution. *BS 6150: 1982 Code of Practice for painting of buildings.*

British Standards Institution. *BS 8203: 1987 Code of Practice for installation of sheet and tile flooring.*

British Standards Institution. *BS 5385: Part 1: 1990 Code of Practice for the design and installation of internal ceramic wall tiling and mosaics in normal conditions.*

Building. Paints and protective materials in buildings. Issue 21/28 (December, 1984).

Building Research Establishment, UK. *Sheet and Tile Flooring made from Thermoplastic Binders.* Digest 33 (1971).

Building Research Establishment, UK. *Damp-proofing Solid Floors.* Digest 54 (1971).

Building Research Establishment, UK. *Shelling of Plaster Finishing Coats.* Technical Information Leaflet 14 (1971).

Building Research Establishment, UK. *Clay Tile Flooring.* Digest 79 (1976).

Building Research Establishment, UK. *External Rendered Finishes.* Digest 196 (1976).

Building Research Establishment, UK. *Developments in Paints and Surface Coatings.* Overseas Building Note 169 (1976).

Building Research Establishment, UK. *Plastering on Dense Concrete.* Technical Information Leaflet 24 (1977).

Building Research Establishment, UK. *Painting Walls: Part 1: Choice of Paint.* Digest 197 (1982).

Building Research Establishment, UK. *Painting Woodwork.* Digest 261 (1982).

Building Research Establishment, UK. *Hardcore.* Digest 276 (1983).

Building Research Establishment, UK. *External Walls: Rendering – Resisting Rain Penetration.* Defect Action Sheet 37 (1983).

Building Research Establishment, UK. *External Walls: Rendering – Application.* Defect Action Sheet 38 (1983).

Building Research Establishment, UK. *Painting Walls: Part 2: Failures and Remedies.* Digest 198 (1984).

Cattell, D. *Specialist Floor Finishes: Design and Installation*. Blackie, London (1987).

Chaplin, R. G. Methods of repairing defective cement:sand screed by in situ penetration hardening. *Construction and Building Materials*, UK, Vol. 1 No. 4 (December, 1987).

Chatfield, H. W. *Science of Surface Coatings*. Ernest Benn, London (1962).

DOE Construction 4, External Wall Tiling with Cement/sand Bedding. HMSO, London (December, 1972).

DOE Construction 5, External Wall Tiling with Adhesives. HMSO, London (March, 1973).

Everett, A. *Finishes*. Batsford, London (1986).

Freeman, I. *DOE Construction No. 14, Building Failures*. Department of Environment, UK (1975).

Hamburg, H. R. and Morgans, W. M. *Hess's Paint Film Defects: their Causes and Cure*. Chapman and Hall, London (1979).

Hinks, J. and Cook, G. Defects in paintwork. *Building Today* (September, 1989).

Lambourne, R. *Paint and Surface Coatings: Theory and Practice*. Ellis Horwood, Chichester, UK (1987).

Morgans, W. M. *Outlines of Paint Technology*. Charles Griffin, London (1969).

Parker, D. H. *Principles of Surface Coating Technology*. Wiley, New York (1965).

Payne, H. F. *Organic Coatings Technology*. Wiley, New York (1961).

Perkins, P. H. *Floors: Construction and Finishes*. Cement and Concrete Association, UK (1973).

Perkins, P. H. *Concrete Structures: Repair, Waterproofing and Protection*. Applied Science Publishers, London (1977).

Property Services Agency. *The Good Screed Guide*. Building Technical File No. 22 (July, 1988).

Pye, P. W. *BRE Screed Tester: Classification of Screeds, Sampling and Acceptance Limits*. Information Paper 11/84, Building Research Establishment, UK (1984).

Ragsdale, L. A. and Raynham, E. A. *Building Materials Technology*. Edward Arnold, London (1972).

Ransom, W. H. *Building Failures: Diagnosis and Avoidance*. Spon, London (1987).

Seeley, I. H. *Blight on Britain's Buildings: a Survey of Paint and Maintenance Practice*. Paintmakers Association (1984).

Thomas, K. The strict procedure for laying clay paving. *Building Today* (November, 1988).

Turner, G. P. A. *Introduction to Paint Chemistry*. Chapman and Hall, London (1967).

Warlow, W. J. and Pye, P. W. *Wet Cleaning as a Cause of Shrinkage of PVC Flooring.* Information Paper IP 25/79, Building Research Establishment, UK (1979).

Warton, J. and Pye, P. W. *The Rippling of Thin Flooring over Discontinuities in Screeds.* Current Paper 94/74, Building Research Establishment, UK (1974).

Wehlte, K. *The Materials and Techniques of Painting*, Van Nostrand Reinhold, New York (1975).

14 Dampness in Buildings

Every building is surrounded more or less by natural moisture of one kind or another. Most buildings also contain moisture created internally by normal habitation or use and industrial processes. Good design measures are essential to keep the moisture out of the building, but when these measures are inadequate, dampness can enter the building materials to cause their deterioration.

14.1 Rising Damp

14.1.1 Mechanism of Attack

Rising damp is concerned with the movement of water from the ground to the porous material of the walls. It commonly occurs in walls near ground level as well as in solid ground floor slabs, particularly at junctions with the walls. The mechanism of moisture movement through the porous material takes place in both saturated and unsaturated soils.

Soil which is saturated has its interstitial spaces filled with water and this will usually saturate a porous material in contact with it by hydrostatic pressure, thus allowing the water to flow into the pores. Unsaturated soils also contain water held around the points of contact by surface tension. But water is drawn into the pores of the material by capillary action in the latter case.

After entering the base of a wall, the water will move up primarily by capillarity. The height of rise of moisture depends on the pore structure of the wall, degree of saturation of the soil and rate of evaporation.

Groundwater invariably contains dissolved hygroscopic salts which crystallise out on the wall surface where the water evaporates. When the air is humid, these salts will attract moisture from the laden air to cause apparent 'dampness' on the wall.

Generally, at the base of a wall where rising damp is present, the major factor in the dampness is the actual capillary moisture. Further up the wall, the influence of hygroscopic moisture increases and forms the main component of dampness.

14.1.2 Causes of Rising Damp

The problem of moisture from the ground rising in a porous wall medium has been recognised for a long time. Defective damp-proof courses and poor detailing where such courses are provided constitute the main causes of rising damp (see figure 14.1). Examples include the following:

- Absence of damp-proof courses in very old buildings.
- Bridging of damp-proof course (d.p.c.) internally by a floor screed being laid without a membrane or including a membrane which is not keyed or chased into the d.p.c. in the wall.
- Bridging of d.p.c. by an external rendering which is liable to crack and allow moisture to rise in the crevice formed behind it.
- Bridging by earth deposited against the outside of the wall.
- Bridging caused by mortar droppings and other debris into the cavity of the cavity wall construction.

14.1.3 Remedial Measures

Some causes of rising damp can be dealt with quite cheaply and easily (see figure 14.2). For example, it may be possible to lower earth or pavings which extend above the damp-proof course, or to remove rendering or pointing which bridges the d.p.c. Where there is no damp-proof course or where it is defective, however, more expensive methods involving either installing a new d.p.c. *in situ*, or removing the cause of the bridging by conventional building methods are necessary.

1 Physical Insertion of Damp-proof Courses
An early method relied on cutting out one or two courses of bricks to the full thickness of the wall at the appropriate level and then building in new engineering bricks.

New techniques involve removing a horizontal mortar joint by cutting through the full thickness of the wall, using a tungsten carbide-tipped saw, for lengths of about 1.200 m at a time. Various damp-proof materials can be used, including copper, bituminous felt or polyethylene. It is necessary to overlap all joints by at least 150 mm and the space above the d.p.c. is usually made good and solid with cement mortar.

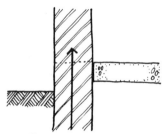

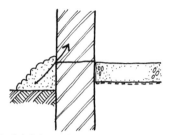

a. No dpc or defective dpc

b. Debris heaped against the wall allows moisture to pass into wall above dpc

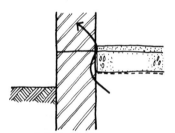

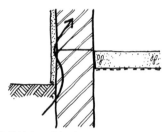

c. Solid floor bridging dpc

d. Bridging of dpc by porous rendering

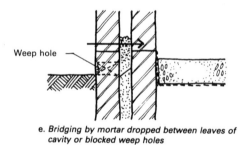

Weep hole

e. Bridging by mortar dropped between leaves of cavity or blocked weep holes

Figure 14.1 Typical causes of rising dampness in external walls

These methods work best on coursed brickwork or stonework. Particular attention should be taken to make sure that concealed services pipes are not damaged in the process.

2 Electro-osmotic Process
Electro-osmosis as a technique of *in situ* treatment of rising damp makes use of the principle of short-circuiting and reducing the surface tension that causes the problem. Two methods have been in use.

The more widely used passive system has copper electrodes inserted in the walls, which are then wired up to the earth. The active system requires an electric current from a DC source passing into the wires

that connect up with the electrodes in the wall. This approach, however, is no longer recommended by the Building Research Establishment, UK.

In both cases, the electrodes provide the electrical charge to repel
rising damp from the ground. However, electrical charges in rising
damp depends considerably on the types of salts present. To be effective, therefore, the current that produces the charges must be adjusted
accordingly along the wall to take into account the salt concentration.
For this reason, the electro-osmotic process is not very effective.

3 Installation of Siphons
In this method, siphons in the form of porous clay ceramic tubes are

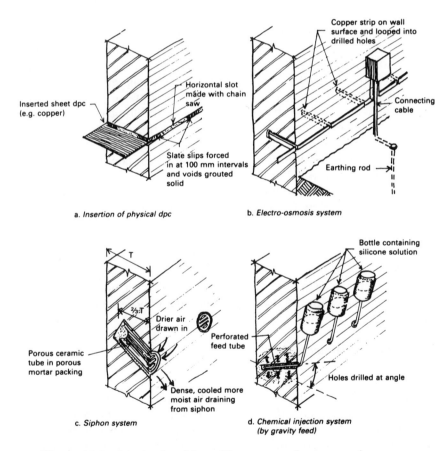

a. *Insertion of physical dpc*

b. *Electro-osmosis system*

c. *Siphon system*

d. *Chemical injection system
(by gravity feed)*

Figure 14.2 Methods of installing a new damp-proof course

inserted into holes in the affected walls. These tubes are held in position by a salt-free porous mortar packing. The holes are then covered with a ventilator.

The technique depends on rising damp being drawn into the siphon tubes by capillarity. The tube is designed and positioned to discharge the humid air developed inside it and replace it by fresh air.

One major disadvantage with this technique is that the pores on the surface of the tube can become blocked with the accumulation of salts during the evaporation process.

4 Chemical Injections

The main types of chemicals used for injection fluids are silicones, siliconates or stearates. Application is either by pressure injection or by a diffusion technique based on gravity.

In the pressure injection method, an aqueous solution of siliconates, such as sodium or potassium methyl siliconate, is pumped into pre-drilled holes at about 150 mm centres, usually along the mortar joint. Injection is done by a lance which is specially designed to maintain a constant pressure during the process. The volume of fluid to be injected will depend on the thickness of the wall and the type of material.

The gravity-feed system requires a series of holes to be drilled at a downward sloping angle at the position of the new damp-proof course. The diffusion liquid is applied from a container which feeds the tube by gravity. It is important that the fluid diffuses into the wall completely in order to be effective. Sufficient time must be provided for all the fluid to flow from the container and to be absorbed by the wall, which may take up to a few days.

The efficacy of the chemical injection system depends on the extent of penetration of the injection fluid through the damp wall. If the solvent is readily miscible with the moisture in the walls, a more effective system can be expected. Other effects of organic solvents include fire risks with the use of flammable solutions, their smell and higher costs.

14.1.4 Other Treatments

1 Replastering

The hygroscopic salts deposited on wall surfaces with the evaporation of water continue to absorb moisture from the atmosphere even after the rising damp has been eliminated. Therefore, for any curative treatment to be completely satisfactory, the old salt-contaminated plaster must be removed and a new plaster applied.

The function of the new plaster is two-fold: to replace the existing contaminated plaster and to provide a barrier to prevent any residual dampness and hygroscopic salts from reappearing on the newly plastered walls. As such, the new plaster must be properly formulated and correctly applied. The replastering process should also be delayed for as long as possible after the installation of the damp-proof course to allow for complete elimination of the salts.

A cement-based plaster of 3:1 sand/cement mix should be used. The protection can be further enhanced by incorporating waterproof additives such as stearates, oleates or styrene butadiene in the mix.

2 Drylining

Drylining can substitute replastering where rising damp has occurred. The timber studs or battens must be pre-treated with preservatives before they are fixed to the wall. The timber members must also be protected from any dampness in the wall by a damp-proof polythene sheet.

Various types of plasterboards can be used, including those which are foam-backed or foil-backed. After fixing the boards to the studs or battens, the tops of the nails are covered with a spot of PVA emulsion paint and the plasterboard joints are scrimmed prior to the application of a top plaster coat.

14.2 Rain Penetration

14.2.1 Effects of Rain Penetration

Rainwater is the most obvious and commonest source of dampness and its penetration through external walls and roofs may take place by means of gravity flow and wind forces, and capillary action in the pores of the materials. The most vulnerable parts of a building are joints between components and the use of porous materials which offer little resistance to penetration, including those used in roofs, cavity walls, parapet walls and around openings.

Rain penetration has the following effects which tend to lead to failure:

- Loss of adhesion and/or cracking of finishes due to chemical reaction with constituents of the background material, for example, in efflorescence or sulphate attack; frost action in temperate countries; and differential movement of finish or background.
- Cracking of components or elements due to moisture movement during wetting or drying out; and chemical reactions such as reinforcement corrosion.
- Increased condensation arising from a reduction of the thermal

resistance of some of the materials and resulting in unsightly mould growth.
- Changes in the appearance of the surface such as staining and streaking.

14.2.2 Causes of Rain Penetration

Buildings are obviously designed in various ways to avoid rain penetration. External walls should be sufficiently thick to absorb rainwater and allow it to evaporate later or be constructed as cavity walls to break the capillary flow of moisture towards the interior. Other measures may include wide overhanging eaves at roof level and the use of impervious membranes for roof construction.

However, despite all the good design practices, problems still occur. The principal causes of rain penetration can be summarised as follows:

- Permeability of porous materials, particularly clay bricks and lightweight concrete used for wall construction, allows some absorption of water. The problem is worse if there are cracks in the mortar joints.
- Cracking of units of materials or between components is liable to occur as a result of movements in monolithic concrete walls and roofing membranes, giving rise to loss of adhesion at joint and unit interface.
- Inadequate provision for drainage arising from under-designed gutters and downpipes, and poor maintenance.

14.2.3 Contributory Factors to Rain Penetration

The amount of rainwater that can penetrate into or through an element such as a wall or roof depends on the exposure of the element to wind-driven rain; the water-excluding characteristics of the units, components and joints making up the construction of the element; and the modes of transmission of the water within the thickness of the construction of the element.

1 Exposure
The likelihood of rain penetration, particularly through vertical surfaces, depends on both the quantity of rainfall and wind speed. In the absence of wind, rain would fall vertically. Any projection on a wall is sufficient to prevent rainwater wetting it. This condition, however, is unusual.

The angle at which rain strikes a wall depends on wind speed and raindrop size. The bigger the size of raindrops, the greater will be the wind speed required to induce the angle of incidence of raindrops on a wall, otherwise the raindrops will fall vertically. A direct relationship, therefore, exists between the amount of rain which falls on a wall surface and the degree of exposure of the site. Clearly, buildings located on more exposed sites, such as those on elevated ground, are more vulnerable to penetrating dampness caused by driving rain.

2 Water-excluding Characteristics
The extent of rain penetration also depends on the water-excluding characteristics of the materials used for the element.

With the use of permeable materials in walls, for example, there is a higher risk of rain penetration. However, this risk can be reduced (see figure 14.3) by the application of one of two principles in the construction, namely:

- Controlled penetration, allowing the penetration of water to a certain depth of the wall which is sufficiently thick so as not to cause any serious problems.
- Breaking the capillary paths that attract moisture movement as in the case of cavity wall construction.

The use of impermeable materials at the exposed surface of an element, on the other hand, enhances greater water run-off on these surfaces and hence reduces the likelihood of rain penetration. However, greater demands are imposed on the design of joints to ensure complete resistance to rain penetration. In the case of flat roof construction, the horizontal impermeable membrane covering results in a slower water run-off, making the design and construction of movement joints critical.

3 Modes of Transmission
There are three main modes of water transmission through an element as a whole which can affect the amount of rainwater penetrating into the building (see figure 14.4). The upward rise of water is entirely by capillarity through the pores of porous materials or along fine cracks at the interface of units of components.

The lateral penetration of water takes place through the combined action of capillarity and wind pressure. The effects of wind pressure are increased as the pressure differences between two sides of an exposed layer are raised.

The last mode of transmission is downward penetration caused almost entirely by gravity.

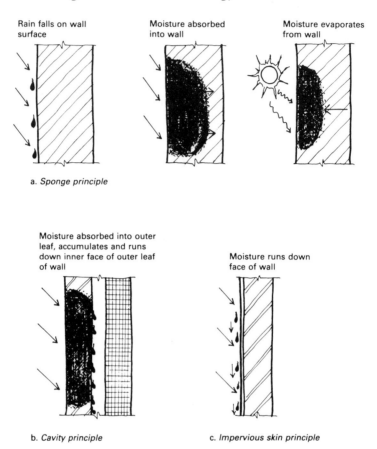

a. *Sponge principle*

b. *Cavity principle*   c. *Impervious skin principle*

Figure 14.3   Methods of water exclusion

14.2.4 Rain Penetration Through Cavity Walls

If constructed properly, the cavity wall is most effective in the prevention of rainwater penetration. Although the outer leaf of the walls may suffer a high degree of water penetration, the cavity can prevent rainwater going into the inner leaf. Many problems can occur, unfortunately, in practice (see figure 14.5).

Any mortar which inevitably falls on the wall ties and cavity trays must be removed. If this is not done, damp patches are likely to occur sporadically.

Ties should not be fixed with a slope from the outer to the inner leaf. It is also possible that ties are not properly bedded laterally so that the drip is not positioned centrally in the cavity, but touching the inner

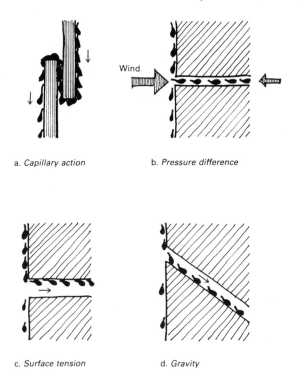

a. *Capillary action*   b. *Pressure difference*

c. *Surface tension*   d. *Gravity*

Figure 14.4   Forces acting to move water through an opening

leaf. These faults will permit water to reach the interior face of the inner leaf.

If metal wall ties are not galvanised, corrosion will most certainly take place in the external leaf. The consequent expansion from corrosion can cause horizontal cracking along brickwork courses around the ties.

Many failures that cause rain penetration can also occur at the junctions between the reinforced concrete frame and the cavity walls. This problem is often caused by the omission of stop-ends and in-adequate lapping or sealing of lengths of cavity trays; and the failure to bring the damp-proof course to the beam and wall face.

Water penetrating along the external leaf and collecting above a damp-proof course at the base of the wall, or above a cavity tray, needs to be removed (see figure 14.6). Weepholes are provided by omitting the mortar in some of the perpend joints between bricks. If these weepholes are not provided, considerable amounts can collect to cause dampness penetration. Sometimes, weepholes are provided but are rendered ineffective because of blockage by mortar droppings and other debris.

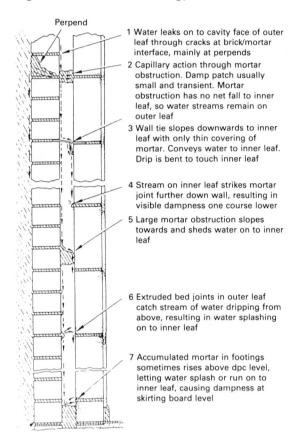

Perpend

1 Water leaks on to cavity face of outer leaf through cracks at brick/mortar interface, mainly at perpends

2 Capillary action through mortar obstruction. Damp patch usually small and transient. Mortar obstruction has no net fall to inner leaf, so water streams remain on outer leaf

3 Wall tie slopes downwards to inner leaf with only thin covering of mortar. Conveys water to inner leaf. Drip is bent to touch inner leaf

4 Stream on inner leaf strikes mortar joint further down wall, resulting in visible dampness one course lower

5 Large mortar obstruction slopes towards and sheds water on to inner leaf

6 Extruded bed joints in outer leaf catch stream of water dripping from above, resulting in water splashing on to inner leaf

7 Accumulated mortar in footings sometimes rises above dpc level, letting water splash or run on to inner leaf, causing dampness at skirting board level

Figure 14.5   Routes for water penetration across an unfilled cavity (Source: Property Services Agency, *Defects in Buildings*, HMSO, London, 1989)

14.2.5 Correction of Faults in Cavity Walls

A useful preliminary test is to wet artificially the outer leaf with a hose and to open the cavity at a point from which it is possible to observe water crossing. If the route for penetration can be identified, it may be possible to take corrective action by removing bricks in the affected area. Also, it is sometimes possible to use a metal detector to determine the position of wall ties. If a tie coincides with a damp patch, it may be worth removing a brick from the outer leaf and inspecting the tie.

If the main cause of the problem is blocking up of weepholes by

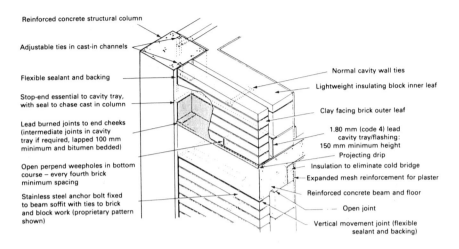

Reinforced concrete structural column

Adjustable ties in cast-in channels

Flexible sealant and backing

Stop-end essential to cavity tray, with seal to chase cast in column

Lead burned joints to end cheeks (intermediate joints in cavity tray if required, lapped 100 mm minimum and bitumen bedded)

Open perpend weepholes in bottom course – every fourth brick minimum spacing

Stainless steel anchor bolt fixed to beam soffit with ties to brick and block work (proprietary pattern shown)

Normal cavity wall ties

Lightweight insulating block inner leaf

Clay facing brick outer leaf

1.80 mm (code 4) lead cavity tray/flashing: 150 mm minimum height

Projecting drip

Insulation to eliminate cold bridge

Expanded mesh reinforcement for plaster

Reinforced concrete beam and floor

Open joint

Vertical movement joint (flexible sealant and backing)

Figure 14.6   Detail recommended by PSA to deal with movement and damp penetration problems associated with brick infill to concrete frames (Source: Property Services Agency, *Defects in Buildings*, HMSO, London, 1989)

mortar droppings or the lack of a damp-proof course, the repair is more extensive and expensive. In the case of repair to some public housing in Singapore, the bottom two courses of brickwork are completely removed and the wall is temporarily supported by adjustable metal props spaced at convenient intervals. The cavity is then cleared; a groove is formed along the outer face of the inner leaf by raking out the mortar joints. The pre-formed cavity tray is then inserted, care being taken to ensure that it is held securely to the inner wall. The final step is to replace the two courses of brickwork, making sure that weepholes are adequately provided (see figure 14.7).

14.2.6 Other Remedial Measures

If the dampness is widespread with many points of entry, then it is probably better to take additional measures to improve the weather resistance of the outer leaf using any one of the following methods:

1 Repointing
If the existing mortar is deteriorating and eroding, then repointing is most likely to be effective. It can be an expensive measure since it may be necessary to chase out existing joints. Raked joints are sometimes associated with penetration problems in exposed walls. These joints

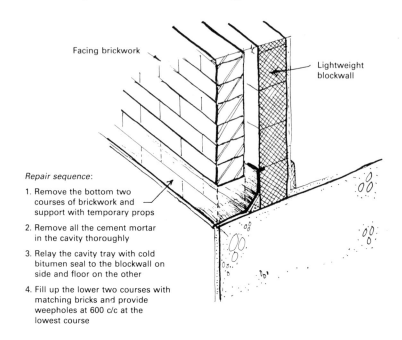

Facing brickwork

Lightweight
blockwall

Repair sequence:

1. Remove the bottom two
courses of brickwork and
support with temporary props

2. Remove all the cement mortar
in the cavity thoroughly

3. Relay the cavity tray with cold
bitumen seal to the blockwall on
side and floor on the other

4. Fill up the lower two courses with
matching bricks and provide
weepholes at 600 c/c at the
lowest course

Figure 14.7   Procedure to rectify water penetration in a cavity wall

can be filled to the front surface of the wall and perhaps finished with a
weather-struck joint. It may also be necessary to re-point before applying water repellents, sealants or paints.

2 Water Repellents
Colourless waterproofing solutions based on 5 per cent silicone or
aqueous siliconates can be used on porous walls. These solutions are
generally cheap and they do not greatly affect the appearance of the
wall.

The main effect of water repellents is to reduce rainwater absorption
and, while reducing the rate of water evaporation off the treated wall
as well, their application improves the overall situation, provided that
the wall does not contain cracks exceeding 0.15 mm in width.

For porous walls, much of the solution will be absorbed by the bricks
at the expense of the brick/mortar interface cracks. Therefore, it is an
advantage to wet the wall before treatment and to brush additional
solution over the mortar joints.

Some treatments may lead to superficial staining when they are
applied to wet materials. It is advisable, therefore, to carry out a trial on
a small area of wall before proceeding any further.

3 Sealants

There are a number of sealants available, most of them being based on acrylic polymers. They are more visible than water repellents since they form a film on the surface which can give it a glazed appearance. These treatments are much less widely used than colourless water repellents.

Sealants act by blocking the pores of the bricks and so will inhibit the movement of water vapour through the surface. Water repellents do not block the pores and so allow the external leaf to breathe, a property which is seen as an advantage.

4 Masonry Paints

There is a wide range of paint types available for masonry which will seal the surface in much the same way as colourless acrylics but will usually be able to bridge the cracks more effectively by filling them. Examples include cement paints and other emulsified formulations incorporating acrylic resins, bitumens, PVA or styrenes.

These paints provide relatively porous coatings so that, while rainwater penetration may be reduced, evaporation of water vapour and drying out can continue, although at a reduced rate. But, because they are opaque, unfilled cracks can be very conspicuous. Another disadvantage is that the paint may not be aesthetically acceptable because of the change in colour of the wall. Paints are also generally more expensive than water repellents.

5 Rendering

A rendering coat will cover up fine cracks and vulnerable areas and normally rainwater will not penetrate to cracks in underlying masonry. However, if the render becomes cracked from drying shrinkage, for example, rainwater is easily admitted. In this case, the hard rendering coat would retard the evaporation of the trapped water and dampness could penetrate through the wall.

Rainwater penetrating behind the render, especially if the render is dense and impermeable, may cause loss of adhesion, further cracking and subsequent disintegration by other factors of deterioration. For this reason, rough rendered surfaces are preferred because rain falling on a smooth surface with little absorption tends to fall unevenly in streaks. A rough surface will break up the flow and avoid such concentrations of water flow; is more damp resistant; and is less likely to craze.

6 Cladding

A cladding in the form of slates or tiles hung vertically on the wall can provide a useful protection against penetrating dampness. The tiles, with moisture-resisting backing such as felt, should be fitted to preservative-treated battens using suitably protected nails.

In certain countries, weatherboarding is used. The materials for weatherboarding include selected timber as well as plastics. Cladding as a remedy against penetrating dampness is expensive and may also present problems of detailing.

14.3 Condensation

14.3.1 Mechanism of Condensation

Air is said to be saturated when it holds the maximum amount of moisture that it can contain at that temperature. When air which is not saturated is cooled, it reaches a temperature called the dew point at which it can be saturated. Any further cooling of the air below the dew point will result in the precipitation of liquid water as condensation.

There are, therefore, two principal ways whereby condensation can occur: by increasing the amount of water vapour in the air at a constant temperature until saturation is reached, and by cooling air containing a constant amount of water vapour until, at dew-point temperature, it becomes saturated.

In tropical climates like that experienced in Singapore, materials seldom attain a low enough temperature to get below the dew point. When this condition does happen, it is often due to cold temperatures being created within an air-conditioned building, with resulting condensation appearing on the outside of the building enclosure. In temperate climates, however, hot and cold air temperatures are reversed and the problem of condensation inside a building becomes more serious.

14.3.2 Surface and Interstitial Condensation

There are two forms of condensation, namely surface and interstitial. The former type occurs on visible surfaces when the inner surface of the structure is cooler than room air. It occurs mainly in kitchens, toilets and bathrooms which are subject to periods of high temperatures and high humidities. Because these periods are relatively short, they do not normally raise the average surface temperatures so that condensation tends to occur on walls as well as on cold water supply pipes and certain parts of windows (see figure 14.8).

In temperate climates there is a tendency for the interior temperature to be higher than the exterior. The higher vapour pressure developed in the warm interior can drive water vapour through porous materials towards the colder exterior which then condenses when it

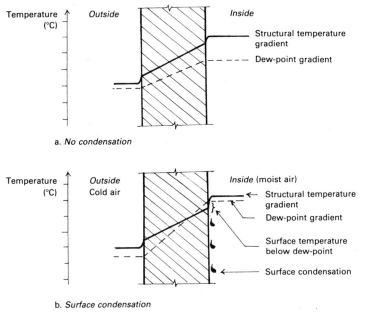

a. *No condensation*

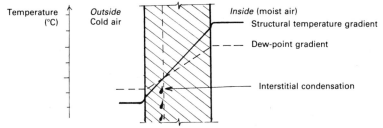

b. *Surface condensation*

c. *Interstitial condensation*

Figure 14.8 Temperature profile and its effect on condensation

reaches suitable conditions. This form of condensation occurring in a permeable structure is known as interstitial condensation.

14.3.3 Effect of Condensation

One of the inevitable consequences of condensation is the formation of growths of fungi and bacteria. These growths flourish on surfaces in buildings once the humidity rises above 70 per cent relative humidity. The fungal hyphae will then grow on the damp surfaces and produce and liberate spores which are responsible for the characteristic black, green and white colours.

Proprietary fungicidal washes can be used on surfaces where persistent mould growth occurs. If decorative finishes are badly affected or damaged, they are best removed first.

14.3.4 Controlling Condensation

Various measures are available to reduce the problem of condensation in buildings, including ventilation, structural insulation, use of moisture vapour barriers and heating.

1 Ventilation
In all cases of condensation, it is important that there is adequate ventilation to remove the humid air out of the building. The best way is to use an extractor fan in the humid room such as the kitchen or bathroom. Some extractors are controlled by sensors which operate only when the humidity levels rise.

Another measure entails the installation of a thermostatically controlled blower in the roof space where it draws in air already slightly heated by solar radiation. The air movement is sufficient to remove the vapour-laden air and control condensation.

2 Insulation
Under normal circumstances, the envelope of a building is required to act as an insulating medium to protect the occupants from the cold, in addition to its other functions. The main aims of insulation are, therefore, to keep surface temperatures above dew point, improve the thermal transmittance or *U*-values, reduce heating costs and ultimately enhance comfort for the occupants.

The various methods of providing insulation to arrest the problem of condensation include:

- Providing cavity wall insulation with such materials as expanded polystyrene, polyurethane foam, mineral fibres or glass fibres.
- Improving the insulation of walls and partitions internally by dry-lining techniques with the use of a special composition of plasterboards and an insulant such as expanded polystyrene or polyurethane.
- Installing double-glazing to windows and incorporating an effective air gap between the glazing units.

3 Moisture Vapour Barriers
The risk of condensation in or on the enclosing elements of a building depends on the vapour and thermal resistance of these elements. If insulation is to be used in the construction, it will inevitably result in an increase in the humidity so long as vapour-laden air can penetrate through the structural element beyond the insulation. One method of

controlling this problem is to restrict the diffusion of vapour-laden air into the structure by the use of vapour barriers.

For example, in cool climates, humidity in the roof space may produce condensation under the impermeable roof covering in a flat roof construction. For this reason, it is essential that moisture barriers should be positioned at or close to the warm side, with substantial insulation provided between the vapour barrier and the cool surface.

4 Heating and Dehumidification

Heating as a means of controlling condensation is the most effective but also the most expensive in terms of running costs. The principle is to improve conditions by increasing air and surface temperatures and by reducing relative humidity.

In a dehumidifier, humid air is passed over a cold coil which causes condensation on to its surface. The condensate is then collected and discharged to the outside. The dehumidified air is then allowed to pass over a warm coil where it will be heated up. Like other heating systems, dehumidifiers are expensive to operate.

14.4 Other Sources of Dampness

14.4.1 Entrapped Moisture During Construction

In structures which are constructed *in situ*, as opposed to being of precast or prefabricated construction, the water content can represent a high proportion of the weight of materials. If sufficient time is not provided to permit this water to dry out, particularly when there is a need to speed up the construction process, dampness may take place in the structure. The retention of moisture within the thickness of a construction may cause:

- A reduction in thermal insulation.
- Decay and deterioration of organic and moisture-sensitive materials such as timber, metals and their products.
- Blistering and tearing of roofing membranes.

14.4.2 Faulty Plumbing and Rainwater Discharge Systems

Plumbing systems in a building need attention to make sure that joints are tight and all metallic fittings are protected against corrosion by regular preventive maintenance. Internal damp conditions may be accelerated with faulty plumbing systems which are concealed in walls and floors.

Gutters and downpipes used to discharge rainwater from the roof of a building must be correctly designed to prevent overflowing. Metallic parts may be affected by corrosion arising from atmospheric pollution or by contaminated water. Regular maintenance to clear any blockage by fallen leaves and other debris is also vital.

14.4.3 Moisture from Occupation of Buildings

Such sources of moisture come from cleaning, washing, and cooling activities inside the building. Floors should be designed to slope towards gullies in kitchens, bathrooms, toilets and laboratories. In these cases, the floor finishes should be resistant to constant wetting. Any leak occurring through defective floors and drains can cause internal dampness in the structure below. See table 14.1.

Table 14.1   Typical moisture production within a five-person dwelling (Source: British Standards Institution, *BS 5250: 1989 Code of Practice for control of condensation in buildings*)

Regular daily emission sources	Moisture emission per day/kg or litre
Five persons asleep for 8 h	1.5
Two persons active for 16 h	1.7
Cooking	3.0
Bathing, dish washing, etc.	1.0
Total, regular sources	7.2
Additional sources	
Washing clothes	0.5
Drying clothes	5.0
Paraffin heater (if used)	1.7
Total, additional sources	7.2
Combined total	14.4

Note 1. The table does not include moisture introduced or removed by ventilation.

Note 2. The high moisture input from clothes drying shows the importance of designing for its control.

Note 3. The considerable emission during cooking, which is of short duration, indicates a need for local control.

Note 4. The water vapour emitted by flueless oil stoves significantly increases condensation risk. (Flueless gas appliances also produce a considerable quantity of water vapour.)

14.5 Diagnosis of Dampness

14.5.1 Inspection

Dampness is a natural condition in the environment. Diagnostic methods are devised (see table 14.2) to detect the presence of excessive damp so that appropriate remedial measures can be taken in time.

The initial survey usually starts with a visual inspection of the external conditions. This inspection will reveal obvious symptoms of dampness which will assist the surveyor when the internal inspection is carried out subsequently. Brief site notes and sketches will also serve as useful reminders (see figure 14.9).

For the normal survey for dampness, the surveyor will need certain items of equipment such as a torchlight, mirror, crowbar, moisture meter, measuring tape, ladder and timber probe. For a more detailed survey, other items such as a metal detector, camera, binoculars, hygrometer, boroscope and carbide meter are included.

14.5.2 Moisture Meters

Moisture meters are commonly used to detect the presence of dampness. They rely on the measurement of electrical resistance between two prongs pressed into the material. The higher the amount of current passing through the meter, the lower will be the level of resistance because water is a good conductor of electricity.

Electronic moisture meters are popular because they are small and light in weight, easy to use and do not cause any visible damage to the materials and finishes. However, because of the widely differing conductivities of various salts in building materials, these instruments have limited applications for quantitative measurements. For example, readings registered by the meter on walls decorated with aluminium foil-backed plasterboard can be exceptionally high and have nothing to do with dampness.

14.5.3 Carbide Meters

In this method, a sample of masonry is first obtained by drilling the wall, mortar or plaster. The sample is weighed and then made to react with some calcium carbide in a special pressure vessel. The resulting gas pressure generated can be measured on a dial gauge. The quantity of gas produced is directly proportional to the moisture content of the sample collected.

Although carbide meters can measure the actual moisture content of a sample, they do not directly indicate whether the source of the

a. *External survey*

b. *Internal survey*

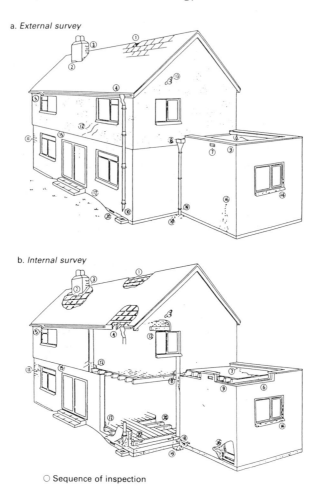

○ Sequence of inspection

Figure 14.9   House inspection for dampness: inspection procedures
(Source: *House Inspection for Dampness: a First Step
to Remedial Treatment for Wood Rot*, Information
Paper IP 19/88, Building Research Establishment, UK,
1988)

moisture is capillary or hygroscopic. To determine this, it is necessary
to divide the sample into two equal portions. With the first portion, the
total moisture content can be obtained in the usual way from the dial
gauge reading. The second portion is placed in a container maintained
at 75 per cent relative humidity for about 2 days and then tested in the
meter to obtain the hygroscopic moisture content at 75 per cent relative humidity. The difference in the two readings is the capillary moisture content of the sample.

347

Table 14.2 *Diagnosis of dampness problems* (Source: Oxley, T. A. and Gobert, E. G., *Dampness in Buildings*, Butterworths, London, 1983)

Evidence	Condensation	Rising damp	Penetrating damp
Moisture readings at the margin (especially the upper margin) of the damp areas	*Gradual* change from wet to dry	*Sharp* change from wet to dry	Usually a *sharp* change from wet to dry
Moisture readings in skirting and floor in direct contact with wall	*Low* readings	*High* readings	*High* reading in lower part of wall affected
Are there many mouldy patches?	Yes. They may be relatively dry at the time of survey	Very rarely	Sometimes
Is mouldiness especially noticeable behind pictures and furniture or in corners or enclosed spaces?	Yes	No	No
Soil salts, including nitrate, in wallpaper or in a scraping from the wall surface	Absent	Present[a]	Absent
Moisture readings taken at various depths in the wall using deep wall probes	High at the surface, lower at depth[b]	High all through	Generally high all through. Higher towards the source and often lower towards wall surface

continued on p. 348

Table 14.2 continued

Evidence	Condensation	Rising damp	Penetrating damp
Sources of water vapour[c] additional to those normally met (e.g. flueless gas or oil heaters, much drying of laundry) are present	Probably one or more of these is present	These are not affected by water vapour sources, but may themselves act as a source, aggravating condensation	

[a] Rising damp may not produce a typical salts deposit if it is derived from residual water of construction in a concrete floor slab.

[b] Dampness in the thickness of a wall may be due to interstitial condensation, but in this event the inner surface of the wall is usually dry.

[c] Further evidence that dampness is due to condensation is available if it is shown that the damp areas are likely, at times, to be colder than dew-point measured during the survey. Due allowance must be made for the possibility that conditions are somewhat different at times when survey is impossible, for example, when a space is occupied and warmed only for a few hours each day.

14.5.4 Oven-drying Method

The most accurate method of determining the moisture content of the material is to take a sample, weigh it, dry it to constant weight in an oven at a suitable temperature (about 100°C) and then re-weigh. The dampness is expressed by the loss in weight by drying as a percentage of the oven-dry weight of the sample under test. Like the carbide meter, this method needs to be modified to find out both components of the dampness reading.

Related and Further Reading

Addleson, L. *Building Failures*. Architectural Press, London (1989).

Atkinson, G. *Avoiding Problems due to Difficult Sites and Minimising Dampness*. Building Technical File No. 31 (October, 1990).

British Standards Institution. *CP 102: 1973 Code of Practice for protection of buildings against water from the ground*.

British Standards Institution. *BS 6477: 1984 Specification for water repellents for masonry surfaces*.

British Standards Institution. *BS 5617: 1985 Specification for urea–formaldehyde (UF) foam systems suitable for thermal insulation of cavity walls with masonry or concrete inner and outer leaves*.

British Standards Institution. *BS 5618: 1985 Code of Practice for thermal insulation of cavity walls (with masonry or concrete inner and outer leaves) by filling with urea–formaldehyde (UF) foam systems*.

British Standards Institution. *BS 6576: 1985 Code of Practice for installation of chemical damp-proof courses*.

British Standards Institution. *BS 4255: Part 1: 1986 Rubber used in preformed gaskets for weather exclusion from buildings: specification for non-cellular gaskets*.

British Standards Institution. *BS 5250: 1989 Code of Practice for control of condensation in buildings*.

British Standards Institution. *BS 6375: Part 1: 1989 Performance of windows: Part 1 Classification for weathertightness*.

Building Research Advisory Service, UK. *Condensation: Causes and Cure*. Building Technical File No. 12 (January, 1986).

Building Research Establishment, UK. *Damp-proofing Solid Floors*. Digest 54 (1971).

Building Research Establishment, UK. *Damp-proof Courses*. Digest 77 (1971).

Building Research Establishment, UK. *Condensation*. Digest 110 (1972).

Building Research Establishment, UK. *Chemical Damp Proofing Courses for Walls*. Technical Information Leaflet 36 (1972).

Building Research Establishment, UK. *Corrosion of Wall Ties in Cavity*

Brickwork. Technical Information Leaflet 22 (1974).

Building Research Establishment, UK. *Diagnosing Rising Damp.* Technical Information Leaflet 29 (1977).

Building Research Establishment, UK. *Built-in Cavity Insulation for Housing.* Digest 277 (1983).

Building Research Establishment, UK. *External Masonry Cavity Walls: Wall Ties – Selection and Specification.* Defect Action Sheet 19 (1983).

Building Research Establishment, UK. External Masonry Cavity Walls: Wall Ties – Insulation. Defect Action Sheet 20 (1983).

Building Research Establishment, UK. *External Masonry Cavity Walls: Wall Ties – Replacement.* Defect Action Sheet 21 (1983).

Building Research Establishment, UK. *Cavity Insulation.* Digest 236 (1984).

Building Research Establishment, UK. *Rising Damp in Walls: Diagnosis and Treatment.* Digest 245 (1986).

Building Research Establishment, UK. *External Masonry Walls: Eroding Mortar – Repoint or Rebuild.* Defect Action Sheet 70 (1986).

Building Research Establishment, UK. *External Masonry Walls: Repointing – Specification.* Defect Action Sheet 71 (1986).

Building Research Establishment, UK. *External Masonry Walls: Repointing.* Defect Action Sheet 72 (1986).

Building Research Establishment, UK. *Cavity External Walls: Cold Bridges around Windows and Doors.* Defect Action Sheet 77 (1986).

Building Research Establishment, UK. *External Masonry Walls: Partial Cavity Fill Insulation – Resisting Rain Penetration.* Defect Action Sheet 79 (1986).

Building Research Establishment, UK. *Brick Walls: Injected Damp-proof Courses.* Defect Action Sheet 85 (1986).

Building Research Establishment, UK. *Brick Walls: Replastering following Damp-proof Course Injection.* Defect Action Sheet 86 (1986).

Building Research Establishment, UK. *Cavity Parapets – Avoiding Rain Penetration.* Defect Action Sheet 106 (1987).

Building Research Establishment, UK. *Cavity Parapets – Installing of Copings, Damp-proof Courses, Trays and Flashings.* Defect Action Sheet 107 (1987).

Building Research Establishment, UK. *External Cavity Walls: Wall Ties – Selection and Specification.* Defect Action Sheet 115 (1988).

Building Research Establishment, UK. *External Cavity Walls: Wall Ties – Installation.* Defect Action Sheet 116 (1988).

Building Research Establishment, UK. *House Inspection for Dampness: a First Step to Remedial Treatment for Wood Rot.* Information Paper IP 19/88 (December, 1988).

Building Research Establishment, UK. *Solid External Walls: Internal*

Dry-lining – Preventing Summer Condensation. Defect Action Sheet 133 (1989).

Building Research Establishment, UK. *Surface Condensation and Mould Growth*. Digest 297 (1990).

Building Research Establishment, UK. *Installing Wall Ties in Existing Construction*. Digest 329 (1990).

Burberry, P. Condensation and how to avoid it. *AJ Energy File* (3 October, 1979).

Freeman, I. *DOE Construction No. 14, Building Failures*. Department of Environment, UK (1975).

Gratwick, R. T. *Dampness in Buildings*. Crosby Lockwood, London (1974).

Kyte, C. T. Laboratory analysis as an aid to the diagnosis of rising damp. *Chartered Institute of Building*, No. 35 (1984).

Marsh, P. *Air and Rain Penetration of Buildings*. Construction Press, London (1977).

Moore, J. F. A. *The Performance of Cavity Wall Ties*. Current Paper 3/81, Building Research Establishment, UK (1981).

Newman, A. J. *Rain Penetration through Masonry Walls: Diagnosis and Remedial Measures*. Report, Building Research Establishment, UK (1988).

Oliver, A. C. *Dampness in Buildings*. BSP Professional Books (1988).

Oxley, T. A. and Gobert, E. G. *Dampness in Buildings*. Butterworths, London (1983).

Pountney, M. T., Maxwell, R. and Butler, A. J. *Rain Penetration of Cavity Walls: Report of a Survey of Properties in England and Wales*. Information Paper IP 2/88, Building Research Establishment, UK (February, 1988).

Ragsdale, L. A. and Raynham, E. A. *Building Materials Technology*. Edward Arnold, London (1972).

Ransom, W. H. *Building Failures: Diagnosis and Avoidance*. Spon, London (1987).

Richardson, B. A. *Remedial Treatments of Buildings*. Construction Press, London (1980).

Roger, P. Chemical damp-proof courses under the microscope: most rising damp isn't. *Building Trades Journal*, No. 15 (1984).

Seeley, I. H. *Building Maintenance*, 2nd edn. Macmillan, London (1987).

Southern, J. R. *Summer Condensation on Vapour Checks, Tests with Battened, Internally Insulated, Solid Walls*. Information Paper 12/88, Building Research Establishment, UK (1988).

Vekey, R. C. de *Corrosion of Steel Wall Ties: Recognition, Assessment and Appropriate Action*. Information Paper 28/79, Building Research Establishment, UK (1979).

Vekey, R. C. de   *Performance Specifications for Wall Ties*. Information Paper 4/84, Building Research Establishment, UK (1984).
Vekey, R. C. de   *Ties for Cavity Walls: New Developments*. Information Paper 16/88, Building Research Establishment, UK (1988).

15 External Works

External works describe primarily the areas immediately surrounding the building, and provisions include minor roads in a housing estate, paved areas, boundary walls, railings, fencings and turfed areas. The main causes of failure related to external works include poor design, bad workmanship, soil settlement, chemical attack on materials, weathering elements, mechanical damage and vandalism.

15.1 Flexible Roads

Flexible road construction is so called because it allows a small amount of vertical movement of the road structure under load. A flexible road usually consists of four layers of road construction materials built up on the formation (see figure 15.1).

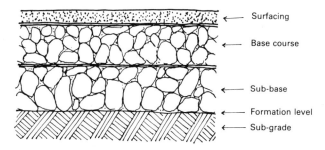

Figure 15.1 Components of a typical flexible road

15.1.1 Defects in Flexible Roads

Flexible roads are usually designed to take account of traffic growth. However, a road can only achieve its designed life period and carrying

353

capacity if the actual job of construction is properly done and all the materials are of required specification and correctly used.

Some of the common defects in flexible roads include the following:

1 Cracking

Cracking is caused essentially by movements which exceed those that the material can accommodate. In flexible roads laid on cement-bound bases, a pattern of well-spaced cracks frequently forms on the bituminous surfacing corresponding to cracks previously formed in the base. These cracks are difficult to cure permanently although surface sealing gives a temporary remedy.

Cracked surfaces allow water penetration which may lead to weakening of foundations. The penetration of water will also accelerate deterioration owing to the effect of frost and de-icing salts in temperate countries.

2 Crazing

Finer crazing may result when a bituminous surfacing is unable to absorb thermal movements. This may, in the first instance, be due to the use of bitumen or tar which has a low penetration rate. Another possible cause is the loss of fluxing oils by solar radiation.

Crazing is a surface defect and does not initially lead to water penetration. The problem may be temporarily alleviated by means of surface treatments. Deeper crazing, however, necessitates replacement of the material.

3 Deformation

Surface deformation in roads is the result of prolonged or severe mechanical stress. It is quite common in deceleration areas of roads such as near roundabouts, traffic junctions or bus stops.

The main cause is due to the use of either too much binder, too soft a binder or incorrect aggregate grading. In most cases, the defect leads to corrugations on the surface. The corrugations then exacerbate the problem as upward-sloping sections of each undulation become subject to higher stresses under a given vehicle load. To effect a cure it is necessary to replace the surfacing with one that is designed to have extra stiffness.

A more serious form of deformation may occur in which the roadbase is also affected. This is caused by structural failure of the pavement as a whole and results in large depressions in the road surface. In such situations, the surfacing and roadbase must be removed and replaced to an uprated specification.

4 Embedment
Embedment refers to the sinking of chippings into the binder and, in some cases, the underlying material. The cause of embedment is possibly the excessive use of binder or the presence of a soft substrate. Where this defect occurs, a further surface dressing can be applied with relatively low binder content, together with increased chipping size.

5 Bleeding
Bleeding of asphalt surfaces may be caused by using asphalt which is too soft. It may also be caused by consolidation of the surface. Bleeding can pose a danger to motorists in that it can cause skidding problems.

6 Groundwater
Pavement distress can result from adverse groundwater conditions. Waterlogged ground, for example, allows excessive movement of the structure and leads to premature damage and destruction. The remedy requires removal of the water near its source by providing adequate drainage.

15.1.2 Patch Repair of Flexible Roads

Generally, patching covers the repair of separate randomised areas like potholes, but not the replacement of continuous lengths of the pavement covering the whole width or partial width of the road.

There is a wide range of bituminously bound aggregates suitable for patching purposes, including cold, warm and hot-laid materials such as cold asphalt, tarmacadam/bitumen macadam and hot-rolled asphalt.

The recommended procedure for patching flexible roads comprises the following steps:

1 Preparation
Defective areas of surfacing should be broken up to the limits marked out with straight lines to form rectangular patches. The cavity and the surrounding area should then be cleaned after excavating and removing the loose material.

2 Cavity Treatment
The cavity should be tack coated on the base and sides with cold emulsion if cold or warm-laid materials are to be used, or with filled bitumen to the sides and cold emulsion to the base if hot-laid materials are to be used.

3 Base Course
The cavity should be filled with a suitable material and then compacted. The operation should be repeated until the compacted material is at the level of the top of the base course.

4 Wearing Course
The cavity above the base course level should be filled and compacted so that the material is level with the surrounding pavement.

5 Sealing
Sealing should be applied to all open-textured materials as soon as possible after completion of the patching.

6 Surface Treatment
This consists of dry or coated chippings to hot and cold asphalts.

7 Pavement Cleaning
Any loose and/or waste materials should be brushed aside and collected for disposal.

15.2 Rigid Roads

A rigid road does not deflect within itself under traffic. Concrete is usually used for the construction of a rigid road. The main structure of the pavement is a concrete slab (wearing surface), base course and road base combined (see figure 15.2).

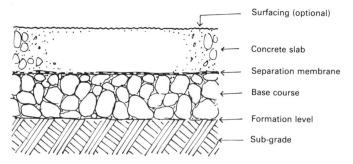

Figure 15.2 Components of a typical rigid road

15.2.1 Defects in Concrete Roads

Defects in concrete roads can be due to two basic causes. The first is deterioration of the pavement itself brought about by freezing and thawing, alkali–aggregate reaction, scaling and the use of poor-quality materials. The other cause affects the structural adequacy of the structure evidenced by unevenness, cracks, faulty joints and other symptoms.

1 Structural Cracks

Structural defects usually manifest themselves mainly in the form of cracks in the slab. The main types of cracks are:

- Transverse cracks caused by excessive bay length, dowel bar restraint or inadequate reinforcement.
- Longitudinal cracks caused by excessively wide bays being cast, omission of bottom crack inducer at longitudinal joint, compression failure or settlement.
- Diagonal cracks caused by settlement or heave of the sub-base or subgrade.

Narrow cracks in reinforced slabs do not require immediate action but can be remedied by sealing. Wide cracks can be remedied either by full depth repair of the slab or by means of replacement of the defective concrete bay (see figure 15.3).

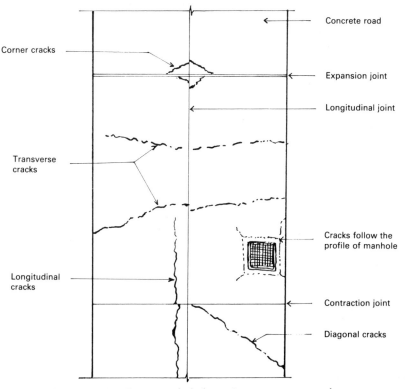

Figure 15.3 Structural defects in concrete roads

2 Shrinkage Cracks

These cracks usually occur within the first few hours after the slab has been constructed. The cracks are typically short and oblique in direction and are comparatively shallow at the initial stage. They occur because of volume changes which take place at the surface following rapid evaporation of the water.

The remedies include surface sealing with either a low viscosity resin or a latex emulsion; or full depth repair; or demolition and replacement if the problem is very serious.

3 Surface Scaling

The most common cause of scaling is frost attack, the likelihood of which is increased when deicing salts or chemicals are used. Other causes include the use of mixes which are too wet and dirty aggregates containing silt or clay. To increase the resistance of concrete to this type of damage it should have a sufficiently large quantity of cement, low water: cement ratio and be air-entrained.

The remedy consists of a thin bonded surface repair method using either cementitious mortar or fine concrete (see figure 15.4).

4 Inadequate Skidding Resistance

The skidding resistance of a concrete road depends on the type and depth of the surface texture, and the resistance of the aggregates in the

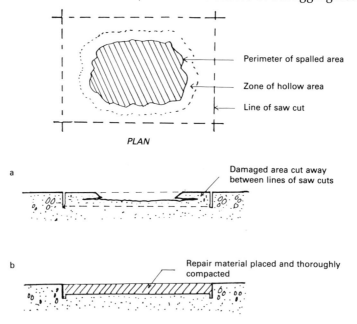

PLAN

— Perimeter of spalled area

— Zone of hollow area

— Line of saw cut

a   Damaged area cut away between lines of saw cuts

b   Repair material placed and thoroughly compacted

Figure 15.4   Thin bonded surface repair procedure of surface scaling

road surface to polishing and abrasion. The reduction of skidding resistance to undesirably low values results from the loss of surface texture and polishing that is caused by the action of traffic on the surface.

The skidding resistance of worn surfaces can be restored by grooving or mechanically roughening the existing surfaces or by the application of a surface dressing consisting of an epoxide resin-based binder and calcined bauxite chippings.

5 Spalling Around Joints

Any spalling on the road will allow water and detritus to enter the joint which in turn will lead to further deterioration.

The main causes of shallow spalling are the presence of weak concrete in the arrises, the infiltration of incompressible detritus into the joint grooves and mechanical damage to the edge of the slab.

Deep spalling at joints usually extends at least down to the centre of the slab and may go deeper. This defect is caused by dowel bar misalignment; excessive bond along the free ends of the bars; and ingress of solids into the joint cracks.

Shallow spalling around arrises can be rectified by means of a thin bonded repair method (see figure 15.5).

6 Faulty Joint Seals

It is essential that joint seals are maintained well so that silt, grit, stones and water are prevented from entering the joints. The accumulation of detritus in the joint will impair its free movement and this may result in spalling at the joints and compression failures.

The main materials for joint seals include hot applied bitumen, cold applied polysulphide, polyurethane or silicone, and compression seals such as polychlorophene and neoprene. Sealants tend to harden and become brittle with age. They need to be replaced regularly.

The main causes of joint failure include:

- Inadequate preparation of the sealing grooves, including failure to use a suitable primer, failure to scour the sides of the grooves to form a good key, and failure to clean the grooves.
- Groove dimensions are not sufficient to allow for movements expected at the joints.
- Overfilling of grooves leading to damage caused by traffic.
- Poor workmanship, for example, remelting the sealing material or allowing the material to overflow on to the slab.

The remedy involves removing the old sealant, thoroughly cleaning out, preparing groove to receive new sealant and finally resealing with suitable material.

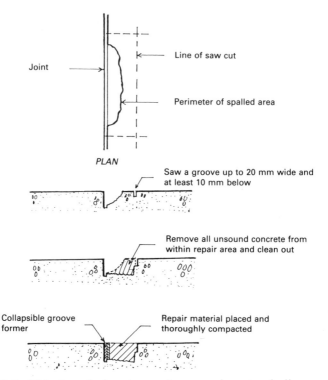

PLAN

Joint

Line of saw cut

Perimeter of spalled area

Saw a groove up to 20 mm wide and at least 10 mm below

Remove all unsound concrete from within repair area and clean out

Collapsible groove former

Repair material placed and thoroughly compacted

Figure 15.5   Thin bonded arris repair procedure to shallow spalling at joints

15.3 Paving Slabs

The range of precast concrete slabs or flags is very wide; they are available in many sizes and shapes to add attraction to the external areas. The flags should be laid broken-jointed on a well-compacted granular bed and bedded on lime–sand mortar. The falls on the footways should be a minimum of 1 in 24 towards the kerb. After laying, the joints can either be grouted with a cement sand mortar or left open.

The main faults occurring in the use of flags for footpaths include:

- Vertical misalignment of flags which may cause pedestrians to trip over.
- Cracking, often as a result of settlement of bed or subgrade.
- Uneven bedding, causing the flags to 'rock'.
- Mechanical damage from vehicular traffic and other sources.
- Damage caused by tree roots.

Damaged or broken flags should be broken up and replaced with new ones as soon as possible after dealing with the cause of damage. For example, the base and subgrade should be examined and remedied before relaying the flags.

15.4 Fences and Gates

Fences are fabricated principally from timber or steel to serve as boundaries or demarcation between different properties. Gates are usually made from similar materials to match the fencing used.

The main problems encountered with fences and gates include:

- Rotting of timber, particularly at the base of posts in contact with groundwater.
- Weathering of timber members, leading to warping and distortion of slats, boards, rails and posts.
- Loosening of joinery.
- Corrosion of chain-link fencing components, including steel posts, braces and barb-wires.
- Corrosion of metal gates and ironmongery.
- Sagging of gates, resulting in difficulty in opening and closing.
- Flaking of paintwork.

Regular maintenance of the fences and gates is important, especially when these components are constantly subject to the detrimental effects of weathering. For example, metallic parts should be periodically lubricated or painted to slow down the process of corrosion.

15.5 Boundary Walls

Boundary walls require an adequate foundation, damp-proof course, a coping and careful bonding in order to perform well.

The common defects found in brick boundary walls include:

- Loose or split copings.
- Efflorescence of brickwork caused by hygroscopic and soluble salts.
- Sulphate attack on mortar joints.
- Settlement of subgrade or foundation, giving rise to cracking of the wall.
- Cracking along long lengths of a wall due to failure to provide expansion joints.

The repair work necessary to rectify the above defects is similar to that generally used for other brickwork.

15.6 Drainage

Surface water on roads and paved areas is directed towards drainage channels or gullies. The water collected is then discharged into the main drainage system.

As a general rule, all paved surfaces over 6 m² should be drained and given a minimum fall of 1 in 60. This will help to discharge the water quickly and effectively, and avoid the formation of puddles.

The main problems with external drainage systems include:

• Blockage of gullies and surface drains by deposits of fallen leaves or silt as well as rubbish.
• Damage of drains by the penetration of tree roots.
• Cracking of drains caused by loss of support due to settlement of soil.
• Missing gully covers as a result of theft.

Regular maintenance is vital to minimise the problems. For example, inspection chambers and manholes should be periodically inspected and drains cleared regularly. Metal covers to manholes may rust and require repainting.

15.7 Trees and Turfed Areas

Trees, turfing and landscaped areas must be regularly maintained for better appearance and also to avoid potential hazards.

The conflict between trees and buildings can take many forms. In extreme cases, the trunk or branches may break and cause direct physical damage to properties but, more commonly, there can be complaints of obstruction of light, blockage of gutters from fallen leaves or unsightly secretion from the trees. Trees can also damage overhead telephone or power lines and even interfere with television reception.

In addition, tree roots can block drains, and damage paths and pavings, walls and buildings by their growth. The effects of tree roots in shrinkable clay soils also lead to structural damage to buildings.

The scope of lawn maintenance usually covers the following:

1 Weeding
Weeds interfere with plant growth and also mar the landscape. Any fertiliser or water applied around the plant will be first taken up by the fast-growing weeds, thus depriving the plants of nutrients.

When carrying out weeding, the weeds must be removed together with the roots. This is to ensure that new weeds will not grow from the roots left behind.

2 Soil Loosening

The soil must be in a friable and loose condition for the roots to spread in search of nutrients and water, and at the same time allow water, air and nutrients to penetrate the soil to reach the active roots. Loose soils will facilitate the escape of damaging carbon dioxide produced by root respiration. They will also allow excess water to be drained away, otherwise the soil will become waterlogged.

In soil-loosening, only the top layer of the soil should be loosened and turned over. This can be done with a hand fork.

3 Fertilising

After weeding and before soil-loosening is carried out, the required amount of fertiliser is applied, the soil loosened and then turned over. The soil should then be watered gently to allow the fertiliser to dissolve and penetrate into the lower depths of the soil to reach the roots.

The fertiliser should be applied a little at a time but at frequent intervals. The best procedure is probably to apply rock phosphate once a year and at other times to use ammonium sulphate in dilute solution.

4 Liming

Liming is usually carried out for turfed areas to raise the pH value of the soil to about 5.5 so that microbial activity is increased. Overliming will cause the soil to become too alkaline and this condition is often detrimental to most plants.

5 Watering

Water is one of the requirements for vigorous growth of plants as well as being one of the raw materials for photosynthesis. Watering is usually restricted to certain periods of the year where there is no rainfall.

The best method of watering is to have a hose and an automatic sprinkler that distributes a spray over a considerable area to give the soil a good soaking.

6 Pruning

Trees have to be pruned to give better air circulation and promote new growth.

Pruning is done with special tools such as chain saws, pruning knives and tree loppers. Cuts are usually made just above a node and should be done at an angle so that water will not collect on the cut surface. In all cases of pruning, cuts above 25 mm diameter should be painted over with a wound-sealant compound to reduce infection.

7 Pesticides and Fungicides

In order to maintain plants in good health, it is necessary, among other things, to ensure that pests and disease-causing agents are controlled. One of the ways of keeping diseases and pests in check is by means of chemicals specifically manufactured for this purpose.

Preventive control is to treat the plants with chemicals even before there are any signs of pest infestation or diseases. Curative control, on the other hand, is to spray the chemicals after the pests or diseases have been detected.

15.8 Pest Control

Most property owners employ a professional pest control specialist on a contract basis to keep their premises free of household pests. The criteria for the selection of the specialist include his experience, trade association and affiliation, and recommendation from known customers.

Common pests that need to be controlled include:

1 Ants

Ants usually nest in the soil or in masonry or woodwork of buildings. They are irritating and many inflict painful bites.

Preventive measures usually rely on the use of a chemical called chlordane.

2 Cockroaches

Cockroaches feed upon a wide variety of foodstuff and are known to carry diseases. Pesticides can be sprayed into cracks and other infested areas to control them.

3 Mosquitoes

Mosquitoes lay their eggs in water where they hatch into larvae and live until they change into adult mosquitoes. These pests hide and breed in lawns and bushes and cause many diseases such as malaria and yellow fever.

Control measures should be directed at the larvae rather than at the adult mosquitoes.

4 Rats

Good sanitation and proper handling of food and garbage are essential for controlling rats. Locations where rats may enter into buildings should be blocked with light metal mesh. All openings around piping and conduits should be closed. In addition, poisons such as 'warfarin' and zinc phosphide may be used.

Additional good housekeeping and sanitation methods are required to control pests. These include the following:

• Sealing cracks in foundations and external walls.
• Checking the seal or caulking around air-conditioning units, windows, doors and other openings.
• Storing garbage in tightly covered containers.
• Eliminating all possible breeding grounds for mosquitoes, particularly stagnant water.
• Repairing all cracks and holes in floors, walls and ceilings.

Related and Further Reading

Asphalt Institute, USA. *Asphalt in Pavement Maintenance.* Manual Series No. 16 (MS-16) (March, 1983).

British Standards Institution. *BS 4092: Part 1: 1966 Domestic front entrance gates: metal gates.*

British Standards Institution. *BS 4092: Part 2: 1966 Domestic front entrance gates: wooden gates.*

British Standards Institution. *BS 1446: 1973 Mastic asphalt (natural rock asphalt fine aggregate) for roads and footways.*

British Standards Institution. *BS 1722: Part 8: 1978 Mild steel (low carbon steel) continuous bar fences.*

British Standards Institution. *BS 1722: Part 9: 1979 Mild steel (low carbon steel) fences with round or square verticals and flat standards and horizontals.*

British Standards Institution. *BS 5837: 1980 Code of Practice for trees in relation to construction.*

British Standards Institution. *BS 594: 1985 Hot rolled asphalt for roads and other paved areas.*

British Standards Institution. *BS 1722: Part 1: 1986 Chain-link fences.*

British Standards Institution. *BS 1722: Part 3: 1986 Strained wire fences.*

British Standards Institution. *BS 1722: Part 5: 1986 Close-boarded fences.*

British Standards Institution. *BS 1722: Part 7: 1986 Wooden posts and rail fences.*

British Standards Institution. *BS 1722: Part 11: 1986 Woven wood and lap boarded panel fences.*

British Standards Institution. *BS 1447: 1988 Mastic asphalt (limestone fine aggregate) for roads and footways and pavings in building.*

British Standards Institution. *BS 1722: Part 2: 1989 Rectangular wire mesh and hexagonal wire netting fences.*

British Standards Institution. *BS 5889: 1989 One-part gun grade silicone based sealants.*

British Standards Institution. *BS 1722: Part 10: 1990 Anti-intruder fences in chain-link and welded mesh.*

British Standards Institution. *BS 5212: 1990 Cold applied joint sealants for concrete pavements.*

British Standards Institution. *BS 7263 Precast concrete flags, kerbs, channels, edgings and quadrants. Part 1: 1990 Specification. Part 2: 1990 Code of Practice for laying.*

Jaffa, G. Fencing – a new hurdle for maintenance costs to clear. *Building Maintenance and Services*, UK (May, 1978).

Kendrick, P. S. and Wignall, A. *Roadworks – Theory and Practice.* Heinemann, London (1981).

Mildenhall, H. S. and Northcott, G. D. S. *A Manual for the Maintenance and Repair of Concrete Roads.* Department of Transport, and Cement and Concrete Association, UK (1986).

Seeley, I. H. *Building Maintenance*, 2nd edn. Macmillan, London (1987).

Index